MIDDLE
PUGET SOUND
AND HOOD CANAL

Afoot & Afloat

MIDDLE
PUGET SOUND
AND HOOD CANAL

Afoot & Afloat

MARGE AND TED MUELLER

THE MOUNTAINEERS • SEATTLE

THE MOUNTAINEERS: Organized 1906 "... to explore, study, preserve, and enjoy the natural beauty of the Northwest."

4   3   2
5   4   3   2

Published by The Mountaineers
1011 S.W. Klickitat Way, Suite 107, Seattle, Washington 98134

Published simultaneously in Canada by Douglas & McIntrye, Ltd.
1615 Venables Street, Vancouver, British Columbia V5L 2H1

Published simultaneously in Great Britain by Cordee
3a DeMontfort St., Leicester, England LE1 7HD

Copyedited by Joan Gregory
Designed by Judy Petry
Photos by the authors
Maps by Marge Mueller

Cover photo: The beach at Potlatch State Park. Inset: The locks, Seattle
Frontispiece: Duwamish Head at low tide
Title page photo: Striped nudibranch found on the beach at Duwamish Head

Printed in the United States of America

Library of Congress Cataloging in Publication Data

Mueller, Marge.
    Middle Puget Sound and Hood Canal afoot and afloat / Marge and Ted Mueller.
        p.   cm.
    ISBN 0-89886-236-1
    1. Outdoor recreation--Washington (State)--Puget Sound--Guide
-books.   2. Outdoor recreation--Washington (State)--Hood Canal-
-Guide-books.   3. Marinas--Washington (State)--Puget Sound--Guide
-books.   4. Parks--Washington (State)--Puget Sound Region--Guide
-books.   5. Parks--Washington (State)--Hood Canal Region--Guide
-books.   6. Puget Sound Region (Wash.)--Description and travel-
-Guide-books.   7. Hood Canal Region (Wash.)--Description and travel-
-Guide-books.   I. Mueller, Ted.   II. Title.
GV191.42.W2M84   1990
917.97--dc20   89-77763
                                                                    CIP

Contents

APPENDICES 243

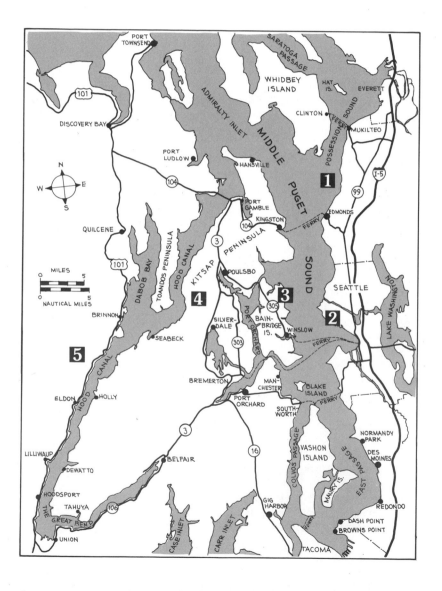

Preface

The *Afoot and Afloat* series operates on the premise that one of the great attractions of the water and shores of Puget Sound is its diversity. This series describes not only the broad natural and historical range of the Sound, but also the many activities that are associated with it. It is our hope the *Afoot and Afloat* series will lure the beachgoer to some heretofore undiscovered cranny and expand his understanding of this environment.

While this series focuses more on the surroundings than on the facilities to be found, it is understood that facilities often enable visitors to enjoy the marine environment, so brief descriptions of marinas and campgrounds are included.

Where is "Middle Puget Sound"?

This book includes the waters lying between the southern tip of Whidbey Island and the northern end of Vashon Island. While it is not part of the Sound, Hood Canal is included as an added bonus, since it adjoins the area called Middle Puget Sound.

The broad seaway on which the major population centers of Western Washington front, and on which thousands of boats travel daily, ought to have a nice all-inclusive name. Unfortunately, it doesn't. In precise geographic language "Puget Sound" applies only to the channels south of a line drawn from Port Townsend on the Olympic Peninsula to Admiralty Head on Whidbey Island. That leaves a whole chunk of Washington's inland waters without a name. True, some of these—the Strait of Juan de Fuca, Saratoga Passage, Rosario and Haro straits—have specific names, but the area still lacks an official, overall name that weather reports, government agencies, the populace in general, and beleaguered writers, especially, can use.

From time to time various labels have been proposed to the State Board of Geographic Names. The most recent suggestion was "Whulje" (loosely translated as "big salt water"), the original Indian name for this inland sea. While the word has a lot going for it, historically, it doesn't trip lightly over the tongue, and it was rejected.

Officialdom aside, however, many local people (as well as most state agencies) commonly consider Puget Sound to be all of Washington's inland waters that run north from Olympia to the Canadian border, and west to the Pacific Ocean. Since that designation was used for our companion volume, *North Puget Sound, Afoot and Afloat,* it follows that the areas described in this book must be considered "Middle Puget Sound."

*   *   *   *   *

The locations in this book were surveyed over a period of several years and rechecked just prior to publication; however, changes to facilities do occur. The authors and The Mountaineers would appreciate knowing of any such changes so future editions can be updated. Please address comments to the authors in care of: The Mountaineers Books, 1011 S.W. Klickitat Way, Seattle, WA 98134.

Marge and Ted Mueller
April 1990

Introduction

Middle Puget Sound boasts more population and more boats than any other section of Washington's inland waterways. The waterway teems with the activities of giant freighters plowing up and down the channel, ferries churning back and forth, bevies of white-crowned sailboats driven in the wind, cruisers of every size bustling about, and fishing boats bobbing on the tides. From the cities and towns along its shores stream thousands of recreation-seekers, some headed for distant vacation lands, but many looking for nearby diversions.

And the diversions *are* here—beaches and parks draw people for a wide array of activities, ranging from fishing to sand-castle building, from birdwatching to sunbathing. Parks and public shorelands are sandwiched between real estate developments and tucked in obscure crannies of quiet bays. They range from multipurpose facilities of several hundred acres to narrow beach accesses offering only a chance to drag a boat to the water and toss it in.

Getting Around

Time was when the only way to travel around the Puget Sound area was by boat. Forests so thick that even walking was difficult blanketed most of the shoreline; the communities that sprang up as the land was settled were linked by sailing ships and rowboats. Since waterways provided easy channels of travel, time was better spent clearing land for farming or cutting timber for mills than undertaking the Herculean task of road building.

Even as cities grew, the water remained the transportation mainstay; steamboats joined the wind- and muscle-powered vessels, and a network of sturdy little packets moved passengers and goods throughout the channels, sloughs, and navigable rivers. These workhorses, known as the Mosquito Fleet, were active on the sound for nearly seventy years, until the road system finally reached all communities, and the state took over the operation of the ferry system.

Thanks to today's extensive highway network, it is not necessary to use a boat (ferries excluded) to reach most of the fine saltwater recreation sites on Middle Puget Sound and Hood Canal. The exceptions are the public beaches managed by the Department of Natural Resources (the DNR beaches)—many of these can be approached only by boat.

LAND ACCESS

On the east side of Puget Sound, the major north–south freeway is Interstate 5; for most recreation sites outside of urban areas this book uses I-5 as a reference point. In some cases the predecessor to I-5, old Highway 99, is referred to when it is closer to the beaches than I-5 and offers a more convenient approach. In urban areas directions generally are given starting from major arterials in the vicinity. Although the authors are Seattle-based, we try to avoid the provincialism of assuming all readers of this book use Seattle as a reference point.

The Kitsap Peninsula can be reached from the south end by leaving I-5 in Tacoma and heading north on State Highway 16, reaching the peninsula via the Tacoma Narrows Bridge. Still another route is available via US 101 from Olympia to Shelton, then to the Kitsap Peninsula on state highways 3 or 106.

The east side of Hood Canal is only minimally accessible by road. A county road extension of State Highway 300 west of Belfair skirts the north edge of the canal's "hook" as far as Tahuya, then turns inland and wanders, sometimes paved, sometimes not, through dense forest to touch the east side of the canal at only a couple of small bays with no public access. This is real primitive country! Not until the vicinity of Seabeck, near the north end of the canal, are public recreational sites again accessible by land. North of Seabeck the huge Bangor Naval Base locks up shore access until Lofall, the old Hood Canal ferry terminal.

The west side of Hood Canal can be reached from the south through Olympia and Shelton via US 101, a very scenic highway running along the complete length of the west shoreline of the canal. From the north end of Kitsap Peninsula, the Hood Canal Floating Bridge (on Highway 104) provides a route to the west side of the canal.

FERRY ACCESS

By far the most convenient means of reaching the Kitsap Peninsula, Bainbridge Island, and Hood Canal from the east side of Puget Sound is the Washington State Ferry System. Two ferry routes leave from the Colman Terminal, Pier 52, on the Seattle waterfront. One crosses the sound, then winds through narrow Rich Passage to arrive at Bremerton on the Kitsap Peninsula; the other runs straight across the sound to Winslow, on the east side of Bainbridge Island.

A ferry leaving the east side of Puget Sound at Fauntleroy, south of Seattle's Lincoln Park, reaches the Kitsap Peninsula at Southworth, with an intermediate stop at Vashon Island. North of Seattle, a ferry route runs from Edmonds, on the east side of the sound, to Kingston, on the north end of the Kitsap Peninsula.

The ferries are easy to use; simply drive to the terminal area, inform the cashier of your destination if leaving from Colman Terminal or Fauntleroy (all other terminals have only one destination), purchase a ticket, and

Washington State Ferry leaving Kingston

follow attendants' instructions. Fares are collected for car, driver, and passengers on westbound runs, but only for car and driver on eastbound ones. At terminals lacking a separate passenger loading ramp, passengers will be boarded and discharged from the car deck before any auto traffic moves. Bicyclists will also enter and leave the car deck of the ferry ahead of vehicle traffic.

On holidays and busy summer weekends, don't expect a guaranteed spot for your car or camper on the next departing ferry. Vehicular loads are often too heavy for even the largest superferries, and delays of one or more sailings can be expected. Bring a book, some games, a picnic snack, and a sense of humor, and relax while cooling your heels with the crowd in the large asphalt holding lot.

A passenger-only ferry operated for a brief time between Bremerton and Seattle, and two more were planned and built for other routes; however, as of the writing of this book, operating funds were not available from the state for these boats, and both were figuratively and literally "dead in the water." They may be put in operation in the future.

BOAT ACCESS

Boating is a pleasant way of getting around Middle Puget Sound, and for those who choose to travel this way, ample boating facilities are available. Many of the state, city, and county parks have mooring buoys, floats, and launch ramps. When these facilities are not provided, boaters usually can anchor out and approach the shore in dinghies, kayaks, or other boats small enough to be beached. No fee is charged for day-use of dock, floats, or buoys; however, boaters using state parks are required to pay for overnight tie-up.

A number of bays are totally surrounded by private property. Dropping a hook for a lunch stop or overnight stay in these bays is permitted, but private shores should be respected.

Boats cruising on Puget Sound are subject, of course, to such details as depth of keel, levels of tide, and submerged reefs and rocks. Kayaks and other small paddle-propelled boats can travel with impunity, strong winds and tidal currents excepting. Boats moored in the sheltered freshwater of Lake Washington and Lake Union, or those headed from the sound into freshwater destinations, must work their way through the locks at Shilshole Bay. The trauma of doing this is directly related to the number of inexperienced or indifferent skippers waiting to go through in the locking. (Locking procedures are described in detail in chapter 2.)

Public Recreation Sites on Middle Puget Sound and Hood Canal

PUBLIC PARKS

Public shorelands on Middle Puget Sound and Hood Canal fall under the jurisdiction of a number of different governmental agencies. Most

Picnicking at Tawanoh State Park

parks are owned and maintained by either city, county, or state park departments, although a few owe their existence to one of several local port authorities.

Facilities vary widely from park to park. Camping is available at Seal Rock Forest Camp and at many of the state parks. County parks on Middle Sound are day use only; a few are minimally developed or poorly maintained. Roughly half of these county parks have launch ramps. Facilities at public shoreline accesses provided by various port authorities tend toward launch ramps and fishing piers, with some limited picnicking facilities. A quick reference chart listing the facilities of each of the parks is in the back of this book.

Because of their nearness to large population centers, city parks can have a downside. They tend to be quite crowded on weekends, holidays, and sunny summer days. Several suffer a summer inundation of younger people and, unless tightly policed, attendant problems of crowds of cars, raucous music, alcohol, and drugs. Seattle's downtown waterfront parks, unfortunately, have their share of vagrants who have drifted here to sleep off their last hangover and harass passersby into contributing to their next.

DNR BEACHES AND OTHER PUBLIC TIDELANDS

Aside from parks, substantial stretches of public beach are owned by the Washington State Department of Natural Resources. Most of these shorelands are public only up to mean high water line; property above that is privately owned. As a result, most DNR beaches are not accessible via land unless they are a continuation of a beach in front of some other public property.

At one time the DNR attempted to mark the boundaries of public beaches with distinctive black-and-white posts at high water line, but they abandoned the effort because of problems they had maintaining these markers. Similar black-and-white posts are now used to identify offshore geoduck leases—do not confuse these with DNR markers.

A number of publications available from the DNR give general locations and boundaries of their public beaches. Use care to avoid trespassing on private property; adjoining private beaches are usually liberally posted as such, but do not assume unposted property is public. This book attempts to give you guidelines for locating boundaries, where possible.

In addition to beaches owned by the DNR, several other public beaches are administered by the Washington State Parks and Recreation Department as State Park Recreational Tidelands.

LAUNCHING FACILITIES

Public launching facilities are available at some city, county, and state parks; a few more are provided by the Washington State Department of Fisheries and some of the various port authorities. These are all paved ramps; however, the depth of water at the end of the various ramps, and the condition of the beaches beyond them varies widely. Some lead out to shallow beaches that become extensive mudflats at low tide, making them usable only at high water. At other launch sites there are sharp drop-offs not far beyond the end of the ramp. Exercise care using any launch facility until you are familiar with it.

The condition of the ramps themselves also varies widely, with some receiving only cursory maintenance. The best ramps are multilane, with adjoining boarding floats provided for the convenience of loading supplies and passengers; one such facility is found at Marine Park in Everett. Several of these larger ramps are divided into two sets of lanes; one set is reserved for launching boats; the other set is for retrieving them. At most ramps users are charged a launching fee, either collected by on-site support personnel or voluntarily deposited at a nearby collection station.

Marinas and beach resorts also have launching facilities; most have slings adequate for handling power boats up to 30 feet or more. Launching facilities at some resorts may not be available during off-season months. Commercial facilities are subject to economic vagaries—resorts and marinas may go out of business or be expanded to accommodate sudden popularity.

MARINA FACILITIES

Middle Puget Sound has the largest and most elaborate marinas in the state, with every amenity for boat, captain, and crew: fuel, groceries, ice, fishing equipment and bait, restaurants, shops, marine repair and supplies, water, power, restrooms, showers, laundry, and, frequently, attractions for stir-crazy kids. But not all marinas fit this description; there are also a number of sleepy boat houses, mouldering in disrepair, that rent a few kicker boats each day to neighborhood anglers. The description of each area in this book begins with an information list that attempts to cover facilities available at the time of publication.

Commercial or port authority-run marinas normally set aside one or more docks for transient (or guest) moorage, available for a daily fee. Transient moorage fees generally cover use of all marina facilities with the exception of dockside power, which is available for an additional fee. Some marinas accept advance registration, either by mail, telephone, or boat radio. If arriving without prior arrangements, check in at the fuel dock or marina office immediately upon arrival to be assigned and pay for a vacant slip.

A few marinas have a tidal grid—a "poor man's drydock,"—consisting of a stable platform below the water level and some adjoining pilings to which boaters tie their craft. As the tide goes out, the keel of the boat settles on the platform and the pilings support it for the duration of the low tide; the boat is thus exposed for maintenance and repair. Numbers painted on the side of the pier or pilings (the "grid") indicate the depth of the water at the platform. Use of a tidal grid or other special-purpose facilities requires prior arrangement with the marina office.

Recreation on Middle Puget Sound and Hood Canal

A wide variety of recreational opportunities are available on Middle Puget Sound and Hood Canal, ranging from boating, paddling, beach-combing, shellfish harvesting, fishing, scuba diving, birdwatching, swimming, and sunbathing to bicycling, hiking, and camping. Several museums and a bounty of historical markers recall the exploration, settlement, and key events in the growth of the region. Recreation is here for all ages and all levels of energy, with appeal to tourists and residents alike.

BOATING

A quick look at the forests of masts in the Everett or Shilshole Bay marinas, or at the parking lots full of boat trailers at any of the larger launch sites, will quickly establish the fact that Puget Sound residents do like their boating. Billowing sails and throbbing motors don't tell the whole story, however; peek into any small, secluded bay and you will probably find a group of kayakers quietly paddling in search of shoreline sights that the crews of larger boats may never take time to find. Boating is diverse, but regardless of the size or shape of your aquatic transportation, certain fundamentals and cautions apply to all using these waterways.

Chartering and Renting. Boating in the area is readily available to those who do not own a boat; over two dozen firms offer charter services for boats ranging from small weekenders to large luxury yachts. Charter operators will insist on a demonstration of adequate boat handling and navigation skills before renting their vessels to an unknown sailor, and, if not impressed with the candidate's abilities, may require a quick boating course or the company of a paid crew to protect their investment.

On a lesser scale, a deposit fee will rent a small outboard-powered craft from any of several boathouses and resorts in the area for a day's fishing at the local hot spot. The required lifejackets usually can also be rented.

Paddling. Each passing year sees greater interest in the sport of kayaking, and it is rare to spend a day on the water without spotting several of these sleek, muscle-powered craft poking into shallow backwaters where only they have the draft to venture. More experienced kayakers may even make a cross-sound trip, provided weather and tidal current conditions are favorable.

Kayak and canoe rentals, as well as training in their use, are available at several locations around the sound; outdoor groups in the area also provide training courses, and the safety and camaraderie of group-sponsored outings.

Boating Safety. Because of the sheer number of boaters enjoying the waters of Puget Sound and Hood Canal, it is inevitable that some of them will disregard the requirements of safe boating. One needs only to approach the locks at Shilshole Bay on a busy summer weekend to realize

Feeding ducks in the locks

some boaters lack the skills, courtesy, and sobriety necessary to make an outing pleasurable for their fellow boaters. Anyone starting into boating should take one of the boating safety courses provided by the local U.S. Power Squadron. Information on time and location of these courses can be obtained from the U.S. Coast Guard.

Although a boat on Middle Puget Sound or Hood Canal is never more than a couple of miles from the nearest shoreline, navigational hazards and potential bad weather still mandate that every boater be thoroughly familiar with the skills of coastal navigation and possess the tools and navigational charts required to put this knowledge to use. The illustrative maps in this book are intended for general information only. They are not intended to replace a *good navigational chart*. A list of current NOAA charts for this area is in the back of the book.

Vessel Traffic. Middle Puget Sound is heavily used by commercial vessels, naval vessels, ferries, fishing boats, and recreational boats, making it seem downright crowded at times. As any boating course graduate knows, there are rules-of-the-road specifying who stays clear of whom under what conditions; however, don't risk life, limb, and the hull of your boat assuming another captain knows those rules and will follow them. A sailboat skipper shouting "Starboard tack!" at a large power vessel closing at high speed may end up getting his satisfaction in maritime court—after he has been fished from the icy sound.

To bring more order to large vessel traffic, the Coast Guard has installed a Vessel Traffic Service on Puget Sound. North- and southbound traffic lanes have been designated down the center of the sound, and these are marked on all navigation charts of the area. The ½-nautical-mile-wide traffic lanes lie on either side of a ¼-nautical-mile-wide separation zone, which has mid-channel buoys marking ever point at which the lanes alter direction. Radar stations are located at key points on the sound to track vessel traffic; all radar signals feed into the Coast Guard VTS center on Pier 36 on the Seattle waterfront.

Vessels over 300 gross tons, vessels carrying passengers for hire, vessels engaged in commercial towing, and dredges or floating plants are required to participate in the vessel traffic control system. Communication with the VTS center takes place over VHF channel 14; boaters concerned with location of large-vessel traffic can monitor this frequency for information. Smaller commercial and recreational vessels generally don't participate in the VTS; however, they will probably appear on the center radar, depending on their size and radar reflectance. These boats may contact the center in emergencies, and the center will provide assistance, if possible.

Another potential traffic problem, especially at night during commercial salmon fishing season, is the dozens of fishing boats with nets deployed; at times they seem to blanket the sound. Proper lights on fishing boats and nets should identify areas to avoid, but a sharp lookout is required to spot these lights and avoid running into nets.

Weather. Summer favors Puget Sound and Hood Canal with mild temperatures, moderate weather, and light winds—the major weather concern is avoiding a painful sunburn. However, sudden summer storms do come up occasionally; in other seasons the waters in this area can at times be downright nasty and dangerous. Prevailing storm winds come from the southwest; the shift of wind to that direction, plus a falling barometer, bodes of worsening weather.

This section of Puget Sound has a weather anomaly known as a "convergence zone." Low-level winds from the west off the ocean split as they encounter the Olympic Peninsula; a portion loop south around the mountain range then back down the sound, and a portion loop north through the Strait of Juan de Fuca and then up the sound. When these two fronts of wind meet head-on (generally in the area between Seattle and Everett), a violent local weather front is sometimes created, with localized high winds, rain, and at times thunder and lightning.

The long, open, unobstructed north–south channels of Puget Sound and Hood Canal provide plenty of fetch for strong storm winds to build up substantial seas. When wind-built waves are met by tidal currents from the opposite direction, sharp choppy seas can result, making for uncomfortable, if not unsafe, boating. The best defense against being caught by adverse weather conditions is a regular monitoring of the NOAA weather channel, VHF channel WX1 (FM 162.550 MHz).

Fog. The temperature differential between the always-cold sound and summer-warmed beaches creates ideal conditions for formation of fog, especially in late night and early morning hours. Although this fog generally lifts by midday, a planned early departure may have to be delayed, or navigation skills will be severely tested in the blank white wall of surrounding mist.

Rocks and Shoals. Most serious navigational hazards in this area are marked with lights, buoys, or other navigational markers. However, with a potential tidal variation of 16 to 20 feet at extreme tides, normally submerged and safe rocks and reefs can come dangerously close to the surface at extreme minus tides, and underwater shoals and bars can become a four-hour or more resting place for the sailor who doesn't keep a wary eye on the chart, tide table, and depth sounder. When anchoring for the night, check tide levels at the time and for the duration of your stay to make sure you have enough water under you during that period, and that the proper length of anchor rode has been payed out.

Tidal Current. Tide level and tidal current are related, but definitely not synonymous. The tide refers to the change in the depth of the water due to gravitational influences of the sun and moon and other more esoteric things such as barometric pressure. In Puget Sound there are two highs and two lows in any tidal cycle of roughly twenty-five hours. As the vertical water level rises and falls, the volume of water at any point must move in and out of the area, resulting in horizontal tidal currents. The direction and velocity of the current are determined not only by the tidal cycle, but also by the channel involved and by any shoreline or underwater obstructions.

Tidal currents in Middle Puget Sound range from virtually zero along the east shoreline to two knots or more in Admiralty Inlet near Foulweather Bluff. In the narrower channels, such as Agate Passage, Rich Passage, and the Port Washington Narrows, tidal currents of up to four knots can be expected. The impact of such currents on small low-powered boats or hand-powered kayaks is obvious—you can be going full-steam ahead into a strong current and still be moving backwards.

Tidal current tables are printed annually and are keyed to stations identified on the NOAA small-craft chart portfolio. A combination of the charts and current tables will give a good approximation of current strength and direction that you can expect to encounter in a given area.

WALKING AND HIKING

Hiking is probably a misnomer for the foot-bound recreation described in this book, since trails in the parks included here rarely exceed a mile or so one way, and elevation gained and lost is seldom more than 100 to 200 feet. Such short walks have their interest and charm, however, as more time can be spent observing the surrounding sights, smells, colors, flowers, and wildlife when there is less pressure to cover a long distance. There certainly is a wide variety of things to see on these walks. Even urban Discovery Park, for example, is visited by over 221 species of birds, and includes a dozen varieties of trees, an equal or greater selection of

The beach at Picnic Point County Park

shrubs, 40 or more types of herbs, ferns and mosses, more than 50 species of beach life, and a showcase-lesson in Puget Sound geology in its beach bluffs.

Beach walks of up to a couple of miles in length can be found in some locations where DNR beaches are accessible from public uplands. Many beach walks are very dependent on tide levels; a wide, gently tapering beach can disappear within four or five hours beneath an incoming tide. Since many beaches lie below steep bluffs or impenetrable brush, note the time of the next tide change and plan your walk to avoid getting trapped in some uncomfortable or unsafe place by the incoming tide. Tide tables are available at bookstores and marine supply stores, and daily predictions are published in most area newspapers.

Descriptions of beach hikes can be found in Harvey Manning's *Footsore* series of books published by The Mountaineers. Areas in Middle Puget Sound and Hood Canal are covered in *Footsore 1, 3,* and *4.*

BICYCLING

Nearly all the areas covered in this book are well suited for bicycling, and many are quite popular for both one-day and extended bicycle trips. Since traffic tends to keep to the inland highways and freeways, many of the shoreline roads are lightly traveled.

On weekends the ferries to Bainbridge Island disgorge dozens of bicyclists intent on some variation of a loop trip around the island. Most of the roads on Bainbridge have wide shoulders usable for bicycle lanes, and the roads around the perimeter of the island are reasonably level, although some crossing the island can be a real bear, climbing and dropping over successive ridges and valleys.

Highway 101 along Hood Canal is also popular for longer trips and, with a few exceptions, has shoulders wide enough for safe and comfortable bicycling. Highway 106 along the south side of the bend of Hood Canal is another well-used bicycle route; however, the road is narrow and twisted and traffic is generally heavy, so more caution is advised on this trip.

A number of bicycle tours in this area are described in detail in the two books *Bicycling the Backroads Around Puget Sound* and *Bicycling the Backroads of Northwest Washington*. Both are by Bill and Erin Woods, and are published by The Mountaineers.

In Washington, bicyclists are required to use the right side of the road, the same as vehicular traffic, and to travel single file, or, on wide roads, no more than two abreast. Bicyclists are not permitted to stack up a line of traffic behind them; if one starts to build, cyclists should pull over to the nearest safe spot and permit traffic to pass. Courtesy is the byword, and consideration by bicyclists for the requirements of auto traffic will increase chances that such consideration will be reciprocated.

CAMPING

Forest Service campgrounds and those state parks offering camping provide both tent and RV camping at individual sites; some also provide a group campsite, available by reservation only. A host of private resorts in the area also offer camping; most resorts stack campsites side-by-side with little individual privacy. As of 1988, none of the state parks in this area require reservations; camping is on a first-come, first-served basis. Fees are collected nightly for all campsites, and campgrounds are closed after 10:00 P.M. Picnic areas cannot be used for overflow camping.

BEACH EXPLORATION

Although most of the beaches in this area are heavily used, low tides still uncover a wide variety of saltwater plants and animals for examining and photographing. Park regulations prohibit removal of any beach life except for food use; consideration for other future beach explorers as well as for the environment dictates that nothing be taken from any of the beaches. All plants and animals play a vital role in the environment and food chains; their removal can only lead to deterioration in the beach ecology. Even empty shells and pockmarked driftwood may serve as future homes for small marine creatures, and are better left on the beach than stuffed in a forgotten sack on someone's back porch.

HARVESTING SEAFOOD—FISHING, SCUBA DIVING, AND BEACH FORAGING

Licenses and Limits. The Washington State Department of Fisheries requires a personal-use fishing license for taking any food fish in the state. In addition, a salmon-catch record card is required for any migratory salmon fishing. With the exceptions of shrimping in Hood Canal and digging razor clams, harvesting shellfish or crab is permitted without a license. It is the responsibility of the individual to be aware of all regulations regarding size, limits, methods of harvesting, seasons, restricted sites, and license requirements.

A saltwater sport-fishing pamphlet published by the Department of Fisheries, and a freshwater game fishing pamphlet, published by the Game Department, outline license requirements and other regulations. The annually published guides are available from the respective departments and are also found in most sporting goods stores.

Scuba Diving. To take food fish, scuba divers must have a saltwater fishing license. It is unlawful to fish for or take salmon, octopus, or crabs using underwater spearfishing gear. With the exception of regulations regarding lingcod, all bag limits, size, season, and area restrictions for fishing apply to scuba divers as well.

Digging Holes on the Beach. State regulations require that holes dug on a beach for purposes of gathering clams *must always* be refilled. The incoming tide may take three or four cycles to fill holes; in the meantime small marine animals trapped in the pile are subject to smothering, and those on top, exposed to the sun, may die of dehydration.

Oyster Gathering. It is unlawful to remove oyster shells from the beach; the shells are hosts for oyster larvae which will die if the shells are re-

Oysters on a Hood Canal DNR beach

moved. Take a bucket and an oyster knife to the beach with you and shuck oysters where you find them.

Paralytic Shellfish Poisoning (Red Tide). When the Washington State Department of Health periodically issues a "red tide warning" and closes particular beaches on Puget Sound, the public usually reacts with confusion or skepticism. A clearer understanding of the phenomenon of red tide will lead to a greater respect for its dangers.

The name "red tide" itself contributes to some of the public's confusion, for it is not always visibly red, it has nothing at all to do with the tide, and not all red algae are harmful. Paralytic shellfish poisoning (PSP) is a serious illness caused by *Gonyaulax catenella*, a toxic, single-celled, amber-colored alga present in small numbers at all times in the water. During the spring, summer, and fall, certain environmental conditions may combine to permit a rapid multiplication or accumulation of these microscopic organisms. Most shellfish toxicity occurs when the concentrations of *G. catenella* are too sparse to discolor the water; however, the free-floating plants sometimes become so numerous that the water appears to have a reddish cast—thus the name "red tide."

Bivalve shellfish such as clams, oysters, mussels, and scallops, which feed by filtering sea water, may ingest millions of the organisms and concentrate the toxin in their bodies. The poison is retained by most of these shellfish for several weeks after the occurrence of the red tide; butter clams can be poisonous for much longer.

When the concentration of the toxin in mollusks reaches a certain level, it becomes hazardous to humans who eat them. The toxins cannot be destroyed by cooking, and cannot be reliably detected by any means other than laboratory analysis. Symptoms of PSP, beginning with the tingling of the lips and tongue, may occur within a half hour of ingestion. The illness attacks the nervous system, causing loss of control of arms and legs, difficulty in breathing, paralysis, and, in extreme cases, death.

Shellfish in all counties on Puget Sound are under regular surveillance by the state Department of Health. PSP (or red tide) warnings are issued and some beaches are posted when high levels of toxin are detected in tested mollusks. Warnings are usually publicized in the media; the state toll-free hotline, listed in appendix A, has current information as to which beaches are closed to shellfish harvesting. Crabs, abalone, shrimp, and fin fish are not included in closures since there have been no recorded cases of PSP in the Northwest caused by eating those animals.

Pollution. Pollution, both chemical and biological, has so thoroughly contaminated beaches in King County that harvesting of bottomfish, crab, or shellfish is not recommended along any of its shores. Similar problems afflict beaches and bays in metropolitan areas of Kitsap and Snohomish counties, and in some limited areas of Hood Canal. Fish and shellfish from these areas have been found to have high levels of pollutants in their body tissues. A continuous diet of such animals can pose a health hazard.

Safety Considerations

Boating and beach travel entail unavoidable risks that every traveler assumes and must be aware of and respect. The fact that an area is described in this book is not a representation it will be safe for you. The areas described herein vary greatly in the amount and kind of preparation needed to enjoy them safely. Some areas may have changed since this book was written, or conditions may have deteriorated. Weather conditions can change daily or even hourly, and tide levels will also vary considerably. An area that is safe in good weather at low or slack tide may be completely unsafe during inclement weather or at times of high tide or maximum tidal current. You can meet these and other risks safely by exercising your own independent judgment and common sense. Be aware of your own limitations, those of your vessel, and of conditions when or where you are traveling. If conditions are dangerous or if you are not prepared to deal with them safely, change your plans. Each year many people enjoy safe trips in the waters and on the beaches of Middle Puget Sound and Hood Canal. With proper preparation and good judgment, you can too.

Emergency Assistance

The overall legal authority in all unincorporated areas of the state rests with the county sheriff or county police. Within city limits, the local city police force has legal authority. Port authority police have jurisdiction on port property only, although in most cases they are cross-deputized in other local police forces. Emergencies or complaints should be referred to the authority having jurisdiction; telephone numbers are listed in appendix A in the back of this book.

Within state and county parks, the park manager or ranger assumes emergency assistance responsibilities. Not all parks have resident managers; appendix A provides the locations of managers responsible for unmanned parks.

The U.S. Coast Guard has primary responsibility for safety and law enforcement on Puget Sound and Hood Canal waters. Marine VHF channel 16 is constantly monitored by the Coast Guard and should be the most reliable means of contact in case of emergencies on the water. The Coast Guard monitors Citizens Band channel 9 at some locations and times, but has no commitment to a full-time radio watch on this channel. Several volunteer groups do an excellent job of monitoring the CB emergency frequency and will assist with relaying emergency requests to the proper authorities.

Port of Everett Marina

1. Possession Sound and Edmonds

Boating spots are usually thought of in two categories—places you go to, and places you leave from. The wonderful change-of-pace destinations like the San Juan Islands, Port Townsend, or Poulsbo fall in the first group. In the latter category are spots boaters don't usually think of stopping at unless the motor suddenly develops palsy, or (worse yet) it's discovered that all the food for the weekend is still sitting at home on the kitchen table.

To Puget Sound boaters, marinas along Possession Sound usually fall in this second group—they are too close to home to offer a convenient first night's stop, or too much like home to provide a real change of pace. A stop along Possession Sound can, however, be a real bonus. Boaters can add one more pleasurable day to the weekend by leaving the home slip in Seattle or points south on Friday afternoon and pausing somewhere along Possession Sound for the night before continuing north. Or they can use this as a last stop on a vacation trip before making the final leap for the locks.

For those not in transit to vacation getaways, Possession Sound offers beaches aplenty for a day's enjoyment wading in the waves, sculpting sand castles, lolling against sun-splashed driftwood, or digging for tasty morsels. For small craft Possession Sound beaches and marinas offer ideal launch points for local exploration or fishing. Scuba divers also relish the opportunity to probe the underwater world within a short jaunt from home.

George Vancouver anchored off Gedney Island in June of 1792, after exploring the southern reaches of Puget Sound. In taking possession of all the inland waters in the name of King George III of England, he gave this arm of Admiralty Inlet its name.

"Possession Sound" is a somewhat pretentious name for this body of water, which is, in truth, just one more wandering arm of Puget Sound itself. It bulges into Port Gardner, a broad basin at the southern confluence of Saratoga Passage and Port Susan. A large part of the east side of this basin is a mud flat at the mouth of the Snohomish River, baring at low tide. A dredged channel leads into Everett, the major city on this body of water.

GEDNEY (HAT) ISLAND

A long, subterranean shelf reaches south from Camano Head to Gedney Island, in the middle of Possession Sound. This is a popular year-round salmon fishing area. To provide more habitat for fish, and thus im-

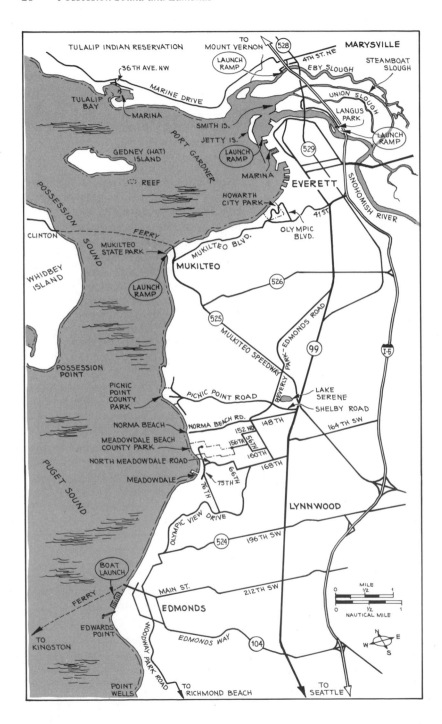

prove fishing and scuba diving in the area, an artificial reef of massive chunks of broken concrete has been placed just off Gedney Island. The reef, marked by buoys, lies ½ mile south of the island.

All of the island is private; the small marina lying behind a breakwater on the northeast side is for the use of island residents only. Avoid cruising too close to the south or east sides of the island, as shoal water extends some distance from the shore.

Tulalip Bay

The Tulalip Indian Reservation spreads along the shore between Kayak Point and Everett. The center of the reservation shoreline is marked by the small, shallow indentation of Tulalip Bay. The north side of the entrance to the bay is dotted with submerging rocks; the hull of the *Hicira*, a gas scow that burned and sank in 1919, lies in these rocks. When entering the bay, favor the north side once past the entrance rocks to avoid drying shoals found near the center of the bay.

TULALIP BAY MARINA

Facilities: Boat launch (ramp), transient moorage, groceries, bait, fuel, picnic tables, restrooms (no showers)

A recently constructed marina lies behind a short rock jetty at the center of the eastern shore of Tulalip Bay. The marina is heavily used by tribal

Tulalip Bay Marina

fishing boats, but unused slips are open to visiting boaters. Check with the marina office or grocery store for available moorage. A steep, concrete, single-lane launch ramp with an adjoining boarding float is located at the south end of the marina area; ample parking is in the vicinity.

To reach the marina by land, take Exit 199 from I-5, signed to Marysville/Tulalip. At the intersection with 4th Street NE, turn west and follow the main highway (which becomes Marine Drive) for 5 miles to 36th Avenue NW, where signs lead to the marina. Historic St. Ann's Catholic Mission, built in 1894, sits prominently on the hillside above the marina.

The Snohomish River

Between Marysville and Everett the Snohomish River meanders soundward, divided into a braided network of sloughs, backwaters, and

Ebey Slough, Snohomish River

channels. The main channel of the Snohomish River is navigable by large boats for about ¾ mile east of the I-5 overpass. A railroad swing bridge and several highway bridges—some fixed, some opening—cross the channel. The least vertical clearance of the fixed bridges is 56 feet. Several marinas are located near the mouth of the river, at Ebey Slough, Union Slough, and on the main channel. All have haulouts and marine repair, but none provide guest facilities.

Small boats put in along the channel can explore the maze of quiet sloughs, or cruise out to the bustling activity of Port Gardner. Paddle-powered trips should be planned with the tidal current in mind.

Snohomish County officials have recently recognized the ecological value of these wetlands and have begun purchasing areas at the western tip of Smith Island and lying between Ebey and Steamboat sloughs. It is planned that as money becomes available some 2,200 acres of marshland will be placed in the public domain, and that the area will provide recreation for fishermen, kayakers, hikers, and birdwatchers. A wide variety of gulls, ducks, shorebirds, and herons can be seen in the estuary, and deer, river otter, raccoon, and coyote live in the grassy marshes.

EBEY SLOUGH LAUNCH RAMP

A public launch ramp on the most northerly of the Snohomish River sloughs provides access to the many channels of the estuary. To reach it, leave I-5 at Exit 199 to Marysville. In Marysville turn south on Beach Street, the first intersection after leaving the freeway. Follow Beach Street south to a T intersection with 1st Street and then head west. Just after the street ducks under I-5, a single-lane launch ramp is on the left, facing on Ebey Slough. There is a dirt parking area under the freeway with space for three or four cars with trailers. Park well off the road, as logging machinery and trucks make heavy use of the road during working days.

LANGUS WATERFRONT PARK

Park area: 15 acres; 500 feet of shoreline
Facilities: Boat launch (ramp), float, restrooms, picnic tables

This City of Everett park on the main channel of the Snohomish River offers a newly constructed two-lane concrete launch ramp with adjoining boarding floats, landscaped picnic sites, parking, and public restrooms. The south end of the park also has a wide concrete float used for fishing or for launching racing shells into the river. Picnic tables lining this short stretch of open shoreline provide a place to munch a sandwich and watch birds or boats, whichever is your fancy.

A narrow, rough dirt road along the top of the dike, better suited for walking than driving, leads downriver from the park along the water's edge for nearly a mile. A few small pocket beaches along the dike provide more spots to relax and watch the river creatures and activities.

To reach the park, leave I-5 at Exit 195 in Everett, or Exit 198 south of Marysville. From Everett follow Marine View Drive to where it joins old Highway 99 and crosses the river. After crossing the bridge, take the first exit to the right, go one block and turn right again on Ross Avenue. At a Y intersection bear left on Smith Island Road, signed to the park; this road passes the large area for the dry storage of boats at Dagmar's Landing. At another Y intersection at 12th Street NE, a little over ¼ mile south of Dagmar's, bear right, and in ½ mile reach the park.

If exiting I-5 from the north, Exit 198 leads east to old Highway 99. Turn south on 99 (State Avenue) and follow it to where it crosses Union Slough. Take the first road to the right after crossing the slough and follow the signs.

The park is tucked between the river and the freeway. The steep dirt embankment next to the freeway is heavily used by riders of dirt bikes and ATVs. Be forewarned—this is not a place to find tranquility on a summer weekend. At other times the banks of the river and surrounding marshy lands make a wonderful nature and birding walk.

Port Gardner and Everett

Many communities along Puget Sound were founded on the basis of a rumor and pure speculation. When railroad magnate Jim Hill visited Everett in February of 1892, he commented on the boom, claiming he had seen only four tree stumps that hadn't been given a town name. Unlike the many waterfront communities that died on the vine without the stimulus of industry and investor's money, Everett grabbed the brass ring on the speculative merry-go-round when in 1893 it became the West Coast terminus of the Great Northern Railroad.

Although Everett had been one of the last towns to be established on Puget Sound, in the years immediately preceding the arrival of the railroad it grew from a handful of settlers to over 3,000 persons rushing to make their fortunes in the anticipated economic boom. These first entrepreneurs cleared patches of land and lived in tents and hastily erected shacks—a local coffin maker found his wares were more in demand for bunks than for burials. The frenzied growth was fueled in 1889 by the discovery of gold and silver at Monte Cristo in the mountains a few miles to the east. By 1892 construction was underway in Everett on a huge smelter that would handle the rich ores soon to arrive from the high Cascades.

Once its future was assured by the railroad, Everett settled down to a period of population growth and industrial expansion, although the output of the Monte Cristo mines was much more modest than had been anticipated. The depressions of 1893 and the 1930s affected the town, as they did all of the country, but the small metropolis on Port Gardner was able to ride out its difficulties and continue as an industrial center.

The most tragic chapter of Everett history was written in 1916 when a labor dispute between the Industrial Workers of the World, known as the "Wobblies," and the lumber mill owners resulted in a confrontation between 250 union members and a group of deputized policemen. In a moment of anger a shot was fired, triggering a volley of gunfire that ended only when at least five men lay dead, and sixty others were mortally wounded or injured. The event became known as the "Everett Massacre."

One of the most striking features of the town is its harbor. Back in 1895 town founder Henry Hewitt got the bright idea to divert the Snohomish River south along the waterfront to give the city a freshwater harbor. He planned to build a dike and a series of locks that would force the Snohomish River into a new channel. (This was obviously before the days of environmental impact statements.) The rock dike was built; however the mighty Snohomish was not to be domesticated, and it retaliated by dumping silt in its new channel, making it unusable for navigation. These engineering problems, coupled with financial difficulties, caused the project to be abandoned. A cut, called Steamboat Gap, was made through the dike at its north end, permitting the silt to collect in two settling basins. With locks now out of the question, the city was left with a rock breakwater serving nicely to shelter its harbor (still salt water).

Another major change to the Everett waterfront is underway, and this one has had to run the gauntlet of environmentalists and other interests. In 1990 the Navy began construction of a carrier battle group base, the first phase of which will accommodate six ships. The major problem that con-

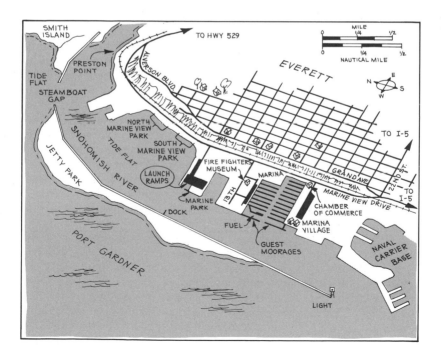

cerns environmentalists is the safe disposal of contaminated wastes dredged from the harbor during the building process. The Navy base, when completed, will occupy about 200 acres along Port Gardner Bay.

PORT OF EVERETT MARINA

Facilities: Transient moorage with power and water, restrooms, showers, laundry, pumpout station, groceries, restaurants, shopping, marine supply and repairs, boat charters and rental

Over the years the Everett waterfront has seen a shift from a purely commercial status to a recreational one. Today the 2,000 slips in the Port of Everett boat harbor qualify it as the second largest marina on the West Coast, surpassed only by Marina Del Rey in California. The marina, lying behind the rock jetty, north of the commercial wharfs, is easily spotted; just watch for a forest of aluminum spars.

Two lighted markers are at the entrance to the dredged channel, at the south opening of the breakwater. Boats should enter well from the south to avoid the huge shoal, marked by buoys, lying off the end of the Snohomish River and extending from Tulalip Bay to the southern end of the jetty. The main channel of the Snohomish River flows behind the dike, and the current can be quite strong, especially when it is combined with an outgoing tidal flow.

The marina basin lies between two 2,000-foot-long earth-fill piers. A network of floats extends from each of the piers, and a marine repair area with haulout slings is at the head of the basin. The Everett Yacht Club was once on the north side, but it is now closed. On the south pier is Marina Village, a collection of nice shops and restaurants done up in modern "olde-timey" decor; the harbormaster's office is on the east side of this complex.

Guest moorages are at the entrance to the basin on the two concrete floats that serve as a breakwater. When the river current is strong, docking at these outer floats can be wicked. The finger piers on the inside of the floats are fairly stable, but boats tied to the outside of the floats will be buffeted by the current and boat wakes. For boaters moored on the north section, it is more than a mile-long walk around the basin to facilities on the south, although it is just a short row—if you brought your dinghy. Visitors on the north side can pay for moorage at the gas dock to save a trip to the marina offices on the south side.

Regular bus service connects Marina Village with downtown shopping and services. In addition, an old-fashioned trolley, complete with polished brasswork and a clanging bell, offers hourly transportation. Merchants can provide information on schedules.

Downtown Everett has stores and services to meet every need. The rustic Public Market, at the corner of Grand and California streets, is an old warehouse now filled with restaurants, antique shops, arts and crafts stores, and other interesting places to browse. Shopping areas in the town

Port of Everett Marina

are easily reached from the waterfront by bus or old-fashioned trolley.

By land the Port of Everett marina is reached by leaving I-5 at Exit 193 (if traveling from the soouth), or Exit 194 (from the north), and driving west about 1½ miles to Marine View Drive. Turn north and in about 1½ miles more the marina complex is reached.

The Swiss chalet-style mansion at the entrance to the marina is worth a stop, whether visiting by land or water. The building was originally constructed in 1927 on the Everett waterfront as an office for the Weyerhaeuser sawmill. In 1938 the company moved it around Preston Point to a site up the Snohomish River just east of where the freeway crosses the channel. When the company outgrew the building, they donated it to the city, and it was barged back downriver to its present site, which should certainly qualify it as the most-traveled building around; it is also one of the most beautiful. It now serves as an office for the Chamber of Commerce (which has information about other interesting sights in Everett).

On the north side of the marina, on 13th Street is a fire fighters museum housed in an old fire station adjacent to a more modern one. The building is filled with memorabilia such as vintage hoses, nozzles, switchboards, fire helmets, and several old fire engines. The museum is not staffed, so its historic treasures are viewed from the outside through large windows.

NORTH AND SOUTH MARINE VIEW PARKS

Park area: 4.5 acres; 1,200 feet of waterfront
Facilities: Park benches
Attractions: Viewpoint, walking

The City of Everett has turned a ½-mile stretch of shorefront along Port Gardner Bay into a pretty little viewing and strolling area. Although they are considered two separate parks, North and South Marine View are really two parking areas joined by a blacktop path with numerous benches along the route. Up-close views are of rafts of thousands of logs waiting for the mill (or an extensive log-strewn mud flat at low tide), and lots of ducks, gulls, and cormorants. The more distant scene is of Possession Sound and blue-collar boats going about their daily work, or pleasure cruisers headed for a day's leisure.

North Marine View Park is on West Marine View Drive, just as the street drops down from the bluff at the north end of the city; ¼ mile farther is the parking area for South Marine View Park. From here walks can continue south to the boat launch area of Marine Park or on to the Port of Everett Marina.

MARINE PARK

Park area: 21 acres; 710 feet of shoreline
Access: Land, boat
Facilities: Boat launch (ramps), floats, picnic tables, restrooms

This is, hands down, the best boat launch facility on Puget Sound. In a region that hypes itself as a boating capital, there should be many more like this. Located at the end of 10th Street, the concrete-surfaced launching area is thirteen lanes wide, with a short boarding float between each pair of ramps. The adjacent parking lot has space for 300 vehicles and trailers. The ramps are well maintained, have a good slope, and have protection from weather. To facilitate use of the ramps, those on one side are marked for launching boats only; those on the other are reserved for retrieving boats. A small float protecting the west side of the launch area from river currents can be used for overnight moorage, but for only one day per week.

A pretty little grassy park on the bank south of the launch ramps offers picnic tables, benches, and nice views of both Jetty Park and boating activity in the channel. A large, modern, metal sculpture adds to the "first class" atmosphere.

The first weekend in June, the park is the site of "Salty Sea Days," a nautical festival featuring pirates, parades, log rolling contests, a barbeque, kayak races, fireworks, and numerous other fun events.

Boat launch at Marine Park

EVERETT JETTY PARK

Park area: 160 acres; 13,200 feet of shoreline
Facilities: Picnic tables, latrines, dock

For years people took the rock jetty that created the Everett harbor for granted—it served nicely to shelter the moorages, it was a handy final resting place for old barges (which also served to stabilize the sand and silt), and it was an ideal seagull parking lot. Recently the secret got out about what a great spot the jetty is, and now it is the darling of the Everett waterfront—and if you don't have your own boat to get there, the city will take you!

The Jetty Park dock is across from the boat launch area at Marine Park, making it convenient for small boats to cross the ¼-mile-wide channel; if traveling in paddle-powered craft, be aware that the current can be strong at times. Kayakers will enjoy a circumnavigation of 2-mile-long Jetty Island, exploring hulks of beached barges and passageways around old pilings and logs. Throughout the summer, a city boat leaves from the guest dock at Marina Village at regular intervals, taking visitors on the 5-minute ride to the jetty. A nominal fee is charged for the trip.

Summer tides flowing over the long sandy shoals on the west side of the island are warmed to near-bathtub temperatures on sunny days; the sand is the best around for castle construction. Picnic tables are scattered in the beach grass at the top of the dike.

A large colony of sea lions frequents the island in winter and spring before heading south to breeding grounds in southern California. They can often be seen hauled out on the beached barges at the southern end of the dike. Observe them from a distance, as they have little fear of man and can be dangerous.

HOWARTH CITY PARK

Park area: 28 acres; 3,960 feet of shoreline
Access: Land, boat
Facilities: Picnic tables, restrooms, hiking trails, tennis courts, horseshoe
   pits, children's play equipment
Attractions: Beachcombing, hiking, fishing

In the late 1800s, when railroads first arrived at Puget Sound and made their way to welcoming pioneer settlements, the logical route for tracks was the path of least resistance. Inland were forests, ravines, and hills, so the tracks were laid along the shoreline—between Seattle and Everett some thirty miles of beach front is consumed by railroad beds. As it traveled along the shore, the railroad cut across numerous small spits, leaving them exiled from the rest of the land. Several of these spits eventually became community parks, with elaborate pedestrian viaducts crossing the tracks. In fact, it almost seems the architects were vying with one another to create the most unique design.

One of these parks, on the south side of Everett, spans not only the shoreline, but also an adjoining gully and blufftop. To find this park, leave I-5 at Exit 192 and drive west on 41st Street SE, which eventually joins Mukilteo Boulevard. At a small shopping center, turn north on Olympic Boulevard and follow it as it circles through a residential area to a viewpoint marking the north end of the park; here are stunning views out over Possession Sound. The road then hairpins down to the lower entrance of the park. You may choose not to turn at the eastern intersection of Olympic Boulevard and continue west on Mukilteo Boulevard for another mile, to where the west end of the loop of Olympic Boulevard can be caught at upper Howarth Park.

At the lower entrance to the park, a road goes north, down the gully of Pigeon Creek No. 2, to a parking lot. From this entrance a trail also follows the bank of the creek through thick brush and past some tiny waterfalls to reach the parking lot. From the west end of the lot, a trail crosses the creek, climbs stairs to the railroad overpass, and at the west end winds down a staircase around a castlelike tower to the beach. The grass-and-sand flat of the park is on a landfill behind a riprap bulkhead. Small boats can be landed on the beach in calm weather.

To the south, stairs and a trail climb up the gulch to a viewpoint on a

Howarth City Park

curve of Olympic Boulevard, 100 feet above, and to the upper portion of the park. Upper Howarth Park is the more "civilized" section, with grassy expanses, tennis courts, horseshoe pits, and play equipment for kids.

Mukilteo

Facilities: Ferry terminal, fishing pier, groceries, restaurants, stores, bait, boat rentals, gas, marine supplies and repairs
Attractions: Boating, fishing, beach walking

The early Indians called this point of land "Muckl-Te-Oh," meaning "good camping." That this was a favored spot of the local Indians undoubtedly prompted Governor Isaac Stevens to choose it as one of three meeting sites on Puget Sound used for signing the treaty in which the Indians gave up their lands and agreed to live on reservations. Over 2,000 Indians from twenty-two different tribes met here in January of 1855 to be read the Point Elliot Treaty and have their chiefs place their marks on the document. Considering that they relinquished all the territory from Seattle north to the Canadian border and east to the crest of the Cascades in exchange for some meager reservation lands and a monetary pittance, the Indians might now more appropriately call the site "Bamboozle."

A year after the signing of the Point Elliot Treaty, Morris H. Frost, a customs collector from Port Townsend, and J. D. Fowler, who had been running a saloon on Whidbey Island, established a trading post at Mukilteo to exchange flour, blankets, gunpowder, and other white man's goods for the Indian's furs. When reservation lands were finally allotted and the Indians moved onto them, settlers began to establish claims at Mukilteo. By 1875 ten streets had been laid out, and the new town had a modern steam-operated sawmill, salmon saltery, brewery, telegraph station, school, and several taverns and hotels.

By 1910 the town was booming, capitalizing on growth in nearby Everett. A powder mill established here was the largest on Puget Sound, surpassing in size the Dupont Powder Company south of Tacoma. At its peak it turned out 400,000 tons of explosives monthly for shipment throughout the West for use in land clearing, logging, railroad building, and mining. In September of 1930 the town boomed in quite another way, when the powder works was destroyed by a series of shattering explosions and fireworks forcing the temporary evacuation of the town.

Mukilteo Lighthouse

Earlier that same year the lumber mill had closed its doors, and when the vacant mill buildings were burned to the ground eight years later in a spectacular fire, the industrial life of Mukilteo came to a resounding end. Today the town leads a quiet life as a suburb of Everett and a terminal for the ferry to Whidbey Island.

Mukilteo is reached by turning off I-5 at Exit 189 and driving west on Highway 526, and then north on 525. The ferry landing is at the bottom of the hill. Turn right to the town's shopping area, or left at the bottom of the hill to the state park.

The Mukilteo lighthouse, first manned in 1906, is west of the ferry terminal, next to the state park. The lighthouse, with its handmade lens, dating from 1858, is open to public tours Saturdays and Sundays, noon to 4:00 P.M.

The shore below the railroad tracks can be walked north from Mukilteo for 3 miles to Howarth City Park, or for another 2 miles into Everett. Plan the walk for low tide, when the most beach is exposed. To begin the walk, drive ½ mile east from the ferry terminal past a series of oil storage tanks to a small parking lot and public access. If there is no space for cars here, leave them at the state park and walk the road to the beach access. In early days, before good roads were built inland, it was common to walk the tracks to get to Everett. In ¾ mile Powder Mill Gulch is passed; here was the site of the explosives factory—before it scattered itself all over Possession Sound.

MUKILTEO FISHING PIER

An L-shaped public fishing pier, operated by the Port of Everett, is on the east side of the ferry landing. In addition to fishing it is also a good place to watch the comings and goings of the ferries. The pier can be reached via a walkway angling off from the side of the ferry pier. A nearby boathouse has bait and tackle for sale.

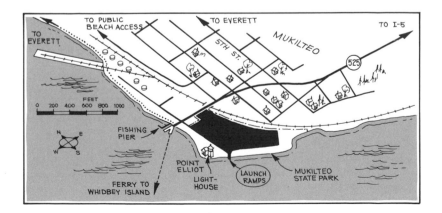

MUKILTEO STATE PARK

Park area: 14 acres; 1,495 feet of shoreline
Access: Land, boat
Facilities: Boat launch (ramp), picnic tables, fireplaces, restrooms, concession stand
Attractions: Boating, fishing, beach walking, scuba diving

This day-use park consists primarily of a three-lane boat launch ramp, with adjoining boarding float, and a large parking lot. When entering the park, turn left—traffic goes clockwise, rather than the expected counterclockwise. Although heavily used, the boat ramp, unfortunately, is considered one of the worst on Puget Sound. Launching is difficult, since the point is exposed to westerly and southwesterly winds. When winds are strong, boaters would be wise to drive north to Everett to launch. The ramp is also difficult to use at low tide because of the very gradual slope at its upper level. About 15 feet beyond the last piling of the boarding float, the ramp drops off sharply.

The nicest part of the state park is the picnic area stretching along the shore south from the launch ramp. Here are tables, fire stands, and a wide gravel beach for sunbathing. The chilly water is only for the brave, or for those rare hot days when even Puget Sound water is inviting. Since the point picks up winds sweeping down Possession Sound, it is a grand spot for flying kites.

PICNIC POINT COUNTY PARK (SNOHOMISH COUNTY)

Park area: 15 acres; 1,200 feet of shoreline
Access: Land, boat
Facilities: Picnic tables, fireplaces, Sani-cans
Attractions: Fishing, swimming, scuba diving

Picnicking is not required, but if you forget the lunch you'll regret it, since you'll want to stay all day. Picnic tables are on a grassy maple-shaded flat, complete with a trickling stream. The sandy beach below fans ever-outward, offering endless possibilities for sunbathing, castle building, Frisbee throwing, or swimming. Scuba divers who explore the seabed, which slopes gently down to 70 feet, find crabs, flounders, skates, sea pens, moon snails, and other sand-loving critters.

The park is midway between Mukilteo and Edmonds. From old Highway 99 north of Lynnwood, turn west on Shelby Road, which in about 1¼ miles crosses Beverly Park–Edmonds Road and becomes Picnic Point Road. Follow this to its end at a parking lot next to the railroad tracks. An elaborate concrete and steel pedestrian bridge crosses the tracks.

Picnic Point is another of the small spits cut off from the world by railroad tracks. For some time, visitors crossed the tracks to reach the park, but several years ago the death of a child who was hit by a train here sparked the building of the overpass.

Picnic Point County Park

NORMA BEACH AND MEADOWDALE

The small communities of Norma Beach and Meadowdale lie on the shore midway between Everett and Edmonds. For anglers, these places are significant because of their proximity to Possession Bar, a huge underwater shelf extending from the southern tip of Whidbey Island. The bar offers year-round fishing for a wide variety of fish, although salmon is the most sought-after prize.

Two commercial boathouses at Norma Beach and Meadowdale have boat rentals, launching, gas, and supplies for anglers. Meadowdale Marina also has a fishing pier (fee). There are no public beaches at either marina.

MEADOWDALE BEACH COUNTY PARK
(SNOHOMISH COUNTY)

Park area: 95 acres; 1,000 feet of shoreline
Access: Land
Facilities: Picnic sites, picnic shelter, restrooms, hiking trail

This jewel-like park, lying between Norma Beach and Meadowdale, was only recently developed and opened to the public. A 1¼-mile hike down the long wooded stretch of Lunds Gulch is required to reach the beach and its adjacent picnic area, although a lower access road and parking area are available for the handicapped.

To reach the main (upper) park entrance, turn west from old Highway 99 at either 148th Street SW or 168th Street SW. Use either street to reach 52nd Avenue West, then follow 52nd to either 152nd Street SW or 160th Street SW. Go west four blocks on either street to 56th Avenue West, which may be used to reach 156th Street SW. In two blocks 156th arrives at the park's upper parking lot.

To reach the handicapped access, leave old Highway 99 at 168th Street SW, and follow it west to 66th Avenue West. Turn north on 66th, then west on North Meadowdale Road to 75th Avenue West. Follow 75th north to the park and the handicapped parking lot.

A kiosk at the upper parking lot has a map of the park and its trail. Just below the parking lot is the upper picnic area—a small, groomed flat with a few trees, but no tables or other facilities. The trail descends through second-growth alder, then switchbacks steeply down to the floor of the gully where the moisture provided by Lunds Gulch Creek and side streamlets promotes growth of cedar, ferns, and salal.

On the floor of the gulch are several old cedar stumps, some up to eight feet in diameter, that have springboard notches—deep grooves cut for the springboards on which loggers stood when cutting the original trees. Most of these huge stumps now nurture new trees growing from their tops.

Meadowdale Beach County Park

The trail breaks into the open a few hundred yards above the beach, and the ranger's residence and lower picnic area are reached. Planks laid across the stream bridge the creek as it flows under the railroad tracks, enabling use of the underpass for beach access. Views are out to the south end of Whidbey Island, and north and south to the boathouses at Norma Beach and Meadowdale.

The sand and gravel beach tapering gently out into the sound is ideal for wading; swimmers should be cautious as there are sudden drop-offs in the water. The park can be reached only by very shallow draft boats, because of the shoal waters.

Edmonds

From its elaborate underwater scuba diving park to its flower beds of blazing color, Edmonds has put a lot of effort into making its waterfront inviting as well as functional. The waterfront complex begins and ends with parks—and even has parks in between. In the center of everything is the ferry terminal, with its giant boats sailing hourly to Kingston on the Kitsap Peninsula. Numerous postcards and travel brochures have carried photographs of this ferry gliding into a scarlet sunset against the black silhouette of the Olympic Mountains.

By water, the Edmonds harbor is 9 nautical miles north of Seattle's Shilshole Bay or 13 nautical miles south of Everett. To drive to Edmonds, leave I-5 at Exit 177, which is signed to Edmonds and the Kingston ferry. Highway 104 (Edmonds Way) goes directly into town. Stay left to avoid ending up in the waiting lanes of the ferry terminal.

A marshland west of the highway, just as the road enters town, is a twenty-three-acre wildlife sanctuary. The marsh was partially filled to build the shopping mall, but fortunately this section was saved in its natural state. The forest of cattails attracts large numbers of red-winged blackbirds.

The Edmonds business district, with its wide range of stores and services, is within walking distance of the waterfront. The small complex on the waterfront has several stores, including one selling fresh seafood. Harbor Square, a larger shopping center west of Edmonds Way (Highway 104) at the foot of Dayton Street, sells everything from marine supplies to lingerie, and includes the town's only hotel. Old Milltown, which has shopping with turn-of-the-century atmosphere, is at Dayton Avenue and 5th Avenue South. Because of the area's popularity with scuba divers, air fills and other needed supplies are available in the town.

Walk two blocks north from Milltown, past a prettily spurting fountain, to find the Chamber of Commerce and Edmonds Museum (open Tuesdays, Thursdays, and Sundays, 1:00 to 4:00 P.M.), just north of the corner of 5th Avenue North and Main Street. The Chamber of Commerce is in an interesting old log cabin.

In 1870 a severe storm chanced to force the canoe of logger George

Brackett onto the beach here. Brackett was so impressed with the spot that he purchased land north of Edwards Point and built a wharf and general store. The town's main claim to historic fame came in 1890 when, falling two short of the seventy-two signatures necessary for filing the petition to incorporate the town, Brackett added the names of two of his oxen, Bolivar and Isaac, to the document. When, thanks to his oxen, the town was incorporated, he became its first mayor.

A more recent source of fame for the town are the many Olympic athletes the town has produced. Twelve Olympic competitors have come

Scuba divers at Edmonds Underwater Park

from Edmonds (perhaps a record for a city of this size); one of the waterfront parks has been dedicated in their honor.

PORT OF EDMONDS MARINA

Facilities: Transient moorage with power and water, diesel, gas, boat launch (sling), restrooms, showers, ice, bait, tackle, groceries (limited), boat charters and rentals, marine supplies and repair, picnic tables, restaurant

Although the guest facilities at the Edmonds marina are small, they are exceptionally nice. The entrance in the center of the rock breakwater, marked with daymarkers and lights, is backed by a second breakwater that channels traffic north and south from the entrance. Most of the 900-slip yacht basin is covered and private. Transient slips are immediately south of the inner breakwater, along the bulkhead north of the fuel dock; power and water are available. Noise from the hoist just south of the fuel dock may jolt boaters out of their slumber when eager fishermen begin to launch their boats just after daybreak. The travel lift and the launching facilities at the south end of the basin are for the use of boats kept in the dry storage areas.

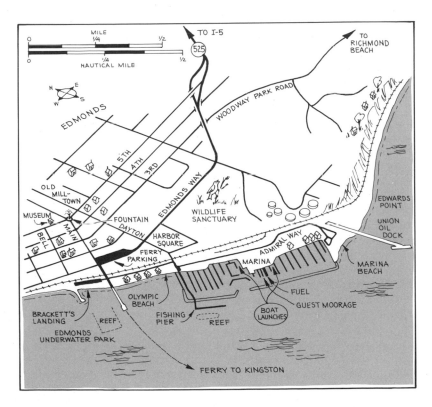

The Port of Edmonds office, on the shore by the fuel dock, has restrooms with showers. Bait, marine supplies, and some limited groceries are available at a small marine store a block to the southeast. Other necessities can be found in downtown Edmonds, within easy walking distance of the marina. A nice little promenade, with picnic tables, benches, and flower boxes, is above the moorages, offering balcony views of the activity below or out across the jetty to the frosty peaks of the Olympics. From here sunset views can be exquisite.

EDMONDS UNDERWATER PARK
(BRACKETT'S LANDING)

Park area: 27 acres; 1,800 feet of shoreline
Access: Land, boat
Facilities: Restrooms, changing rooms, shower, underwater reef,
   tidepools, diver rest floats, informational display
Attractions: Swimming, scuba diving, beach walking, sea lions

The underwater park north of the Edmonds ferry terminal is unquestionably the most popular dive site on Puget Sound. It began accidentally when a 500-foot-long dry dock was sunk here in 1935, long before anyone (except perhaps Jules Verne) had even dreamed of scuba diving. The wreck, with its thickly encrusted marine life, became a focal point for divers, and in 1971 the area was declared a marine preserve. Since that time eight major structures have been added, including two large tugboats, concrete culvert stars, and a reef of earthmover tires. Five diver rest floats are spaced around the park.

Sea lions who have discovered this marine preserve take over the floats in winter and spring. They are a fascinating sight from shore or from the decks of the ferry, but fishermen and scuba divers view them with a jaundiced eye, as they deplete the fish life and pose a threat to divers. By mid-spring most have departed for breeding grounds in California and Mexico.

Boats, including canoes, kayaks, or dinghys are not permitted within the boundaries of the park. Divers arriving by boat can anchor offshore in 30 to 35 feet of water. Future plans call for two mooring buoys to be placed at the outer harbor line.

Since the area is now protected, fish have become quite tame, and divers may see huge rockfish, wolf eels, lingcod, cabezon, and a wide variety of other fish, as well as octopus. The Edmonds Parks and Recreation Department has a brochure available showing a map of the underwater area, and listing regulations and safety precautions.

For nondivers the park is an interesting spot to watch the activity, or at low tide to explore tide pools and marine life on the rock jetty; remember this is a marine refuge and all the plants, animals, and habitat are protected. Parks Department Beach Rangers are at the park during most summer afternoons on which minus tides occur, from two hours before until

Launching a canoe at Edmonds Underwater Park

two hours after low tide. They will provide information about the marine life and beach environment. Groups can schedule lectures by calling the Edmonds parks department. The beach can be walked north for some distance, but it soon narrows to a strip below the rocks of the railroad bed, and at high tide disappears altogether.

PUBLIC FISHING PIER AND OLYMPIC BEACH

Park area: 4 acres; 300 feet of shoreline
Access: Land
Facilities: Fishing pier, restrooms, bait, tackle, snack bar, informational
    displays, picnic tables

The Edmonds fishing pier was the first such facility on Puget Sound to be built exclusively for fishing. It has served as a model for numerous other piers constructed since then. The L-shaped concrete pier begins on the northeast side of the yacht basin, inside the rock jetty, then crosses the breakwater and turns south to follow its outside edge. On the pier are several bait-and-fish-cleaning areas, informational displays, and benches for

Salmon sculpture at Edmonds Public Fishing Pier

watching the action. The lighted pier is open twenty-four hours a day.

A reef of tires has been placed 50 feet offshore from the pier to provide habitat for fish as well as for the marine life they feed on. The pilings of the pier and the rock jetty serve to direct the movement of the fish along the length of the pier to waiting fishermen's hooks. Scuba diving is not permitted in the vicinity of the fishing pier.

On the rock breakwater a school of fanciful salmon glitter and leap in the wind—they are a work of art created from recycled metal scraps such as can lids, forks, and fishing lures.

Olympic Park, named for the town's athletes, is a stretch of manicured grass with picnic tables north of the fishing pier. The soft grass or sandy beach below the bulkhead are ideal for sunbathing or watching the ferries and feeding the city's official bird—the seagull.

MARINA BEACH AND UNION OIL DOCK

Park area: 7 acres; 978 feet of waterfront
Access: Land, boat
Facilities: Picnic tables, fireplaces, children's play structures, Sani-cans, *no water*
Attractions: Paddling, fishing, swimming, scuba diving

At the south end of the Edmonds waterfront, Admiral Way curves around the boat storage sheds and deadends at a gem of a little park. Although the water may be chilly, the sandy beach is so inviting one cannot

Sailboarding in winter off Marina Beach

help but want to wade into the waves. Above the beach is a nice assortment of driftwood to provide seats and backrests for an afternoon of lazing. Grassy mounds next to the parking lot are a favorite spot for flying kites.

There is no drinking water at the park, and the only restrooms are two Sani-cans in the parking lot next to the boat shed. A short road going to the south side of the park provides a spot close to the beach where car-top boats can be launched.

Scuba divers frequently put in here and swim out to explore the old pilings of the Union Oil tanker pier. The bottom drops off rapidly to depths of 100 feet, offering experienced divers an opportunity for deep dives a short distance from shore. Exercise extreme care, and stay under the dock and away from any ships moored alongside. Jagged scraps of metal on the bottom also pose a hazard. The dock is private, and is off limits. The beach south of the dock is park property that is maintained in a natural condition.

2. The Seattle Area

The city of Seattle stretches along the east shore of Puget Sound for over twenty miles, filling shore, bluff, and ravine with residences and commercial enterprises. The town once fronted only on Elliott Bay, but today it has extended so far north and south that it dominates much of Middle Puget Sound, and its skyscrapers and Space Needle have become a navigational landmark from miles away.

Amid the metropolitan sprawl are an array of public facilities and accesses—some sublime, some fascinating, and some deliberately obscure. Here can be seen nearly every facet of the city—historical, natural, recreational, and scenic, as well as workaday.

The Northern Shoreline

RICHMOND BEACH COUNTY PARK (KING COUNTY)

Park area: 40 acres; 900 feet of shoreline
Access: Land, boat
Facilities: Picnic tables, fireplaces, restrooms, changing rooms, water
Attractions: Beachcombing, swimming, scuba diving, tidepools

For a quick getaway on a sunny afternoon from the metropolitan areas along the east shore of Middle Puget Sound, Richmond Beach is the ideal destination—however, if it is a weekend, you may find that hundreds of others had the same idea. Since this is the nicest beach north of Golden Gardens, it is heavily used; but once you've found a place to park your car, the beach has space for a good-sized throng.

To reach the park by land, turn west off Aurora Avenue (Highway 99) onto NW 185th. As 185th heads downhill it becomes NW Richmond Beach Road. At the intersection of 20th Avenue, turn south and follow the road to its end at the park. Drive slowly on the road winding down to the parking lot, as some vicious bumps have been put in the road to discourage speeding.

From the parking lot an asphalt path wanders through a wooded glen where there are some picnic tables and the requisite babbling brook. Beyond here the trail follows an overpass crossing the railroad (from which there is a great view of the sound), and then descends to the beach. The shore is backed by grassy sand dunes and a string of driftwood. Shoal areas on either side of the point are exposed at moderate tides, extending the

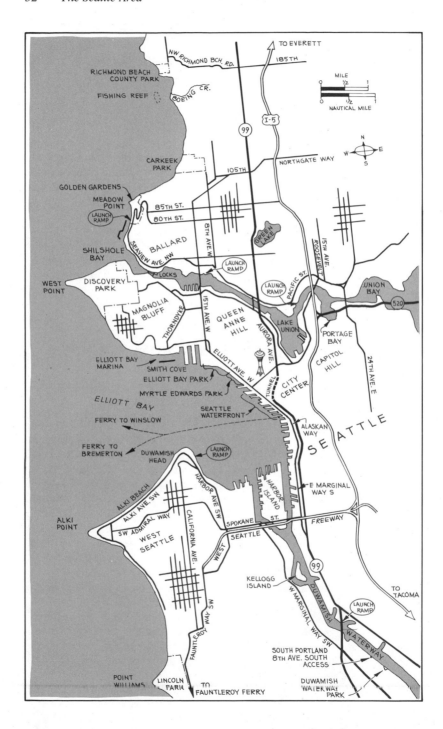

Low tide at Richmond Beach

beach far to the north and south; at extreme low water tidepools and the scattered remains of an old wreck lying just offshore are exposed. The most inviting beachcombing is south, below a wild, 100-foot bluff.

During the 1930s many old sailing ships, reaching the end of their days, were towed to Richmond Beach and burned. Copper and brass were later salvaged from the ashes. Corroded iron fittings frequently uncovered on the beach may be from these old vessels.

The gradually sloping bottom is excellent for beginning scuba divers, who find sea pens, starfish, hermit crabs, and snails. Hand-carried boats can be launched here, although it is a bit of a walk from the parking lot.

BOEING CREEK FISHING REEF

About one mile south of Richmond Beach is the deep, wooded ravine of Boeing Creek. An artificial reef, marked by buoys, has been placed offshore here to improve fishing in the area. The reef is 3½ nautical miles from the launch facilities at either Edmonds to the north, or Seattle's Golden Gardens to the south. There is no upland access.

CARKEEK PARK

Park area: 217 acres; 2,000 feet of shoreline
Access: Land, boat (shallow-draft boats only)
Facilities: Picnic tables, shelters, fireplaces, restrooms, trails, softball
diamond, model airplane field
Attractions: Hiking, nature trail, picnicking, views, beachcombing

Carkeek, the most northerly of Seattle's parks fronting on Puget
Sound, combines two worlds: the saltwater and the forested. The saltwater
offerings are nice enough—even though approach by boat is difficult, the
gently sloping sandy beach is sufficiently ample to hold several hundred
sunbathing, wading, sand-castle-building, or beachcombing people.

Ah, but the forest! The park plunges deeply inland along the canyon
of Piper Creek and the side ravine of Venema Creek. Miles of trails wander
along ravine bottoms and up hillsides in a semiwilderness of conifers,
maple, birch, and ferns. Trails loop about, joining each other or the park
roads. A botanical trail at the southeast end of the ravine has been developed where introduced plants have been cleared out and native ones

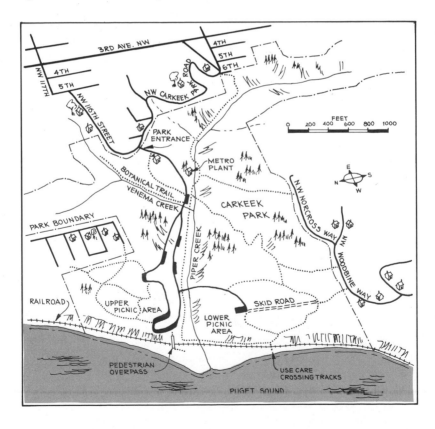

replanted in an attempt to return the area to its natural state.

In the late 1800s the ravine was the site of a sawmill that was fed by the harvest of the surrounding forest. The skid road used to feed logs to the mill site carves the hillside above what is now the lower picnic area of the park. Once the original forest was gone, the land was farmed (remnants of an old orchard can still be found), and a brickyard operated on the south side of Piper Creek. The property was acquired as a park in 1928, although development did not come until some time later.

At one time great numbers of salmon swam up Piper Creek and spawned in the gravel beds of Piper and Venema creeks. A salmon company trapped fish here until the 1930s, but as erosion from civilization's activities covered the gravelly spawning grounds and pollution fouled the water, the salmon runs ceased. A recent effort has been made to restore the creek to its original state and reestablish the salmon runs. Coho salmon were released in the creek in 1980; they are expected to return to spawn in ever-increasing numbers.

To reach Carkeek Park by land, follow any north–south arterial to North 105th Street, then go west on 105th to 3rd Avenue NW. Here turn north and in two long blocks head west again on North 110th Street. In another two blocks, at 6th Avenue NW, find the head of the Piper Creek trail across the street from a shopping center parking lot. To reach the park's entrance, continue driving straight ahead, winding ¾ mile down the steep,

The beach at Carkeek Park

twisting curves of NW Carkeek Park Road to a road heading left into the park. A bit farther down is a small parking area beside a sign identifying the park features and trails; this is the start of many of the park trails.

The beach is reached from the large parking lot on the northwest side of the ravine, where a pedestrian overpass crosses the railroad tracks. On a day with a good breeze, it offers excellent kite flying, or maybe just a pleasant rest against the driftwood logs below the railroad tracks, enjoying the sun and salt breeze.

In recent years the parking lots have been a popular gathering-ground for rowdy young gangs. Parking spaces have been restricted to cut the vehicle capacity, and stricter law enforcement has (one hopes) restored the park to a place to be enjoyed by all for its natural attractions.

Shilshole Bay

GOLDEN GARDENS

Park area: 95 acres; 3,850 feet of shoreline
Access: Land, boat
Facilities: Picnic tables, fireplaces, picnic shelters, restrooms, concession stand, bathhouse, children's play equipment
Attractions: Beachcombing, swimming (no lifeguard), wading, boating, paddling, fishing, boardsailing, scuba diving, birdwatching

In summer, during sunny weather, hordes of Seattle sun-worshipers are lured to Golden Gardens. For over eighty years the beaches at Meadow

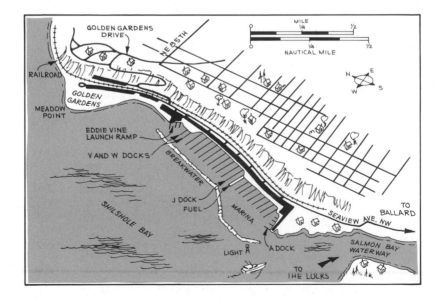

Golden Gardens

Point, north of Shilshole Bay, have seen a succession of youths engaged in the courting rituals of the time, picnickers on family outings, and mothers tending toddlers enthralled with building fantasies in the sand.

Named in 1907 by its owners, Harry and Olive Treat, the beach was then the terminus of a trolley line that offered city dwellers a weekend salt-air retreat—surely it was only coincidence that the route passed through adjoining areas of prime real estate huckstering. A shipyard operated here until 1913. The land was acquired by the city for a park in 1923.

The park is split by railroad tracks; to the east is a wooded sidehill threaded by trails, while west of the tracks is the marvelous sandy beach for which Golden Gardens is so well known. The ¾-mile-long beach is an outward-curving, golden strand of sand topped by silvered driftwood. Icy Puget Sound waters, flowing over the shallow bottom, warm in summer to temperatures pleasant enough for swimming and wading.

The park has two entrances—an upper one at the top of the bluff, and a lower one at the south end of the shore. To reach the upper entrance, take nearly any north–south arterial to NE 85th Street; turn west and follow 85th to 32nd Avenue NW. Here turn north and follow serpentine Golden Gardens Drive NW down to the park; the upper picnic area is passed along the way.

For the lower entrance, find your way to NW Market Street, the main east–west thoroughfare through Ballard, and follow it west past the locks, where it first becomes NW 54th Street, then Seaview Avenue NW. Continue on Seaview as it curves around Salmon Bay past the Shilshole Bay Marina to terminate in the lower parking lot at Golden Gardens, just above the beach. A second large parking lot is located above the railroad tracks off Golden Gardens Drive NW.

Although the beach throng in itself may be enough entertainment for the day, there's also the stream of boats in and out of the north entrance to the marina, the tug and freighter traffic on the sound, and the rugged peaks of the Olympic Mountains. Fly a kite, launch a sailboard, watch a sailboat race, or just wander to the north end of the park and hunker in the driftwood and beach grass for a tan and a semblance of solitude.

It's even a nice place to visit on a blustery winter day when the beach crowd has departed and the bite of wind across the sand brings refreshing memories of our common saltwater origin. Take along binoculars to watch for loons, black brant, and other seabirds on their migratory routes.

EDDIE VINE BOAT LAUNCH

Facilities: Boat launch (ramp), bait, concession stand, fishing pier

Immediately south of Golden Gardens on Seaview Avenue NW is the Eddie Vine boat launch ramp, a 95-foot-wide asphalt ramp with boarding floats along either side. It is busy year-round as a launch point for the hoards of anglers plying the sound. There is ample parking for about 100 cars and trailers in two large lots north of the ramp. A concession stand/bait shop is located just south of the ramp. The wavebreak at the north side of the launch area has a walkway on top to allow it to be used as a fishing pier.

SHILSHOLE BAY MARINA

Facilities: Transient moorage with power and water, diesel, gas, propane, boat launch (cranes, hoist), groceries (limited), ice, fishing piers, bait, tackle, marine supplies and repairs, dry storage, pumpout station, restrooms, showers, laundry, tidal grid, snack bar, restaurants, shops

The vast boat "parking lot" on the north shore of Seattle is a certified tourist attraction, agleam with fiberglass, mahogany, teak, chrome, aluminum, and acres of bright blue canvas. It's the place to bring visitors to show them a little of what boating on Puget Sound is about, or the place for the locals to go to dream about their first boat—or their next one.

Shilshole Bay Marina is the second largest saltwater moorage on Puget Sound, surpassed only by the Port of Everett Marina. A multiyear waiting list for permanent moorage attests to its popularity. Permanent moorage is not the only attraction, as the marina also offers full services for

Shilshole Bay Marina

visiting boaters, as well as nautical-related shops, and restaurants with spectacular views through a forest of aluminum masts in the basin to profiles of distant Olympic peaks.

The marina has provided moorage to Seattle residents and visitors for over thirty years. The U.S. Army Corp of Engineers started work on the enclosing breakwater in 1957; the marina itself was built in several stages by the Port of Seattle over a period of twenty years. Today it has nearly 1,500 permanent slips and about 75 transient moorages, plus areas for dry storage and small centerboard sailboats.

By land, Shilshole Bay is reached by following the main street through Ballard, NW Market Street, west past the locks. The street becomes NW 54th, and then Seaview Avenue NW. The marina lies one mile beyond the locks. A huge parking lot has space for over 1,400 vehicles; some areas are restricted to tenant parking.

From Shilshole Bay, boat entrances to the marina are located at either end of the 4,400-foot-long rock breakwater fronting the yacht basin. The controlling depth in the channel behind the breakwater is 15 feet, and 10 feet in the area of the moorages. Guest moorage is located alongside the central pier inboard of the fueling area. During summer months some slips on J dock are also available for guest moorage. Check with the marina office in the administration building regarding transient moorage.

There is also limited transient moorage at each end of the marina: at the north end, moorage is available along the north side of V and W docks, and at the south end along the head of A dock and at a small float between A and B docks. A self-registration station for boats using the south moorages, or persons using the adjoining mast repair area, is located at building M-7 at the head of A dock. A boat repair yard with hoists is also located here. Six small buildings with restrooms and showers are located along the parking area; the one above L dock also has laundry facilities. A tidal grid at the head of V dock is available for bottom painting and repair, by advance arrangement at the marina office.

Most of the marina shops, restaurants, and facilities are located in the administration building near the center of the marina. Fuel, groceries, supplies, and a pumpout station are at the end of the central pier between I and J docks. For visitors arriving by boat, the Metro bus runs at regular intervals along Seaview Avenue. The Ballard district, with dozens of shops and services, is a few minutes' ride away; downtown Seattle is a little farther.

Walk the promenade along the bulkhead at the head of the docks and choose the boat of your dreams from those tethered at the moorages below; however, except for guest docks, all are locked and accessible only by tenants. Fishing is permitted from the end section of A dock and from the pier forming the wavebreak at the far north end of the marina, south of the launch ramps (once it is repaired).

Salmon Bay and the Lake Washington Ship Canal

The transition from salt to freshwater, from tidal to nontidal, and from the outer shores to the heart of the city takes place in a 6-mile-long, east–west channel dividing Seattle in two. The shores of the Salmon Bay Waterway and Lake Washington Ship Canal are heavily industrialized, with dry docks, shipbuilders, marine repair centers, fuel docks, and a host of other commercial ventures dominating the shoreline, with occasional breaks for private moorages, restaurants, and some public street-end parks. The Fremont Cut, at the eastern end of the ship canal, tapers to a narrow channel bordered with tree-lined concrete bulkheads before it ducks under the Fremont Bridge and opens up to the expanse of Lake Union.

The channel is a treat to travel by water, with close-up views of the bustling, working waterfront. Tugs, fishing boats, crab boats, fish-processing boats, Coast Guard vessels, and barges are crammed hull-to-hull. A Coast Guard buoy tender can usually be seen along the south shore, about ¼ mile east of the locks. Crab traps and other supplies stacked on wharfs await loading onto barges and crabbers headed for Alaska. A homey touch is added by an occasional live-aboard boat, with a tattered

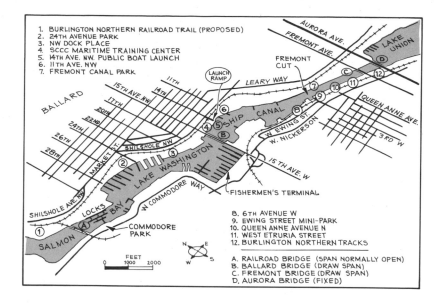

1. BURLINGTON NORTHERN RAILROAD TRAIL (PROPOSED)
2. 24TH AVENUE PARK
3. NW DOCK PLACE
4. SCCC MARITIME TRAINING CENTER
5. 14TH AVE. NW. PUBLIC BOAT LAUNCH
6. 11TH AVE. NW
7. FREMONT CANAL PARK

8. 6TH AVENUE W
9. EWING STREET MINI-PARK
10. QUEEN ANNE AVENUE N
11. WEST ETRURIA STREET
12. BURLINGTON NORTHERN TRACKS

A. RAILROAD BRIDGE (SPAN NORMALLY OPEN)
B. BALLARD BRIDGE (DRAW SPAN)
C. FREMONT BRIDGE (DRAW SPAN)
D. AURORA BRIDGE (FIXED)

lawn chair on deck, a potted evergreen, and a row of bright geraniums.

The canal began in 1871 as a gleam in the eye of the U.S. War Department, which conducted a search throughout the Pacific Northwest for a naval station site for ship repair and resupplying. One prime candidate was Lake Washington, which had the advantages of being protected from enemy naval forces, close to coal supplies from mines just east of the lake, near the terminus of proposed intercontinental rail lines, and adjacent to the area's largest population center—the growing little community of Seattle.

A survey identified several possible locations for a navigable channel and set of locks that would join the nontidal waters of Lake Washington to the tidal waters of Puget Sound. One was on the lake's natural outlet via the Duwamish River to the south. Other routes anticipated a cut through the narrow strip of land between Portage Bay and Union Bay in order to join Lake Washington to Lake Union. From Lake Union, canal routes were proposed either: (1) at Lake Union's natural outlet through Salmon Bay to Shilshole Bay, (2) through Salmon Bay and then south to Smith Cove on Elliott Bay, or (3) from the south end of Lake Union around the southeast side of Queen Anne Hill to the north end of Elliott Bay. The last route seemed the most feasible, since the others would require major dredging in long, shallow outlet coves.

In the end, Lake Washington lost out entirely as the location for the naval station, as Port Orchard on the west side of the sound was chosen instead. City fathers had been set afire by the commercial value of such a canal, however, and continued to push for its construction. For some time little was accomplished other than the carving of a shallow flume permit-

Opening the Fremont Bridge

ting logs to be floated from Lake Washington to Lake Union and Salmon Bay. In 1894 Congress authorized funds to deepen Salmon Bay; the route of the canal was finally cast.

Progress stalled until 1910, when funds were finally authorized for construction of a set of two masonry locks. Chief among the promoters of the canal was the eloquent and convincing officer who headed the local district of the Corps of Engineers, Col. Hiram M. Chittenden, for whom the locks are now named. Construction was begun in November of 1911, and in 1916 the cut was completed between Portage Bay and Lake Washington, lowering the latter by almost nine feet, and affecting the flow of several rivers at its former drainage to the south. The locks began operating that same year, and on July 4th of 1917 were dedicated with proper pomp and circumstance.

The channel is crossed by six bridges. Two are high, fixed spans, the other four are draw bridges that must be opened for sailboats or ships exceeding the clearance. Moving from west to east, measuring from the water to the center of the spans, the Ballard Bridge has a clearance of 45 feet, the Fremont Bridge has 30 feet, the University 44 feet, and the Montlake 46 feet. Boats lacking clearance may request the bridge be raised by sounding a horn blast of one long and one short. The bridge tender will return this signal to indicate his intent to open the bridge. A return signal of four or more short blasts indicates there will be a delay in the bridge opening, either because of time-of-day constraints, emergency vehicle traffic, vehicular traffic build-up from a recent opening, or because the bridge tender wants to group other approaching boat traffic for a single opening.

Bridges will not be opened for recreational vessels on weekdays between the commuting hours of 7:00 and 9:00 A.M. and 4:00 and 6:00 P.M. The bridges are not regularly manned between 11:00 P.M. and 7:00 A.M. Vessels requiring bridges to open during this latter time period must contact bridge operations by telephone at 386-1201, or on marine VHF channel 13, and a bridge tender will be dispatched. (This radio channel may also be used if it is necessary to contact the bridge tender during other hours as well, but it should not be used to schedule routine openings.)

In recent years, traffic congestion caused by frequent bridge openings has triggered experiments limiting the number of openings per hour. If these experiments prove acceptable to both marine and vehicular traffic, these rules may become the accepted method of operation in the future.

The Montlake Cut also has red/green marine traffic lights at either end. When commercial boat traffic such as log booms, which may fill most of the channel, approach the cut, the lights will turn red, and all other approaching traffic must stand clear and not enter the channel until the light again turns green.

HIRAM M. CHITTENDEN LOCKS

Access: Land, boat
Facilities: Boat locks, restrooms, museum, gardens

The locks are the best free show in town, with every year over a million visitors watching the tos and fros of commercial tugs, barges, fishing boats, tour boats, military vessels, and hordes of recreational craft. Although there are other locks in the United States larger than these, none handle more vessel traffic. The locks are in operation continuously; however, the best boat-watching is on the weekend during good weather. To view a combination carnival and comedy-of-errors, come to watch at the end of a three-day summer weekend.

The lock complex, which is operated by the U.S. Army Corps of Engineers, consists of two parallel locks—the larger 825 feet long and 80 feet wide, and the smaller 150 feet long and 28 feet wide. Both are capable of lifting boats a vertical distance of 6 to 26 feet, depending on the level of the tide on the saltwater side. To the south of the small lock is a spillway dam constructed to control the level of the water in Lake Washington and the navigational channel.

The locks are on the southwest side of Seattle's Ballard district; to reach them, follow NW Market Street west. As the arterial curves and becomes NW 54th Street, the entrance to the locks is obvious on the left. A parking lot is along some abandoned railroad tracks, just outside the gate.

At the entrance to the grounds is the Carl S. English, Jr., Ornamental Gardens, a seven-acre arboretum containing both native and exotic trees, shrubs, and flowers. In spring, the rhododendrons and azaleas add a swath of bright color to the nautical scene. A tiered, lawn is designed as a spot for watching the lock traffic, and perhaps enjoying a midday picnic.

A visitor center adjacent to the gardens features displays on the history and operation of the locks, and the Pacific Northwest role of the Corps of Engineers. Visitor center hours are 11:00 A.M. to 5:00 P.M., Thursday through Monday, with guided walks conducted weekends at 2:00 P.M. For groups, guided tours may be arranged with two weeks' advance notice. People arriving at the locks by boat are not permitted to leave their vessels to go ashore, and those on shore may not board boats.

Going Through the Locks. Taking a boat through the locks is an experience every boater should have at least once. The first time through, try to schedule your trip during midweek to avoid the confusion and mob scenes prevalent on weekends and holidays. During the latter periods lock attendants have their hands full trying to bring order to the chaos of boats approaching the lock, many manned by crews of questionable experience and sobriety. Passage time is claimed to be about twenty-five minutes for the large locks, and ten minutes for the small ones, but additional time will be spent waiting for the locks to open, waiting for other vessels to be loaded once you are inside, and waiting for other boaters (surely not yourself!) to untangle their lines and figure out how to tie up.

The following directions should make a trip through the locks less harrowing—and perhaps even fun.

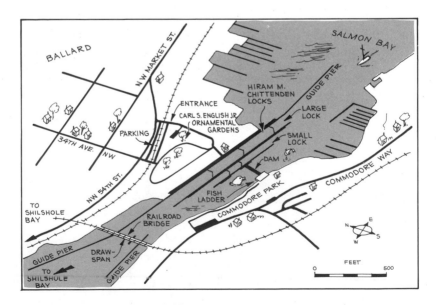

Filling the large locks

Preparations: Boaters planning to go through the locks are expected to have two lock lines, each at least 50 feet long, with a 12-inch eye spliced in one end of each. These will be needed if you are directed alongside the wall in the large lock. Shorter lines will suffice for the small lock or rafting in the large lock; however, you are rarely sure which lock you will be entering or how you will be tied up.

As you approach the locks, ready your lines and tie ample fenders on both sides of the boat. The number of fenders needed depends on the size of your boat and how much you prize its shiny surfaces.

Waiting. Stay well clear of either lock when the red entry light for that lock is lit. Boats waiting for a locking may temporarily tie up to the wooden guide piers outside the locks, or drift about well back from the lock entrances. Be courteous, and maintain your relative place among the group of boats awaiting the locking, or run the risk of dirty looks, profanity, flying objects, or worse from boats you attempt to bypass.

Locking Through. Rule Number One: PAY ATTENTION to the lock attendant! The speed limit for entering the locks is 2½ knots or slower.

When the green light indicates the lock is available for entering, motor slowly and under control, in the order of arrival, and follow the lock attendant's directions for positioning your boat. Government vessels and commercial vessels such as tour boats, tugs, or fishing boats, take precedence over recreational ones; the lock master may direct you to hold off until they are loaded, or he may direct very large pleasure boats to come in first, out of turn, in order to secure them against the wall. Log rafts are loaded last.

The Small Lock. In the small lock, bollards, identified by number, are located on top of a floating wall that accompanies the boats up and down during the locking. Lock attendants will assist you in securing your boat when approaching from freshwater, but when approaching from saltwater, you must be prepared to pick up by yourself the numbered bollards you are directed to.

Once your lines are fastened to the bollards, secure the other ends to your boat cleats and relax as the gates are closed and the lock is filled with water or emptied; however, you should stay alert, in case the floating walls hang up. When the gates are reopened, you will be given directions for casting off and leaving.

The Large Lock. In the large lock, boats are generally rafted several deep, with larger boats placed alongside the wall. Long lock lines are required for the boats against the wall. Attendants will secure the shore end of lines for you. When approaching from freshwater, toss the 12-inch-eye end of each lock line to the attendants; they will put the eye around a bollard. When you are approaching from saltwater, the attendants will drop you light ropes to attach to the eye-end of your lock lines so they may be hauled up. Once secured, immediately check the opposite side of your boat to assist boats directed to raft off you.

If you are rafting off another boat, you can secure your lines and enjoy the ride up or down; however, if you are against the wall with your lines attached to the shore bollards, you will have to man your lines and pay them out or take them in as necessary. In this situation, secure your lines when you first tie up, but when the gates are closed and the lock master announces the lock is about to be filled or drained, loosen the lines, leaving a single loop around the cleat. Adjust the slack in the line, using the cleat for leverage; DO NOT attempt to do this by simply holding the line in your hand, especially if you have boats rafted off you. On any but the smallest boats it will be necessary to have one person available to handle each line.

Filling or Emptying the Lock. After the lock is loaded, the gates will close and water will enter or be drained. During this time there can be dangerous currents and undertows in the lock, and boats may swing around a bit. DO NOT put hands or legs over the side of the boat between the hull and the wall, or between the hulls of two boats. When the gates reopen, the boats close to them will experience a bit more turbulence.

Outside the Locks. One caution for sailboats: the railroad bridge at the west end of the locks is normally open, but it closes as trains approach. Clearance under it is 43 feet at mean high tide, sailboats with taller masts

Sea lions near the fish ladder

will be trapped between the bridge and the locks until the train has passed and the bridge has reopened. Also, if you value your mast, do not be so intent on making a locking or heading out to the sound that you fail to notice the bridge is down.

The U.S. Army Corps of Engineers has a brochure, "Guidelines for Boaters," which has some additional tips on negotiating the locks.

THE LAKE WASHINGTON SHIP CANAL FISH LADDER

Facilities: View areas, restrooms

Since the inland freshwater lakes and streams were vital spawning grounds for over a third of a million salmon and seagoing trout, a fish ladder was incorporated into the original design of the locks. It proved only moderately successful, as the flow through it was freshwater, rather than the mixture of fresh- and saltwater that seems more attractive to fish. The ladder was replaced in 1976 with a new design that included an appropriately salty blend.

The present ladder consists of twenty-one steps, or weirs, that allow fish to move gradually up the grade. A viewing gallery with windows into a portion of the ladder is located along its south side; displays in the gallery identify the various species of fish and explain their migration cycles and the operation of the ladder. Salmon can be seen from June through November, steelhead and cutthroat trout from September through February. The gallery may be reached from the grounds of the locks by crossing the lock gates and the walkway below the dam, or from adjoining Commodore Park.

In recent years a group of sea lions has turned the fish ladder into a briny delicatessen, making a substantial dent in the incoming flow of spawning fish. Concern over depleting runs has triggered an ongoing battle between the Wildlife Department and the sea lions, who are by law a protected species. So far there has been limited success in frightening or luring them away from a free lunch. Visitors (at least those who aren't fishermen) enjoy watching the cavorting sea lions as much as they do viewing the salmon and trout.

COMMODORE PARK

Park area: 6 acres; 1,200 feet of shoreline
Access: Land, boat (small boats only)
Facilities: Restrooms, benches, fire stand
Attractions: Fishing, picnicking, viewpoint, paddling

The fish ladder and locks may be approached from the south side of the canal via Commodore Park, a pretty little park that also provides fishing, picnicking, and ready access for launching hand-carried boats into the saltwater below the locks.

To reach Commodore Park, at the south end of the Ballard Bridge

Kayaker at Commodore Park

head west on West Emerson Place. Pass Fishermen's Terminal and turn north on 21st Avenue West. In two blocks 21st bends west and becomes Commodore Way. The park is on the right in ½ mile.

Stairs lead down to the waterfront promenade; concrete ramps offer easy handicap access. An expansive set of concrete steps drops down to water's edge. Hand-carried boats may be put in here. The concrete walkway heads eastward along the lock spillway to the fish ladder. Near the ladder a series of grassy tiers spill down from the park's loading area to the walkway, forming platforms for viewing the locks traffic, watching feeding sea lions; they also offer a great place for kids to roll and tumble.

Because of the proximity of the fish ladder, this area has particular fishing restrictions. Regulations are posted here and are noted in the pamphlet of sport fishing regulations published by the state Department of Fisheries.

24TH AVENUE PARK

Facilities: Dock

A collapsed and moldering dock, just east of the locks on the north side of the Lake Washington Ship Canal, has recently been reconstructed by the Ballard Neighborhood Coalition, a group of community volunteers. The sturdy, newly-restored, 300-foot-long dock lies off NW Market Street, at the end of 24th Avenue NW, between a marine repair company and a large waterfront restaurant. It is frequently visited by both tour boats and private boaters, who take advantage of its proximity to the heart of Ballard. The shops, restaurants, and historic sites of downtown Ballard are just a stroll away. It is also a fine spot to feed ducks and gulls, or to watch maritime activity on the channel. Fishing is not recommended due to industrial pollution.

FREMONT CANAL PARK

Access: Land
Facilities: Benches, deck, shelter
Attractions: Fishing, sightseeing, mural

An unobtrusive little gem, this mini-park consists of a block-long steel deck just above the concrete bulkhead along the edge of the Fremont Cut. A continuous bench has a small, covered shelter over one end to offer respite from Seattle mists. On the back wall of the shelter a large ceramic tile mural depicts how this spot must have looked in 1875 when, instead of the canal, tiny Ross Creek flowed from Lake Union through the infant towns of Fremont, Ross, and Ballard to reach Salmon Bay. A second, smaller ceramic tile mural by the same artist, Paul Lewing, decorates the back side of the shelter wall.

Parking for a dozen cars can be found next to the railroad tracks at the corner where 2nd Avenue NW turns southeast to become Canal Street

North. Walk across the tracks and follow the path to the stairs and handicap ramp leading down to the deck. Spend a quiet hour feeding ducks, geese, and gulls, wetting a fish line, or enjoying the boats. When locks disgorge boats from their freshwater side, traffic is especially concentrated.

The narrow swath of lawn between the tracks and the canal continues southeast for another three blocks to the abutments of the Fremont Bridge. The 8-foot-high bank down to the canal, steep and mostly overgrown, has a few scramble paths down for views of the canal traffic.

EWING STREET MINI-PARK

Facilities: Benches, viewing platform
Attractions: Fishing, sightseeing, picnicking

Directly across the cut from the Fremont Canal Park is another water's edge mini-park. The entrance is at the junction of 3rd Avenue West and West Ewing Street, by Royal Brougham Pavilion, the fieldhouse for Seattle Pacific University. A large parking area extends east from the street junction, between the pavilion and the water.

The narrow grass strip above the concrete bulkhead, spotted with benches, is a picnic lunch site par excellence, attested to by the many free-loading ducks and geese at the site. A wooden platform on top of a Metro pumping station provides an elevated view of boat traffic in the canal.

Just outside the entrance to the park, a lawn adjacent to the Metro Seattle Environmental Laboratories is also open to the public. A kiosk here describes the field and laboratory activities of the facility. The 30-foot-long concrete float in front of the labs is used by the university crew; public use requires prior permission from the school.

FISHERMEN'S TERMINAL

Facilities: Restaurants, fish market, marine supplies, marine repairs, (all
      moorage is commercial)
Attractions: Sightseeing

Fishermen's Terminal *IS* Seattle's maritime legacy—no phony salty "ambience" here; this is the real, working, fishing fleet. The facility lies ¾ mile east of the locks on a small bay at the southwest end of the Ballard Bridge. Whether approaching by car from the north over the bridge, or from the south via 15th Avenue West, you'll spot the well-marked exit for the terminal.

The docks are filled with weathered fishing boats and equally weathered fishermen mending nets and making other repairs to boats and rigging. The inner floats, which have changed little since the original terminal was dedicated in 1913, are occupied by gillnetters and trawlers; the newer, outer docks hold the larger purse seiners.

Renovations in 1988 added new net sheds, upgraded vessel and equipment storage, refurbished the retail and office areas, and added 600 feet to

Monument in memory of fishermen

the large northwest dock to accommodate huge factory trawlers that have recently joined the Alaskan pollock fishing fleet. This remodeling was viewed warily by older fishing boat owners, fearful that the working nature of the terminal would succumb to gentrification and tourism. So far the Port of Seattle has taken great pains to see that the terminal continues primarily to serve the fishing fleet rather than sightseers—which makes it all the more interesting to sightseers.

The main building has a restaurant overlooking the boating activity, and a cafe and tavern that retain the ambience of the older terminal. Benches around a small grass and concrete enclave just west of the main terminal appeal to a leisurely brown-bag luncher on sunny days. A building just west of the main entrance to the terminal houses a fish market—one can hardly find a place with fresher fare!

With the renovation of the terminal, a sculpture was added to honor the memory of Seattle-area fishermen who have died at sea; their names are listed on an adjoining series of plaques. The 30-foot-high concrete pillar is topped with a bronze fisherman bringing in a catch; a cast bronze bas-relief encircling the base of the sculpture shows thirty-two different marine animals, ranging from salmon to octopus and crab.

OTHER PUBLIC ACCESSES ON SALMON BAY AND THE LAKE WASHINGTON SHIP CANAL

A number of small spots along the shores of Salmon Bay and the ship canal offer some limited accesses to the water. They are described here going from west to east, first along the north shore of the channel, then along the south shore.

Burlington Northern Railroad Trail. After an acrimonious press battle in 1988, the City of Seattle and the Burlington Northern Railroad agreed in principle that the old railroad right-of-way along the northern shoreline would be preserved for a future extension of the Burke-Gilman Trail to Shilshole Bay, whenever rail use of this section of track is discontinued. No firm time frame has been established for this to take place.

NW Dock Place. A reasonably usable street-end access can be found where NW Dock Place and 20th NW join Shilshole Avenue NW, about two blocks west of the Ballard Bridge. The street drops to water level between a pair of private moorages; hand-carried boats can be launched here. The street end has parking space for a few cars, with a one hour limit, however.

SCCC Maritime Training Center. On the north side of the canal, just east of the Ballard Bridge on Shilshole Avenue NW is a Maritime Training Center operated by Seattle Central Community College. The beach at the center is open to public access during college operating hours. A small lagoon rimmed with plantings has a picnic table on shore, and a couple more on a small dock.

Crab boats and crab traps along the Lake Washington Ship Canal

Unfortunately, picnic lunches draw moochers—wall-to-wall Canada geese frequently crowd the area, begging for a handout. Sanitation is not one of their strong points, so bring something to cover the benches if you plan to sit down.

A dirt street end on the west side of the lagoon, underneath the Ballard Bridge, leads to the water's edge. Hand-carried boats can be put in here; some limited parking is nearby.

14th Avenue NW Public Boat Launch. The only public boat launch on this section of the canal is on the north side, one block east of the SCCC Maritime Training Center, east of the Ballard bridge. From NW 45th Street turn south on 14th Avenue NW and in one block, at the intersection of 45th and Shilshole Avenue NW, find a two-lane asphalt launch ramp with a 25-foot-long loading dock along its west side. Note that the dock along the east side of the ramp is private. Parking is very limited in the immediate vicinity, and only street-side parking is available in the adjoining few blocks.

11th Avenue NW. The only other marked public access on the north side of the canal is at the end of 11th Avenue NW, west of the boat launch. The adjoining commercial boat yards have moored boats and a barge in this waterway, leaving skimpy space for public use. Although a hand-carried boat could be launched here, and adjoining street-end parking exists, this is not the best of launch sites. All other street ends on this side of the canal terminate at commercial wharfs or buildings.

6th Avenue West. On the south side of the canal, in the vicinity of Seattle Pacific University, a street end offers a small spot for getting down to the water and possibly launching hand-carried boats. The stub of 6th Avenue West, just past West Ewing Street, ends in a no-bank water access between a couple of private floats. Street-side parking can be found in the vicinity. West from here the shoreline is heavily industrial, and private, all the way to the Ballard Bridge.

Queen Anne Avenue North. Just east of the athletic field behind Seattle Pacific University's Royal Brougham Pavilion, a short stub of Queen Anne Avenue North ends in a landscaped path down to a single park bench at water's edge. There is no parking along the street end; park instead along Nickerson. On occasion, modern-day Tarzans tie a heavy rope to branches of overhanging trees to swing out and splash into the canal waters.

The Fremont Cut, seen from the trail along the Burlington Northern tracks

West Etruria Street. A driveway at the junction of West Nickerson Street and West Etruria Street leads into the parking lots for a group of canal-side office buildings. Although the lots are liberally signed as private, the walkway along this entrance is marked as a public access. Park on Nickerson and walk down one block to a triangular bit of grass above the railroad tracks. A few trees, some park benches, a garbage can, and a water fountain define the perimeter of the park. It's a nice spot for a leisurely lunch, a dash of sunbathing, and views of the canal traffic.

Burlington Northern Tracks. A seldom-used spur of Burlington Northern track follows the south side of the canal, from the Ballard Bridge to where it ducks under the Fremont Bridge and heads down the west shore of Lake Union. The right-of-way between the Ewing Street Mini-Park and the Fremont Bridge provides a pleasant path near the water's edge, just above the concrete bulkhead that lines the canal. West of the Ewing Street park, the tracks are a couple of blocks inland. Use care walking the tracks, as they are occasionally used by trains.

Lake Union

Lake Union, which was known to the Indians as "Kah-chung" (small lake), was given its present name in 1854 by pioneer Thomas Mercer, who predicted its future role in joining Lake Washington to Puget Sound. By as early as the 1880s, the lakeshore saw its first industrialization in the form of sawmills feeding on the harvest of cedar and fir from nearby hillsides. Steamers soon carried goods and passengers to new settlements of Fremont, Brooklyn, Edgewater, and Latona along its northern shore. With the opening of the locks and ship canal in 1917, commercial maritime interests quickly took advantage of the new access, and Lake Union soon became a "working lake," with only smatterings of seedy residential houseboats breaking up the industrialized shoreline.

Ensuing years have found an unplanned hodge-podge of uses taking over sections of the lakeshore. Shacky houseboats have been replaced by tony "floating homes." The threat of high-rise condos, locking off large portions of the shoreline, was barely fended off with new and more enlightened zoning, although some multistory office buildings still sprouted along the western side of the lake. Waterfront restaurants, shops, and other gentrification have recently taken over sections of the shoreline. For better or worse, the lake is shifting away from its industrial heritage. The long-range nature of the lake, debated by city fathers ad nauseum, has yet to be clearly defined, and lakeshore usage continues to respond to the pressures and economics of the moment.

Yet, all this diversity yields an exciting, fascinating mix for those visiting the lake, either by land or water. Houseboats, yacht brokerages, marinas, NOAA vessels, office buildings, marine repair, dry docks, shipbuilders, restaurants—all blend in the colorful potpourri of the shore. At night the lake becomes a glittering well, with the lights of surrounding buildings and downtown highrises reflected in the water. Best of all is 4th of July, when the lake hosts a spectacular fireworks display, and hundreds of boats anchor in the lake, while thousands of people watch from shore.

Most of the restaurants lining the shores of Lake Union have guest docks for patrons coming in by boat. Check with a specific restaurant in advance to verify dock availability, then give your guests (and other restaurant patrons) the unique thrill of arriving for your meal by boat.

So much for the shoreline, but what of the center of the lake? It too experiences the schizophrenia of the shoreline. Chartered seaplanes take off and land amidst the comings and goings of sailboats, cruisers, kayaks, canoes, sailboards, tugs towing log rafts, and every other type of craft imaginable.

Every Tuesday evening during summer, this tight waterway experiences the "Duck Dodge," an impromptu sailboat race, open to all comers, that makes a jovial mockery of the more precise and gentlemanly yacht races on Lake Washington and Puget Sound. Confusion—perhaps terror—is the order of the race. The only known "rule" for the race is that if a boat hits a duck it is disqualified.

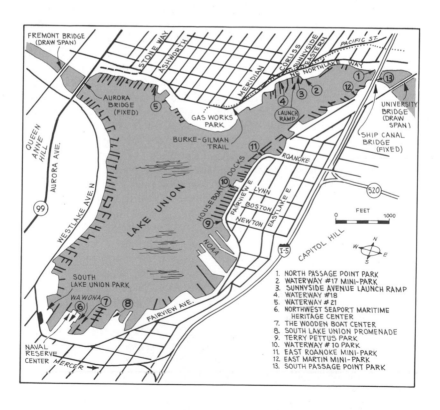

1. NORTH PASSAGE POINT PARK
2. WATERWAY #17 MINI-PARK
3. SUNNYSIDE AVENUE LAUNCH RAMP
4. WATERWAY #18
5. WATERWAY #21
6. NORTHWEST SEAPORT MARITIME HERITAGE CENTER
7. THE WOODEN BOAT CENTER
8. SOUTH LAKE UNION PROMENADE
9. TERRY PETTUS PARK
10. WATERWAY #10 PARK
11. EAST ROANOKE MINI-PARK
12. EAST MARTIN MINI-PARK
13. SOUTH PASSAGE POINT PARK

Lake Union from Gas Works Park

Even non-boat-owners can participate in the lake's aquatic offerings. Several businesses on the lake rent sailboats, sailboards, rowboats, kayaks, and canoes. The depth of the lake is fairly uniform, ranging from 35 to 50 feet. A narrow shoal extending from the peninsula at the north end of the lake, where Gas Works Park is located, is marked by a buoy. A large shoal, also marked by a buoy, is at the southwest end of the lake.

GAS WORKS PARK

Park area: 21 acres
Access: Land, boat (shallow draft)
Facilities: Picnic shelters and tables, play barn, children's play area,
   restrooms, benches
Attractions: Picnicking, kite flying, sunbathing, sightseeing, bicycling,
   walking

This, one of Seattle's premium parks, is a study in the fine craft of turning an eyesore into art. The stark, rusty towers—with their piping, valves, catwalks, tanks, and tall smokestacks that once belched smoke

Flying kites at Gas Works Park

over the landscape—are now seen as an enormous, abstract sculpture. Some cities pay millions to name artists to create such assemblages.

The "park" began as a plant built in 1907 to convert coal to gas for residential use in the vicinity. The coal-conversion process regularly blanketed the area with smoke and soot; this problem, plus other economic considerations, fostered a change of raw material from coal to oil in 1937. The plant remained in service for another twenty years, until pipelines brought cheaper and more plentiful natural gas to the Northwest. The city purchased the abandoned plant and in 1975 converted it to a park.

Although the towers have been fenced off because of safety problems, a large portion of the building housing compressor equipment was retained as a play barn; the giant flywheels, pistons, tanks, and interconnecting piping were cleaned and painted gaudy colors, creating whimsical mechanical creatures, inviting to climb on, over, and through.

The shoreline should be one of the prime swimming beaches in the city, but unfortunately the sediment under the water is so heavily polluted with organic chemicals that wading, swimming, and fishing are prohibited; however, it is a good place to launch a hand-carried boat or raft for a leisurely paddle along the shore.

Queen Anne and Capitol hills bound the lake, forming a natural north–south funnel for winds, guaranteeing the park ideal conditions for flying kites. And fly kites, people do! At nearly any time of the year the skies above the park are laced with fanciful creations: box kites, tiger kites, dragon kites, mylar monsters, and even the basic stick-and-newspaper models.

The park can be reached by turning off the north end of the Fremont Bridge and heading east, or off the north end of the University Bridge and heading west. From either direction, follow NE Northlake Way, which parallels the shore, to the park. The park lies along the route of the Burke-Gilman Trail, and it is heavily visited by cyclists and joggers following the trail.

The park can also be accessed by water via the concrete deck and bulkhead at the extreme south tip of the park. There is no designed docking area, but shallow-draft boats can tie up to the railing that tops the bulkhead. Passing traffic in the lake can make the spot quite bumpy, and nearby waters are rather shallow.

SOUTH LAKE UNION PARK

For years the city has considered several proposals for public parks at the south end of Lake Union. Some were grandiose, others more modest, but all coveted the property occupied by the Naval Reserve Training Center. Recently, through a series of real estate swaps, the city was able to acquire all the property at the southwest corner of the lake—except for the pocket held by the Naval Reserve Center.

Unable to obtain the desired Navy property and under budgetary duress, the city took the least costly route in 1991, and developed South Lake Union Park, which wraps around the Navy property. The grass and park benches of the modest site are fine for sunning or munching a snack after taking in local attractions.

The Northwest Seaport Maritime Heritage Center. A volunteer organization dedicated to the restoration of the historic schooner *Wawona* occupies space between South Lake Union Park and the Naval Reserve Center. Its offices are here, as well as a gift shop, dory displays, and several workshops for people involved with the restoration of the *Wawona*. The three-masted schooner, built in 1897, is moored on the west side of Waterway 4. Volunteers have labored on the project for several years, and the effort will undoubtedly continue for many more.

Originally built to carry lumber, a task she carried out for fifteen years, the vessel was then converted for cod fishing in the Bering Sea. She again saw duty as a lumber barge for the U.S. Army during World War II. Born a sailing vessel, the *Wawona* has never been fitted for engine power throughout her long career. Portions of the vessel not under active restoration are open to public tour; donations are welcome.

The Wooden Boat Center. At the end of Boren Avenue North, a covered wooden pavilion sits just above the dock that houses the Wooden Boat Center. Beneath the pavilion roof are examples of several wooden craft, ranging from Indian canoes to a Bristol Bay fishing boat.

The center itself is a combination museum, classroom in wooden boat construction, and small-boat rental site. In summer, the museum is open noon to 7 P.M. during the week, and 10:00 A.M. to 8:00 P.M. weekends; off-season hours are slightly shortened.

THE HOUSEBOAT COMMUNITY

Although they are not a public facility, the houseboats are such a part of Seattle's inland waterfront that they are looked on as a public treasure. Most of the houseboats are grouped on the east shore of Lake Union and the south shore of Portage Bay; a few are scattered at other spots. The best place to see the houseboats from land is on Fairview Avenue East. Water provides a "front yard" view. These are not RV versions of boats, but bona fide houses that have gone to sea—or lake, in this case.

Houseboats have been on the lake since the early 1900s, when land-built houses were moved onto log rafts. Many of the older houseboats on the lake are still supported by logs, occasionally reinforced by large chunks of high-density Styrofoam. Modern floating homes that are built for this life are on concrete pontoons.

The early houseboats were a disreputable sort—many housed gambling dens and prostitutes. During the 1950s their low rent and funky lifestyle made them the favored housing of students and "hippies." The seventies brought respectability. Prior to that time, sewage from the homes

Houseboats on Lake Union

had drained directly into the lake below. (A favorite saying of houseboaters headed for a plunge in the lake was: "Don't flush, I'm going swimming!") This was eventually recognized as an unsavory practice, and pressure was put on the houseboats to connect to city sewers.

Once their sanitary problems had been resolved, houseboats became "floating homes." With their permanence and respectablity established, and with the increase in the cost of waterfront property, their value skyrocketed. Numerous homes were designed and constructed specifically as floating homes, with architecture rivaling the most posh of land residences; but many of the old houses remain, making the houseboat colony a delightfully colorful mixture of kitsch and class.

LAKE UNION PUBLIC ACCESSES

A number of public street ends and neighborhood parks tucked away along the edges of Lake Union offer a chance for a quiet get-away. They are described here beginning at the north end of the lake and moving clockwise around the shore. Some hold a picnic bench or two, at most. At the least, all offer owners of kayaks or inflatable boats a chance to toss in their vessels and further explore the shoreline. None have restrooms. Public street ends that are high bank, or so brush-infested that no easy access to the water is possible, are not listed here.

North Passage Point Park. This pocket park, lying on the north side of the lake on NE Northlake Way, directly under the I-5 bridge, offers a few picnic tables and arms-length-away views of passing boat traffic. Willows dip gracefully into the water above the shoreline; steps lead down to a water-lapped bulkhead. The north side of the channel is deepest, and the shore below the steps drops off steeply.

Waterway #17 Mini-Park. Just west of the Lakeside Restaurant parking lot at Eastern Avenue North and NE Northlake Way, the shore tapers down to water's edge. A path leads to a gravelled park set with a few benches and tables—an ideal spot for a picnic lunch, wading, or launching a canoe. Parking is available along the north side of Northlake Way.

Sunnyside Avenue Launch Ramp. The only public launch facility on Lake Union for trailered boats is found on the north shore at the intersection of NE Northlake Way and Sunnyside Avenue North. A 45-foot-long wooden dock along the west side of the two-lane asphalt ramp facilitates loading and unloading. Parking for cars and trailers can be found on the north side of Northlake Way. If launching a sailboat, check the mast height; there are overhead power lines at the top of the ramp.

Waterway #18. At the foot of Corliss Avenue North, east of Gas Works Park, dense growth masks a small grass flat above another public waterway. At its west side the brush gives way to a rough roadway leading down to water's edge. A number of boats moor at a long, private float along the

Boat on a marine ways at a Portage Bay shipyard

west edge of the waterway. No amenities here—just a nicely shaded strip of grass with a few bushes at waterline. An ideal spot for an impromptu picnic.

Waterway #21. Marine Logistics Corporation, a shipbuilding company, has improved the shore side of Waterway #21 by building a wooden deck with planters and benches for the public. It is on the north side of the lake, at the intersection of North Northlake Way and Ashworth Avenue North. Here is a chance to view the industrial side of Lake Union, with its busy cranes, tugboats, and floating dry docks. Floats across the outer limits of the waterway prevent any water access to the spot, so it is not possible to launch boats here.

South Lake Union Promenade. The most cosmopolitan of the public accesses is at the south end of Lake Union, east of the Wooden Boat Center. Here a large, new pier holds shops and restaurants. The wooden walkway along the edge of the pier, landscaped with planters of bright flowers, is for public use. The railing along the water has several openings to permit transient boats to tie up and have easy access to the pier.

Terry Pettus Park. This tiny park, landscaped with pines and ivy, is on the east shore of the lake, at Fairview Avenue East and East Newton Street. Stairs lead down to water level, where there is a narrow wooden deck leading out to a concrete float with a swim ladder. The small float and gently sloping beach invite wading or swimming. The park is named for a long-time social activist who led the houseboat community in its struggle for survival in the late 1960s.

Waterway #10 Park. This small park, tucked between the houseboat docks at the intersection of Fairview Avenue East and East Lynn Street is almost a duplicate of Terry Pettus Park. A cluster of pines secludes it from the street. The beach is gentle and sandy, ideal for splashing around or taking a cooling swim on a hot summer day. When the weather is not so nice, mallards abound, begging for a handout.

East Roanoke Mini-Park. Fairview Avenue East is interrupted by a houseboat complex at its junction with East Roanoke Street, but at this corner is a park on a small flat at street level. This portion of the park does not have the float and swimming access that the previous two parks have; however, tucked behind trees to the north of the street end, another section of the park offers benches overlooking a wide channel between two rows of contemporary houseboats.

This is the site of the stillborn over-the-water condominium project that a number of years ago ran afoul of zoning changes in midconstruction. New zoning demanded a water-oriented usage, and after exhausting court challenges, the concrete base platform for the condominum was razed, and the present houseboat community was developed. A small wood float alongside an adjacent restaurant can be used as a temporary moorage if you are visiting the park by water.

East Martin Mini-Park. A street-end waterway on Lake Union between the 3100 and 3200 blocks of Fairview Avenue East is the site of another tiny park, favored by neighborhood folks and the local waterfowl. You may even spot beaver who have taken up residence in the lake. A log bulkhead, small trees, and plantings separate parking from a graveled beachfront that tapers gently into the northeast corner of the lake. Picnic tables rest on a concrete-aggregate pad at the edge of the park.

South Passage Point Park. A companion to its counterpart just across the channel on the north shore, this wide grass slope also lies under the I-5 freeway deck. A few picnic tables dot the park, and concrete steps lead down to a bulkhead at water's edge. This side of the canal is much shallower, making the beach safer for wading than the one on the opposite side. Close-passing boat traffic sparks dreams of yacht ownership; reality is served by the ability to hand-launch small boats.

Portage Bay and the Montlake Cut

Portage Bay is the final link in the chain of waterways between the locks and Lake Washington. At its eastern side is the Montlake Cut, a man-made, concrete-walled canal joining Portage Bay to Union Bay, on the Lake Washington side. The attempt to cut through the neck of land separating the two bays first occurred in 1883, when a small flume was hand-dug in order to move logs from Lake Washington to the mills on Lake Union. Although larger cuts were attempted over the years, all failed, because of insufficient machinery or funds. Only with the federal subsidy for the construction of the locks and Lake Washington Ship Canal was the isthmus finally cut through, causing Lake Washington to be lowered by nine feet.

Today Portage Bay is edged by an eclectic mixture, including the moorages of two large yacht clubs, a city playground, a covey of houseboats, and the lower campus of the University of Washington; a small incursion of marinas, moorages, yacht brokerages, and marine repair businesses are concentrated along the northwest shore, but these may someday succumb to the university's growth.

On the first Saturday in May, Portage Bay plays host to boats celebrating Opening Day of yachting season. Vessels of all types, polished and decorated to a fare-thee-well, gather here, awaiting the noon blast of the Seattle Yacht Club salute cannon, and the following procession through the Montlake Cut, past the reviewing boat of the commodore of the Yacht Club anchored on the east side of the cut. Throngs line the shore to watch the colorful spectacle; an even larger crowd views the parade from boats tied to a long log boom in Union Bay.

PORTAGE BAY PUBLIC ACCESSES

Along the shores of Portage Bay a few public street ends, wedged between private property, provide an opportunity to get down to the water and feed the ducks and geese, watch boating activity, and perhaps swim in warm weather. The southeast corner of the bay is a dense wall of brush and cattail marsh, offering little by land, but giving some opportunity for

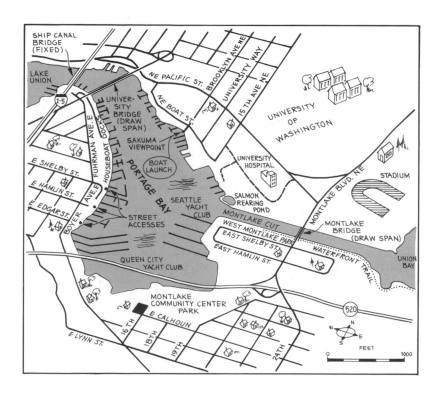

Opening Day of yachting season in the Montlake Cut

paddle exploration amid birds and other water's edge critters. Raccoon can frequently be spotted at dusk; migratory waterfowl gather here in the fall, and ducks and geese nest here in the spring.

East Shelby Street Access. At the corner where Fuhrman Avenue East bends south and becomes Boyer Avenue East, a stub end of intersecting East Shelby Street dead-ends at a small public access with a narrow view across the bay and through the Montlake Cut. Stairs lead down from the street end to a small grass plot bordered by boat and houseboat docks. This is a favorite spot for boat-watching on Opening Day of the yachting season in May. In summer it's a nice place to swim and sunbathe (except for the problem of avoiding droppings from omnipresent Canada geese). Hand-carried boats can easily be launched here. Docks and property on either side of the street end are private; parking is very limited in the immediate area.

East Hamlin Street Access. One block farther south along Boyer Avenue East, a stub of intersecting East Hamlin Street ends at a barricade marked "Street End, No Swimming." Rock stepping-stones lead through shrubbery to a low bank at water's edge. A huge weeping willow leans out over the water, dropping a canopy of branches over half the street end, masking a private little waterside hollow—a secret spot for reading, daydreaming, or perhaps an elfin tryst! The other half of the street end has views across the bay to the Seattle Yacht Club.

East Edgar Street Access. In yet another block, just north of the Queen City Yacht Club, a concrete staircase leads down from Boyer Avenue East through carefully tended flowers and shrubs to another small, grass-covered park. A pair of benches invite a meditative stop, but most views are blocked by the adjacent houseboat and yacht club docks. The shallow water is a favorite spot for summertime wading and swimming. Like other parks along Portage Bay, this is a hangout of ducks and Canada geese, who are a delight to feed, but less than attractive when one wants to find a clean spot to spread a beach towel.

Montlake Community Center Park. A few acres of flat, grassy field atop reclaimed marshes form a park/playfield at the southeast corner of Portage Bay. Most of the shoreline is separated from the soccer and softball fields by thick, brambly marshes. A clearing has been carved through the marsh at the northwest corner of the park, exposing a shallow, open beach for warm weather wading or launching hand-carried boats. The park is on East Calhoun Street, between 16th and 19th Avenues East.

West Montlake Park. Just west of the Seattle Yacht Club, a two-acre lawn fronting the western edge of Portage Bay provides a choice spot for watching the annual boat parade opening yachting season, and the frequent Husky crew races through the cut. A magnificent row of poplar trees lines the grass at water's edge, interspersed with a few benches offering views

Sakuma Viewpoint

over the bay and its busy recreational boating traffic. The gradually tapering beach is a favorite for summer wading and swimming; however, swimmers should use caution, as the beach is unguarded and the heavy boat traffic can be hazardous.

Reach the park by turning east off Montlake Boulevard onto a one-way loop entering the area via East Hamlin Street, and leaving via East Shelby Street. Parking is at a premium along the streets, and may be restricted to residents during times of special activities. The park also marks the western end of the ship canal Waterfront Trail, which heads east from here under the Montlake Bridge.

Brooklyn Avenue NE Mini-Park and Boat Launch (Sakuma Viewpoint). At Boat Street and Brooklyn Avenue NE, just east of a university parking lot, a path leads east to a bulkhead fronting a 40-foot-square grass pocket, masked from the street above by plantings. Trees grow near the shore at either side of the park, and benches line the path above the bulkhead. This is a quiet, secluded spot for lunch and a book, or perhaps sunbathing in season.

At the east edge of the park is a two-lane asphalt road. The launch facility is not adequate for trailered boats, as the surface ends abruptly in rocks a couple feet into the water; the ramp would be adequate for any boat

A fleet of small sailboats being towed through the Montlake Cut

that could be hand-lifted. A sign cautions of rocks and shallow water. Swimming is prohibited.

UNIVERSITY OF WASHINGTON LOWER CAMPUS

The University of Washington campus occupies the north shore of Portage Bay, east from 15th Avenue NE. Most of the waterfront is devoted to oceanographic and fisheries activities. The beautifully landscaped campus is open to the public, and that portion of the shore not occupied by docks and piers is planted with grass and trees fronting the water, offering pleasant spots to relax and share your lunch with the resident mallards.

Just east of the huge, ugly, naval barge, converted several years ago into oceanography classrooms, are the university's fisheries department salmon-rearing ponds. A large circular pond near water's edge serves as a homing pond for university-maintained salmon runs in the fall, for the steelhead run in the winter, and as a rearing pond for young salmon in the spring.

Each May the university releases 150,000 chinook and 60,000 coho salmon from the rearing facilities. The runs are maintained for research and fisheries class projects. Since these salmon are a select breed, and reared in an ideal environment, they generally mature and return to spawn a year earlier than their wild counterparts. The spawning season runs from early October to mid-December; the spawning operation takes place here for two hours each Monday, Wednesday, and Friday starting at 10:30 A.M.

Benches are provided around the edge of the pond for visitors wishing to watch the runs. Fishing is prohibited within 400 feet of the fish ladder leading to the pond.

West from the spawning pond, a wide lawn, once a part of a university golf course, slopes down to the bulkhead above the water. A few benches are shaded by trees; the area is popular for sunbathing, daydreaming about the yachts headed into the Montlake Cut, or cheering on a Husky crew race. A narrow concrete walk tops the bulkhead as it continues beneath the Montlake Bridge to Union Bay. Stairs lead up to street level from either end of the walkway.

Magnolia Bluff

Leaving the freshwater side of Seattle, we return through the locks to Shilshole Bay, saltwater, and the 200-foot-high, handsome bluff that dominates the city shoreline. Although much of Magnolia Bluff is residential, the very best part of the area—the extreme tip—has become a fine, unique park, right in the heart of the city. Here, within a short bus ride from most metropolitan areas, is a grand wilderness for all to enjoy.

DISCOVERY PARK

Park area: 534 acres; 12,000 feet of shoreline
Access: Land, boat (shallow draft)
Facilities: Visitor center, Indian cultural center, hiking trails, bicycle
  paths, nature trail, picnic tables, restrooms, fitness trail, sports fields
  (volleyball, soccer, basketball), tennis courts, museum, children's
  play area
Attractions: Hiking, picnicking, beachcombing, birdwatching, bicycling,
  historical site, lighthouse, nature programs, Seattle Mounted Police
  stables

Discovery Park, the largest and most choice of Seattle's city parks, is also one of its newest. For nearly ninety years the park was locked up as a military reservation, which explains why such prime real estate on Magnolia Bluff went undeveloped for residential or commercial use. Like numerous parcels of land along the sound, the property became available for public use after the government no longer needed it.

In 1894 Magnolia Bluff was one of eleven sites designated as potential military reservations for coast artillery to protect the naval station that had just been built at Port Orchard. The Army concluded that it would be wise to have troops permanently stationed close to the two population centers of Seattle and Tacoma; the proposed Magnolia Bluff reservation seemed an excellent site for an infantry garrison until it might be needed by the Coast Artillery.

From 1896–98 land for the post was acquired, and in the following ten years quarters for officers and non-coms, barracks, a hospital, stables, a quartermaster building, and other units were constructed. At this time the site was officially named Fort Lawton. Although the fort served alternately as a post for infantry and Coast Artillery, no artillery was ever installed. Military activity wound down during the early years of the Depression, and the Army offered the land to Seattle for the price of one dollar; however, the city declined, feeling it could not afford the maintenance costs.

During World War II the fort sprang back to life—more than a million troops were processed here, a prison camp on the fort held 1,150 German POWs, and another 5,000 Italian POWs passed through enroute to Hawaii. After the war, the fort remained a debarcation point for a time, then became a processing station for civil service employees and military headed to the Far East, and finally was a reserve training center. In 1970, the Army surplused 85 percent of the fort property, and the city was able to acquire it for a park.

This was the beginning of the city's headaches. Local Indian tribes demanded the property be returned to them under the provision of early treaty rights; a compromise was reached, and nineteen acres were set aside for an Indian cultural center. Special interest groups, ranging from golf buffs to hang-gliding enthusiasts, came out of the woodwork with plans and demands. The Parks Department, fortunately, maintained the park should be a sanctuary where people could escape for quiet and solitude. Al-

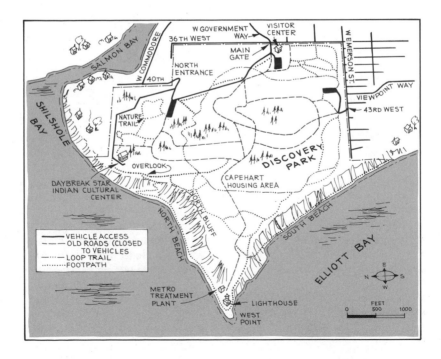

A Discovery Park beach and Mt. Rainier

though some areas were to be developed for conventional recreational use, the bulk of the park was to remain nature oriented.

In October of 1973, the land was formally dedicated as Discovery Park, named for the ship of George Vancouver, the explorer who first charted Puget Sound.

Three entrances lead into Discovery Park: one at a parking area on the south side of the park; another—the main entrance—on the east side of the park, nearest the Visitor Center; and the third on the north side of the park near the Indian Cultural Center.

To enter at the main gate, use exits from Elliott Avenue West at either the Magnolia Bridge, Dravus Street West, or West Emerson Place. From the west end of the Magnolia Bridge, turn right on Thorndyke Avenue West, which later becomes 20th Avenue West, Gilman Avenue West, and then Government Way. From the Dravus Street exit, turn north onto 20th Avenue West and follow the above route. The West Emerson exit leads to this route at Gilman Avenue West

The south parking lot can be reached by driving to the main park entrance as described above, and turning south onto 36th Avenue West, then west on West Emerson, and north on 43rd Avenue West.

The north entrance is reached by turning north from West Emerson Place onto 21st Avenue West, which shortly becomes Commodore Way. Follow Commodore Way to 40th Avenue West, then turn left to reach the park entrance.

In keeping with the park philosophy to keep the grounds as natural as possible, nearly all the roads within the park that had been built for the fort are closed to traffic. Many of the areas must be reached by walking; trails are wide, well maintained, and (for the most part) gentle.

West Point Lighthouse

Visitor Center. The informational hub of the park is the Visitor Center, where most classes and tours begin, and where a wide array of publications and displays are found. It is open Tuesday through Sunday, 8:30 A.M. to 5:00 P.M. Tours of the U.S. Army cemetery can be arranged here. Call directly to the stables of the Seattle Mounted Police, which are located on the grounds, to arrange a visit to those facilities. A ½-mile fitness trail, combining jogging with fifteen exercise stations begins at the Visitor Center.

Discovery Park Trails. Several miles of trails intertwine in the forests, meadows, and on the beaches of the park. Some are genuine footpaths, others follow old roads. Brochures available at the Visitor Center describe the sights along the trails—birds, plants, beach life, and points of geological interest. Take along field glasses, pause frequently, and try to identify some of the 221 species of birds that may be seen at the park.

The 2¾-mile-long Loop Trail begins at the Visitor Center and runs through a grassy meadow (a good place to see wrens, warblers, and thrushes), skirts the crest of a cliff overlooking Elliott Bay, and then circles back to the start. It's an easy trail, with only minimal gain or loss in elevation. Side trails lead down to the beach.

The Wolf Tree Nature Trail, ½ mile long, begins at the northwest end of the north parking lot, and loops through woods, a marsh, and a tiny meadow. A botanical checklist, available at the trailhead, names plants along the way. Naturalist-led tours are available by prearrangement with the Visitor Center.

North Bluff. A wide, grassy field with a trail running its length tops the crest of North Bluff. One could hardly tell that only a few years ago this used to be the site of a row of barracks, so rapidly has nature reclaimed the area. Walk quietly and watch for birds, or even an urban coyote. At the east end of the bluff, a wooden overlook offers sweeping views of the sound with the Olympics beyond. Watch freighter traffic, as well as sailboats racing off Shilshole Bay.

North Beach. Just beyond the North Bluff overlook, a trail heads downhill through forest, first as stairs, then as a steep, dirt path. The forest here is mostly deciduous—maple, elm, and alder with an undergrowth of salmonberry, ferns, and nettles. In less than ¼ mile, North Beach is reached.

The beach is rock and gravel—home for a wide variety of intertidal life ranging from chitons, limpets, barnacles, and mussels to sea stars, urchins, and tiny crab. As the trail heads west along the top of a riprap bulkhead, it is sandwiched between the beach and the fence around the Metro sewage plant.

After many years of controversy, Metro began work in 1991 on a secondary sewage treatment facility at North Beach in the area between the shore and the bluff. Numerous environmental and esthetic compromises were made by Metro, along with a commitment for a $30 million fund to improve and expand waterfront parks. Metro claims that, when finished, the facility, which is a major expansion to an existing sewage plant, will be hidden by landscaping and earthen mounds, and not even a sensitive nose should be aware that it is there. Until it is completed, North Beach will be severely disrupted by the construction, which is not scheduled to be completed until 1997. Until then the trail should be used with discretion, and it is recommended that park rangers be consulted prior to its use.

West Point. The lighthouse at West Point, on the far western tip of Discovery Park, has one of the most scenic settings on the sound. Jumbo ferries lumber by, sailboats with bright spinnakers, racing out of Shilshole, drift by just offshore, and Mt. Rainier rises above the city's skyscrapers. The lighthouse has been overseeing the passing scene since 1881, eight years before Washington became a state. It is now on the National Register of Historic Places. The lighthouse is open to visitors only from noon to 4:00 P.M. on weekends; weekdays are by appointment only.

South Beach. South Beach, stretching more than a mile southeast of West Point, offers a marked contrast to the rocky shoreline of North Beach. Here is sand extending well out into the sound on a minus tide. Driftwood and dune grass define the high tide line at the western end. The beach supports

Sea blubber jellyfish

sea pens, moon snails, nudibranchs, sand dollars, and other sand-loving marine life.

To the east, steep cliffs rising from the beach to the bluff above provide an interesting geology lesson on the formation of the area. Clearly defined bands show the sediments from lakes and streams, topped by dark gray clay that settled out of a huge freshwater lake. Higher up, loose, yellowish sand was deposited by streams and glacial meltwater. This is topped by till—a collection of boulders, rocks, sand, silt, and clay deposited directly by the glacier that last covered this area. Scan the cliffs for the hollows of kingfishers and other birds that have made their nests in the soft sand.

Reach South Beach from the Visitor Center or South Gate by following the Loop Trail to its intersection with the road to the Metro plant, at the northwest corner of the Capehart Housing area, and follow the road downhill to the beach.

Daybreak Star Indian Cultural Center. The Daybreak Star Indian Cultural Center is located just north of the north parking lot picnic area. Here a new, three-story building houses a library, museum, and a gallery of Indian art (some on display only and some for sale). The building also includes a theater where, at scheduled times, authentic Indian meals are served while native singers and dancers depict scenes of their spiritual heritage. A wooden overlook north of the center faces expansive views north over Shilshole Bay to the distant, icy cone of Mt. Baker.

Cormorants on the mooring lines of a ship at Pier 86

Elliott Bay

Elliott Bay, with its deep, protected waters, triggered the birth of the city of Seattle in 1852, and it has continued to nurture the city's growth over the past 150 years. The first settlers in the area landed on the shallow shore at Alki Point in West Seattle; however, it didn't take them long to recognize that a site closer to deep water was essential for creating the port city of their dreams. With a few horseshoes tied to a clothesline, they sounded the east shore of Elliott Bay, and to their delight found the spot that answered all of their needs. Claims were staked out, pioneer families established homesteads, and thus (with a slight oversimplification of time and events), Seattle came to be.

The first commercial venture on the Seattle waterfront was lumber. In the 1850s Henry Yesler built a pier on the southeast end of the bay, adjoining his sawmill, to load ships with lumber for construction of the growing city of San Francisco. By the 1870s coal dug from mines southeast of Seattle had become the mainstay of the local economy, and a coal bunker wharf extended into the bay midway along its eastern shoreline.

In the rush to gain the terminus of a transcontinental railroad, most of the existing waterfront was soon relinquished to railway interests, who then declined to develop it, as it would compete with their Tacoma terminals. Resourceful Seattlites solved this problem by constructing yet another waterfront on pilings farther out over the harbor, the first of many such extensions that eventually molded the current shoreline of Elliott Bay. By the late 1880s, waterfront access was bottled up by the railroads and a host of private piers, each concerned with their own parochial commercial interest, stifling the coordinated growth of the port as a whole.

When Washington became a state in 1889, the constitution included a declaration of state sovereignty over tidelands, with the caveat that tidelands outside harbor lines established by a state commission could be sold to private interests. Seattle harbor lines were drawn, contested, litigated, redrawn, and eventually the harbor fell back into the hands of the waterfront monopoly. A new legislature elected in 1896 strengthened the right of public access to state harbors; however, little was accomplished in breaking the economic stranglehold of the railroads and private owners over Seattle's waterfront.

In the early 1900s the shape of the shoreline underwent major changes as the strong-willed city engineer, R. H. Thompson, decided to eliminate annoying hills and steep streets by washing them into the bay. For more than ten years the landscape suffered a progressive regrade. The unwanted hills gradually filled the area under the plank and piling waterfront, and the land marched out to newly constructed seawalls that today define Seattle's waterfront. A decade later, when the people of King County voted to create the Port of Seattle, the elected commissioners set about developing a master plan for the port's future, and gradually were able to break the railroad-dominated monopoly on the waterfront.

In recent years, the port commissioners recognized a major change in shipping—the shift from bulk cargo to container ships. The aging piers along the downtown waterfront have neither the container loading facilities nor the large areas of waterfront storage that this type of shipping requires. As a result, the port concentrated its development in the tidal landfills

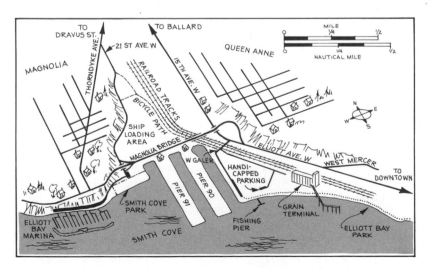

along the East and West Waterways surrounding Harbor Island and at the Smith Cove wharfs.

The world port that the original settlers envisioned has materialized, although certainly not in the form they could ever have anticipated. Today, Seattle is one of the largest container ports in the world. An average of five ocean-going vessels per day call on the commercial piers along Elliott Bay, and the annual value of goods through the port exceeds $25 billion.

SMITH COVE

The giant wharfs of Smith Cove lie along the northern edge of Elliott Bay. The first pier here was built by the Northern Pacific Railroad, which used it for loading coal on ships. Eight years later the railroad constructed two, long, earthwork piers (now Piers 88 and 89), from which railroad-owned steamers linked transcontinental rails to trade with the Orient. Shipments of raw silk valued as high as a thousand dollars a bale were offloaded from ships to waiting special freight trains for a high speed, direct run to the garment factories of the East Coast.

Piers 90 and 91 were constructed at the head of the cove by the Port of Seattle. At the time of their completion, in 1921, these 2,530-foot earth-fill piers were the longest of their kind in the world. The piers were sold to the U.S. Navy in 1942 for use as a major supply depot, but were repurchased by the port in 1976. Today, where bales of silk once stood, now stand the latest treasures of the Orient—Toyotas, Nissans, and Subarus.

Sailing off Smith Cove

SMITH COVE PARK

Park area: 2.5 acres; 500 feet of shoreline
Access: Land, boat (shallow draft)
Facilities: Picnic tables, Sani-can
Attractions: Beachcombing, viewpoint

Squeezed between Pier 91 and the Elliott Bay Marina is delightful little Smith Cove Park. Small, a bit hard to find, and not long on amenities, the park is nonetheless a pleasant waterfront alcove from which to watch the shipping activities of Elliott Bay and enjoy a picnic lunch spiced with a stiff, salt-air breeze.

To reach the park, take the Magnolia Bridge from Elliott Avenue West (or 15th Avenue West, which Elliott becomes north of the bridge). A ramp leaves the bridge and drops to 21st Avenue West just north of the park. Alternatively, take 21st Avenue West south from Thorndyke Avenue, which runs along the southeast side of Magnolia Bluff.

The park can also be reached from a bicycle path that continues north from Elliott Bay Park on Pier 89 along the east side of the Pier 90/91 fence, then around the north end of the piers' loading area to join 21st Avenue West about ½ mile from the park entrance.

Elliott Bay Park

ELLIOTT BAY MARINA

Facilities: Guest moorage, power, water, coffee shop, restaurant,
  groceries, fuel dock, restrooms, showers, laundry rooms, marine
  pump-out station, shops, hazardous waste disposal, chandlery,
  marine repair, observation platform

The most recent major addition to the Seattle waterfront is a 1,200-
slip marina on the north side of Elliott Bay, immediately west of Smith
Cove Park. The marina is protected by a 2,700-foot-long rock breakwater
along the south side of Magnolia Bluff, and a concrete wavebreak at the
west end of the breakwater. Fuel, groceries, and a pump-out station are located at the end of G dock, in the center of the marina. An observation platform that has been built atop the center of the breakwater provides views
across Elliott Bay; it is accessible by boat from the channel behind the
breakwater, or via a shuttle boat from the end of G dock.

Guest moorage is available on A dock, the first dock inside the west
side of the marina. Check with the dockmaster to register for a slip. Buildings at either end of the marina contain necessities such as laundry and
showers; offices and shops are in the building near the end of G dock.

To reach it by land, take the off-ramp from the Magnolia Bridge to
21st Avenue West, and follow it south and west to the marina complex.

ELLIOTT BAY PARK

Park area: 10.5 acres, 4,100 feet of shoreline
Access: Land, boat (shallow-draft)
Facilities: Foot and bike paths, fitness course, benches, picnic table,
  fishing pier, concession stand, bait, tackle, restrooms, children's play
  areas
Attractions: Sightseeing, walking, jogging, bicycling, fishing,
  picnicking, points of interest

The massive concrete silos of the Port of Seattle grain terminal mark
Pier 86, between Smith Cove and downtown Seattle. From here freighters
take on grain, brought here from the nation's heartland, for export to foreign markets. At the base of the terminal, the narrow grass strip of Elliott
Bay Park runs along the shore for nearly a mile.

The park has two paved paths, one for pedestrians immediately above
the rock-ribbed beach, and another for bicycles along the fence at its inland
boundary. The pedestrian path has a number of adjacent fitness exercise
stations, as well as several benches from which to leisurely watch the
marine traffic or a passing sea lion scouting for lunch.

Near the north end of the park, a 400-foot-long, T-shaped concrete
fishing pier extends into the bay. Two orange-striped buoys 100 feet off the
pier mark an artificial underwater reef. Fishing near the reef must be done
from the pier—angling from boats is prohibited here. Fish for surf perch,
flat fish, salmon, cod, cabezon, and rockfish. The pier is open 7:00 A.M.

to 11:00 P.M. daily in the winter, and 6:00 A.M. to midnight in summer.

To reach Elliott Bay Park, turn west off Elliott Avenue West at West Galer, the first intersection south of the Magnolia Bridge. In one block cross the railroad tracks; signs here point to Pier 86, Pier 89, the public fishing pier, and the bicycle path. For handicapped access to the fishing pier, turn south immediately after crossing the tracks and continue to the Pier 86 grain terminal, where a small sign directs you to a narrow road between two fences leading behind the concession stand. Parking is for handicapped and concession employees only.

For all other parking, continue on Galer another block past the entrance to Pier 91, then turn left on 15th Avenue West, which runs along the west side of Pier 89. In three more blocks there is ample parking on both sides of the road end and at the beginning of the path to the park. A bicycle path continues north from here along the east and north sides of the Pier 91 fence, eventually reaching the road leading to Smith Cove Park.

MYRTLE EDWARDS PARK

Park area: 3.7 acres; 2,000 feet of shoreline
Access: Land
Facilities: Picnic tables, benches, Sani-cans
Attractions: Picnicking, jogging, walking, bicycling

The public shoreline and its bicycle and walking paths continue south from the grain terminals in an unbroken swath. The southern portion,

Myrtle Edwards Park

Myrtle Edwards Park, commemorates a past city councilwoman. Benches and picnic tables along the shore offer pleasant resting spots with views to the maritime activities of Elliott Bay and, beyond, Bainbridge Island and the Olympic range.

Near the center of the park is one of Seattle's controversial sculptures, commissioned in 1976 as a part of the city's program providing one percent of development costs for artwork. The sculpture, entitled "Adjacent, Against, Upon," consists of three massive pairs of carved stone slabs and concrete platforms, each slab and platform related, according to the title of the work. Although the work may be too abstract for some tastes, it provides an interesting contrast of human scale versus the monumental.

The park can be reached by walking south through Elliott Bay Park, or by going north from a parking lot at the southern boundary of Myrtle Edwards Park. The metered parking lot is located just north of Pier 70, at the intersection of Alaskan Way and Broad Street.

THE DOWNTOWN SEATTLE WATERFRONT

Access: Land, boat (limited)
Facilities: Shops, restaurants, food carts, picnic tables, parks, restrooms, aquarium, tour boats, transient moorage (limited), view points, points of interest
Attractions: Shopping, sightseeing, picnicking, touring, fishing

The mile-long stretch of waterfront that edges downtown Seattle is a colorful, fascinating melange of commercial and tourist-oriented facilities. Piers are used by cruise ships, tour boats, and the state ferries. Alaskan Way runs the length of the downtown waterfront. Across this street from Pier 59, the Pike Place Hillclimb leads up stairs and terraces to the historic Pike Place Market, one of the best-known public markets in the country. An old railroad track alongside the Alaskan Way Viaduct has been replaced, between Pike Street and Washington Street, by an asphalt footpath bordered by plantings.

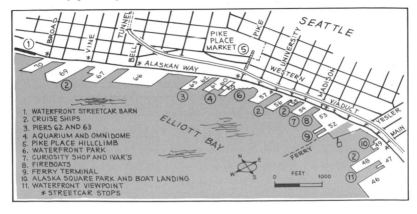

1. WATERFRONT STREETCAR BARN
2. CRUISE SHIPS
3. PIERS 62 AND 63
4. AQUARIUM AND OMNIDOME
5. PIKE PLACE HILLCLIMB
6. WATERFRONT PARK
7. CURIOSITY SHOP AND IVAR'S
8. FIREBOATS
9. FERRY TERMINAL
10. ALASKA SQUARE PARK AND BOAT LANDING
11. WATERFRONT VIEWPOINT
   * STREETCAR STOPS

As the shift to containerized cargo caused the working waterfront to move to Smith Cove and Harbor Island, a number of the warehouses on the downtown waterfront were abandoned. Some have been converted to complexes housing small shops and restaurants, but several lie mouldering. A number of plans have been set forth by city planners for revitalizing the waterfront, in order to better meet the increasing demand for tourist and recreational attractions. Under consideration have been increased pleasure boat moorage, a maritime historical center, a floating park, an outdoor theater, and moorage for large "Love Boat" type cruise ships; however, to date a plan has not yet been put forth that has met with voter support.

Visitors to the area should be aware of one of the problems that can be encountered on the waterfront. The south end of Alaskan Way borders Seattle's Skid Road district, where there is a concentration of homeless vagrants. While most of these people are harmless panhandlers, a few can become aggressive and threatening, especially if encountered in secluded spots. Use care and common sense.

The Waterfront Streetcar. In 1982 the Seattle waterfront gained a novel attraction with the arrival of four 1927-vintage electric trolleys that had been retired from service in Melbourne, Australia. From car barns located north of Broad Street, the picturesque streetcars make their 15-minute run along the waterfront, stopping at several stations along the way. Leaving the waterfront, the streetcar tracks head east through Pioneer Square on South Main Street to 5th Avenue, and the end of the line at Jackson Street. Conductors on the cars enjoy the novelty of the route, and frequently add their personal commentary to make the trip even more fun.

Cruise Ships. The downtown waterfront is the terminal for several cruise ships. For those wishing a quick trip to Victoria, B.C., the *Victoria Clippers,* three 30-knot, 300-passenger jetfoils provide passenger-only service from Pier 69 to Victoria in two and a half hours. Two of the boats operate year-around, and the third, which offers intermediate stops in Port Townsend and Friday Harbor, operates only during summer months. Each of the boats can accommodate a few bicycles and kayaks, in addition to passengers. Check with Clipper Navigation, Inc. for sailing schedules.

Four separate cruise lines are located near the middle of the harbor front: Grayline Harbor Tours and Northwest Tours are between piers 56 and 57; Tillicum Village Tours, which offers trips to an Indian longhouse and restaurant at Blake Island State Park, is between Piers 55 and 56; Major Marine Tours, which provides daily historical tours of Elliott Bay during summer months is at Pier 54. All tours provide narrated commentary about the bay, as well as waterside views of the city.

Piers 62 and 63. These two broad docks are a city park, with picnic tables and ample space for viewing the city skyline and the bay. The dock is surrounded by a low chain link fence, transparent when viewed head-on, but bearing messages when viewed from an angle.

Basket star photographed at the Seattle Aquarium

Piers 59 and 60: the Seattle Aquarium and Omnidome Theatre. Elliott Bay and Puget Sound are important not only for what occurs on their surfaces, but also for what exists below. The Seattle Aquarium, the most outstanding attraction on the waterfront, provides a glimpse of this underwater world. One of the displays, a unique underwater dome, allows visitors to go beneath the waters of the sound and view marine life on all sides and above, much as Captain Nemo would have seen it. On view in traditional glass tanks are nearly every kind of marine life found in Puget Sound, ranging from shy octopus, ferocious-appearing wolf eels, and technicolor nudibranchs. Displays provide information to help visitors better understand the various species and their environments.

Another feature of the aquarium is an operating fish ladder; each year salmon fry are released here to go to sea, and one or two years later they find their way back home to spawn in the "stream" of their birth.

Probably as popular as the fish displays are the tanks containing harbor seals and sea otters. A number of the animals have bred in the aquarium and have raised their young here. The animal families are always a delight for visitors. Additional displays include a "touch tank" where children can examine the crusty skin of a starfish, the squishy body of a sea cucumber, or other characteristics of fascinating marine animals.

In addition to local marine life, a Pacific coral reef exhibit, added in 1986, offers a skin diver's view of the life in these reefs.

Sharing the pier with the Aquarium is the Omnidome Theatre, where wrap-around screens bring the viewers into the film, imparting an eerie sense of not just watching, but actually becoming a part of the scenes shown. The films, which use the breathtaking media technique to its full advantage, have taken viewers on underwater explorations of Australia's Great Barrier Reef, trips around erupting Mt. St. Helens, and space voyages through the universe.

Piers 57 to 59: Waterfront Park. A large, semicircular deck between Pier 57 and 59 forms Waterfront Park. Picnic tables along the terraced deck are favorite haunts of Seattlites who enjoy a splash of salt air as they share their lunches with scrounging pigeons and seagulls. Landscaping, a marvelously splashing fountain, and the ugliest statue in Seattle (Christopher Columbus with a hole through his bronze head) add to the charm of the park. Distinctive, open-air viewing towers can be reached from the deck below via stairs or ramps, or via walkways leading from the second level of buildings on the adjoining piers.

Pier 57 houses a collection of small shops and restaurants. The open end of the pier offers a scattering of tables and benches from which to watch the waterfront activity. This pier end is designated as a public fishing area; rod holders are mounted along its perimeter fence for the convenience of anglers.

Pier 54: Ye Olde Curiosity Shop and Ivar's Acres of Clams. Two commercial enterprises on the waterfront have become Seattle institutions. Ye

Seattle's Waterfront Park

Olde Curiosity Shop, which has been a waterfront fixture since 1899, recently relocated to the north side of Pier 54 when Pier 51, its home of many years, was found structurally unsound. The store houses an eclectic assortment of artifacts, curios, and tourist kitsch—most for sale, but some just for display.

Pier 54 is also the home of one of the best-known waterfront restaurants, Ivar's Acres of Clams. On display in the restaurant are over 500 historical photos of the Seattle waterfront.

Pier 53: Fire Station #5 and Fireboats. Fire Station #5 not only provides fire protection for the land side of Elliott Bay, it also acts as the home base for the two fireboats posted on the bay. In addition to their primary function, the fireboats are frequent participants in marine parades and special events on Elliott Bay. They provide a breathtaking scene when their water cannons send plumes of water arching high into the air.

A historic old fire bell outside the station was originally used in the late 1800s to sound alarms to all fire stations in the north end of the city. Inside the building are two antique fire engines, one a manually powered 1888 squirrel-tailed haywagon pumper, the other an engine of slightly more modern vintage.

Pier 52: The Colman Ferry Terminal. From this Seattle terminus of the Washington State Ferry System, ferries serve Bremerton, on the Kitsap Peninsula, and Winslow, on Bainbridge Island. From balconies in the Col-

Feeding gulls at Ivar's Acres of Clams

man Terminal, visitors can watch the flurry of activity as the huge vessels dock and depart, load and unload.

The Colman dock has had a rather checkered past, perhaps because it has always played a prominent role on the Seattle waterfront. The original dock, built in 1889, was replaced in 1909 by a larger dock that sported a distinctive clock tower at its end. Three years later, a ship plowed into the wharf, severing the clock tower, which floated away in the fog. The clock was rescued the following day, and the tower was rebuilt, but it was partially destroyed by fire after only two years. Again it was rebuilt, and it stood as a waterfront landmark until 1936, when the dock was once more replaced, but without the tower. The present dock and terminal were built in 1966; extensive remodeling begun in 1991 is to be completed by 1994.

When remodeling is completed, all ferry traffic will approach the terminal from the south, along Alaskan Way. The passenger-only ferry slip will be relocated to the north side of the terminal and a plaza will be built to form an immense map of this portion of Puget Sound. A raised platform on the east side of the plaza will be cut to the form of Elliott Bay, and a platform on the west will duplicate the shape of Kitsap Peninsula. Brass markers on the deck will trace the ferry routes between, with bollards marking lighthouses. A tower is planned that will house the restored works of the original old Colman Dock clock. Observation platforms by the ferry slips will offer views of Elliott Bay.

Fireboats on the Seattle waterfront

Washington State Ferry arriving at the Colman Ferry Terminal

Pier 49: Alaska Square Park and the Washington Street Boat Landing. Currently the only public boat access to the Seattle waterfront is found at Pier 49 at the foot of Washington Street. A concrete float, marked on the street side by a historic old pergola, extends about 120 feet out into the bay. The dock provides boaters a somewhat tenuous access to the waterfront, as the floats have no protection from the water side, and the wakes of nearby ferries, as well as other marine traffic along the busy waterfront, make the moorage rather rough. There is a ten-hour maximum time limit for use of the floats, and a twenty-minute limit for one section used for loading and unloading only.

Just south of the floats is tiny Alaska Square Park. Problems with vagrants led the city to replace the park's grass with concrete and asphalt slabs, broken by groupings of rocks and shrubs, and a cluster of rocks around the park's signature totem pole. The resulting park is uncomfortable for inebriated snoozing. Gates that are closed between 11 P.M. and 6 A.M. have helped reduce problems with transients. Even though the park is more secure, it is not advisable to leave a boat unattended at the floats. Even when on board, keep hatches secure at night.

Pier 48: The Working Waterfront Viewpoint. Pier 48 is the start of today's active waterfront; from here south along the East Waterway, at Harbor Island, and along the West Waterway, the bustle of a major working port takes place. On the southeast corner of Pier 48 the Port of Seattle has created displays describing the history and technology of the port.

The Working Waterfront Viewpoint

Viewpoints overlook piers to the south. A footpath marked on the tarmac at the entrance to the pier leads to the area.

Informational displays mounted along the edge of the pier describe the early history and growth of the Seattle waterfront, and the technological changes that have shaped it. Three huge periscopes, about 25 to 35 feet tall, provide views of the working port; a platform offers still another angle on the activity. Gates on the pier at the entrance to the display area, open only during daylight hours, have significantly reduced prior problems with vagrants in the area.

Pier 36: The Coast Guard Museum Northwest and the Vessel Traffic Service Center. The Coast Guard Support Center at Pier 36 has a variety of attractions to interest visitors and keep children enthralled for hours. The pier is home to the United States' two largest icebreakers, which see duty in arctic seas. Two high-endurance cutters stationed here, the *Munro* and the *Boutwell*, are open to visitors on weekends when they are in port. On occasion other interesting vessels that call here are open for tours.

The Coast Guard Museum Northwest, located on the north side of the pier, houses a collection of marine memorabilia, including several models of Coast Guard vessels, historic photos, and vintage uniforms. A post lantern on display was originally located at Alki Point in 1887; it was a predecessor to later lighthouses. A fourth-order Fresnel lens now in the museum was originally installed at Admiralty Head in 1903. It saw duty at the New Dungeness Lighthouse from 1927 to 1976.

The museum is open Monday, Wednesday, and Friday from 10:00 A.M. to 4:00 P.M., and Saturday and Sunday from 1:00 P.M. to 5:00 P.M. Group tours at other times can be arranged by telephoning the museum or the Coast Guard Public Affairs Office.

The Puget Sound Vessel Traffic Service Center, located in the main building on the pier, is also open to visitors from 8:00 A.M. to 4:00 P.M.

daily. This center maintains radar surveillance of about 2,500 square miles of waterways in the Strait of Juan de Fuca and Puget Sound. It controls and tracks over 18,000 commercial vessel movements a month in these waters. A ten-minute slide show describes the operaton of the center; personnel are available to show the vessel tracking room and answer questions about it. On screen can be seen the tracks of ships throughout the sound and straits. A visit to the VTS brings with it a much greater appreciation of the amount of traffic that travels the sound, and the efficiency with which the Coast Guard controls it.

Harbor Island and the Duwamish Waterway

During the late 1800s, when the Federal government was busily quibbling over a route for a ship canal to access Lake Washington, Seattlites grew tired of waiting and took matters into their own hands. In 1890 they obtained approval from the state legislature to construct a canal from the south end of the lake via a cut through Beacon Hill. Although the canal was never constructed, preliminary design work by the Army Corps of Engineers led, in 1895, to dredging of two channels in the Duwamish tide flats. Dredged material that was dumped between the East and West waterways formed the beginnings of Harbor Island. Augmented by ballast from lumber barges and from regrades at Beacon Hill, the island took the shape it has today.

The island lay virtually unused until 1910, when local business interests, spurred by visions of burgeoning trade through the soon-to-be-

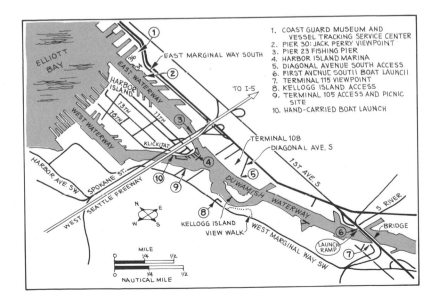

1. COAST GUARD MUSEUM AND VESSEL TRACKING SERVICE CENTER
2. PIER 30: JACK PERRY VIEWPOINT
3. PIER 23 FISHING PIER
4. HARBOR ISLAND MARINA
5. DIAGONAL AVENUE SOUTH ACCESS
6. FIRST AVENUE SOUTH BOAT LAUNCH
7. TERMINAL 115 VIEWPOINT
8. KELLOGG ISLAND ACCESS
9. TERMINAL 105 ACCESS AND PICNIC SITE
10. HAND-CARRIED BOAT LAUNCH

completed Panama Canal, sought East Coast financing to build piers and terminals at Harbor Island. Financing attempts failed, but by the 1920s some commercial development was noticeable, mainly along the edges of the adjoining waterways. A major burst of industrial growth that started shortly before World War II has continued, and turned the island into the bustling industrial area of today.

From its source at the confluence of the Black, White, and Green rivers, the Duwamish River originally meandered eight miles through sixteen serpentine curves to the tide flats of Elliott Bay. In 1906 the White River was diverted to the south, and in 1916 the Black ceased to exist when the completion of the ship canal lowered Lake Washington, its source. Lack of flat land for industry led to extensive reshaping of the Duwamish; between 1913 and 1917 the river had ten of its curves eliminated by the Corps of Engineers, as it was dredged to its present, relatively straight, 50-foot-deep channel.

PIER 30: JACK PERRY MEMORIAL VIEWPOINT

The East Waterway is the heart of commercial activity for the Port of Seattle. The numbers associated with it are staggering: it has 10,634 linear feet of berthing space, 187 acres of adjoining marine terminal yards, can accommodate up to 14 deep-draft vessels simultaneously, and over four million metric tons of cargo are transhipped yearly from its terminals.

The Port of Seattle has developed a public access and viewing site just north of Pier 30, where the hustling activity of the port can be watched close at hand. To reach the access site, follow Alaskan Way south from the central waterfront to where it jogs southwest and then becomes East Marginal Way South. Follow the stub end of Alaskan Way straight ahead to the viewpoint; it is signed at the main road. The short road ends in a parking lot just above the waterway. Between the lot and the waterway is a grass mini-park with a couple of trees, benches, and garbage cans. A sign describes the waterway activities and displays the stack insignias for the various shipping companies that call at the port.

PIER 23 FISHING PIER

Facilities: Covered benches, picnic tables, cleaning stations, Sani-can (restrooms planned for future), water

Sandwiched between a gravel plant and a cold storage plant, with views out to cranes and cargo ships, the public fishing pier at the end of the East Waterway puts a human perspective in this otherwise industrial area.

To reach the fishing pier, take the Harbor Island/11th Avenue SW exit from the Spokane Street freeway. In about 100 yards a couple of unmarked right turns lead into a small parking area, just large enough for half a dozen cars. Look sharply, because the turns are easily missed, and there is no convenient way to backtrack once they are passed. The pier can also be reached by turning west on SW Spokane Street from East Marginal Way

Pier 23 Fishing Pier

South. Additional parking is available under the freeway just after making this turn.

Benches (some covered) and a couple of picnic tables lining the 500-foot frontage of the pier provide pleasant spots to watch the waterway activity while waiting for a hit on the fishline. Signs note that bottom fish, shellfish, and crab may be unsafe to eat, due to pollution.

HARBOR ISLAND MARINA

Facilities: Fuel, groceries (limited), restrooms, shower, viewing pier, transient moorage, pumpout station, deli (nearby)

A pleasant recreational incursion amid the commercial waterfront clamor, Habor Island Marina is the only facility on the Duwamish Waterway for pleasure boaters. To reach it by water, head south from Elliott Bay into the West Waterway and the Duwamish River, pass under the new swing bridge and the high-rise bridge, and continue past a small, private marina to the commercial marina on the southernmost tip of the island.

By land, turn west onto SW Spokane Street from East Marginal Way South, or take the Harbor Island exit from the West Seattle freeway. Follow SW Spokane Street to the stoplight at 11th Avenue SW, just east of the new swing bridge. Here turn left and follow signs to the marina entrance in approximately two blocks.

The upland strip at the head of the docks has been pleasantly landscaped and furnished with benches and a viewing platform where one can relax and enjoy the maritime activities of the waterway.

The relatively new marina has permanent moorage on five docks for about 100 boats. Fuel and some limited groceries are available at the long,

Harbor Island Marina

outside breakwater float that T's off the end of C dock. This float has power and water, and is used for transient moorage. Northwest of the marina, a flat grassy area under the two bridges tapers gently to the edge of the waterway. Hand-carried boats can be launched here, with due caution for marine traffic in the waterway.

DIAGONAL AVENUE SOUTH ACCESS

Around 125 years ago the Duwamish estuary held nearly 2,500 acres of tidal marshes and swamp. Today less than 2% of its marshes and shallows remain. The Port of Seattle has taken a small step to restore some of this lost estuary wetland with the creation of a wildlife habitat area at the end of Diagonal Avenue South. Here a small basin has had fill removed, and shore plants typical of the intertidal habitat have been reintroduced.

Small greenswards on either side of the basin have a few benches from which to observe the wildlife which, it is hoped, will be attracted by the new habitat. A path runs north just above the river bank for a 100 feet or so before ending at a fence that extends into the water.

Two large signs erected by the Port at the parking lot tell of the natural and human history of the estuary. One display compares the physical features and ecology of 1854 to those of 1985. It identifies major changes in the estuary's watershed that collectively reduced by about 75% the watershed area and the volume of water flow through the estuary, and drastically decreased the rivers and streams accessible to andronomous fish (fish that spawn in freshwater, but spend part of their life in saltwater).

A second sign describes the large delta island of Tsuh'-Kahs that existed here prior to dredging of the waterway, and of the Duwamish Indians who hunted and fished here. Several Indian villages existed in the area up

Canada geese at the Diagonal Avenue South Access

into the 1800s, and archeological digs have taken place at the site of one of them. The display also tells how the natives fished, hunted, and caught waterfowl, and how their children played here.

To reach the access, follow East Marginal Way South to about ½ mile south of Spokane Street, then turn west on Diagonal Avenue South, which is signed to the access.

FIRST AVENUE SOUTH BOAT LAUNCH

A launch ramp for trailered boats is provided on the east bank of the Duwamish River, under the abutments of the 1st Avenue South bridge.

Drive about three blocks south of the 1st Avenue South intersection, and turn west from East Marginal Way South onto South River Street. Follow South River to where it ducks under the 1st Avenue South bridge. Immediately underneath the bridge is a two-lane, asphalt launch ramp. The ramp is very steep and tends to be slick when wet. Parking, located in a rough, muddy area under the bridge abutments, is adequate for a dozen cars and trailers.

TERMINAL 115 VIEWPOINT

A small public access on the west bank of the Duwamish, just across the river from the 1st Avenue South launch ramp, offers an opportunity for a picnic snack while watching the boat traffic in the Duwamish or the auto traffic overhead on the bridge. The 200-foot-long beachfront contains a park bench and a trash can for amenities—no restrooms or drinking water. The rocky bank slopes gently down to the water, so hand-carried boats or inflatables could be easily launched here.

To reach the viewpoint, drive south over the 1st Avenue South bridge and take the exit marked "Highland Park Way and South Seattle Community College." After the exit, take the first hard right, which immediately comes to a T-intersection with SW Michigan Street. Head east on Michigan for one block to its intersection with 2nd Avenue SW, then go south on 2nd for one block. At 7100 2nd SW a street runs east, then north, through Alaska Marine Lines lots, and in two blocks arrives at the viewpoint. Parking for four or five cars is available.

DUWAMISH WATERWAY PARK

Access: Land, boat (shallow draft)
Facilities: Picnic tables, fireplaces

A pretty little neighborhood park in the South Park residential area, Duwamish Waterway Park has an open grass field with a few trees, picnic tables, and fireplaces. At its north end the bank slopes gently down to a sandy beach at the river's edge. Pollution in the river and broken glass on the beach make wading a questionable activity; hand-carried boats can easily be launched here, however.

To reach the park follow East Marginal Way South to 16th Avenue South, opposite Boeing Field. Turn south onto 16th, cross the brige over the waterway, then turn west onto Dallas Avenue South. Continue on Dallas for three blocks to its intersection with 10th Avenue South. The park lies ½ block north, bordering on 10th.

SOUTH PORTLAND/8TH AVENUE SOUTH ACCESS

This access is not very attractive at present—just a weed-covered vacant lot with a bank of rubble and concrete slabs—but it is one of the eight sites covered in the Port of Seattle's public access plans that may see improvement sometime in the future. At present it offers views up and down the Duwamish, and a spot to watch the barge traffic in the river.

To reach the access, follow the directions to Duwamish Waterway Park, described above, continuing west for one more block to 8th Avenue South; turn north on 8th and follow it to its intersection with South Portland Street at the river's edge. Limited streetside parking is available in the vicinity.

KELLOGG ISLAND

Kellogg Island was once targeted in Port of Seattle plans as a container cargo storage area; however, the island's priority faded as the growing size of container vessels precluded their travel up the narrow, shallow Duwamish channel. Concurrently, the value of the island as a nesting site for great blue heron, Canada geese, and other waterfowl was recognized by conservation groups, who lobbied to preserve this last wild environment on the lower Duwamish from encroaching commercial development. The discovery that early Indian tribes had used the island for their encampments established it as an important archeological site as well.

It was finally agreed that Kellogg Island should remain in its natural state as a nature preserve in the heart of the industrial Duwamish shorelines.

There are two public accesses to the shoreline west of Kellogg Island. The Port of Seattle created the Terminal 107 Kellogg Island View Path, a 1,500-foot-long asphalt path above the west river bank paralleling the island for its full length. The island can be viewed through the shoreline trees, but there is no access down the 20-foot-high bank to the river. The river bank, brush, and trees along the path are often shared by the island's avian inhabitants—walk quietly, and see how many you can spot.

To reach the north end of this access, follow West Marginal Way South to SW Hudson Street. No parking is available in the immediate vicinity; park somewhere nearby and walk back to the signed start of the path. The south end of the path is also accessible by crossing the railroad tracks just north of the sand and gravel plant at Terminal 107; again, parking in the area is limited. Access to the path may be closed during rail switching on the spur track along West Marginal South.

A second public access is located about two blocks north at SW Edmunds Street. Here a short road stub crosses the railroad tracks to a fence gate; a wide spot has parking space for a few cars. A turnstile north of the gated road permits pedestrian access to the road beyond. The road soon turns south and continues parallel to the river bank through alder and black-

The Duwamish River and Kellogg Island

berry brambles, alive with flitting, twittering birds. The road ends at a low bank above the river, where an easy scramble provides access to the river bank itself.

Kellogg Island lies directly across the narrow channel, in an oxbow of the Duwamish River. Brush and brambles covering the 600-yard-long island provide protection and nesting habitat for great blue heron and some seventy-five other species of birds. Approach quietly on the river bank to observe and photograph; better yet, put in a canoe or small boat at one of the Duwamish access points and paddle slowly around the island. Since the island itself is a wildlife preserve, it is closed to public access.

TERMINAL 105 PUBLIC ACCESS AND PICNIC SITE

Access: Land, boat
Facilities: Picnic tables, shelter, pier

A little park, just south of the tip of Harbor Island, is a nice spot to fish, or just to watch the marine traffic in the busy Duwamish channel. It's especially pleasant on summer evenings when the river traffic is heavier and Mt. Rainier, to the south, is bathed in the glow of a setting sun.

To reach the site, follow West Marginal Way South to a few blocks south of SW Spokane Street, and at SW Dakota Street turn east along a gravel road signed "Terminal 105 Viewpoint." The road continues along the north edge of Terminal 105 to a small parking lot with space for about fifteen cars. A walkway leads to a pair of picnic tables, one under a shelter, and a 40-foot-long concrete pier out into the waterway.

A gravel path heads to the rock riprap beach at the south edge of the park where hand-carried boats may be launched. Signs caution small boats to watch for and avoid commercial vessels in the waterway.

Terminal 105 Picnic Site

West Seattle

West Seattle has always seemed a bit apart from the rest of Seattle—partially because of its physical separation by the broad channel of the Duwamish River, and partially because it is a little bit different (and perhaps better) than much of the city, with its combination of extensive saltwater shoreline, outstanding beaches, and fine water-oriented views.

Although West Seattle (or more specifically Alki Point) was the site of the original settlement in the Seattle area in late 1851, most of the pioneers departed the following year. Their interest was in the deep water along the east shore of Elliott Bay, where they envisioned a port for oceangoing ships. The original West Seattle settlement languished, with little attention paid to it until 1864, when a sawmill was established on the west side of the peninsula at the new community of Freeport; the mill was soon joined by a shipyard and then a cannery. The growing town changed its name to Milton to avoid being confused with another Freeport in Washington Territory.

By 1885 the city of Seattle was becoming congested, by the standards of the day, and the Alki area was platted for homesites. The one problem, however, was that the area was physically isolated from Seattle by Elliott Bay and the Duwamish River. The solution was a ferry, which ran from a pier at the foot of Marion Street in Seattle to a terminal near the site of

Low tide at Duwamish Head

Milton. The ferry continued its eight and one-half minute crossing regularly between 1888 and 1913. (Try getting from downtown to West Seattle in eight and one-half minutes today!)

A railway trestle bridged the tideflats by 1890; in 1902 a planked deck bridge was built at Spokane Street. Over the years bridges were continually added, enlarged, and improved; however, the access never seemed to keep up with the traffic load. The matter was brought to a head in 1978 when a freighter took out the north span of the first bascule bridge, precipitating construction of a new, multilane, high-rise bridge. In 1991 the lower bascule bridge was finally replaced with a new radical-design swing bridge where each half of the concrete span rotates on huge concrete pivots at either side of the waterway—now just wait for the next wayward freighter.

DUWAMISH HEAD

To early Seattlites, the beautiful beaches of West Seattle were a vacation getaway. As early as 1899, the Coney Island Baths opened on the beach west of Duwamish Head, and by 1905 large stretches of the beach were lined with rustic summer cottages. The Coney Island Baths were replaced in 1907 by Luna Park, an amusement site built on a deck over pilings extending into the bay, which boasted a natatorium (indoor swimming pool), dance pavilion, carnival rides, shows, restaurants, and a tavern. In 1931 the park was torched by an arsonist and burned to the water. Recreation shifted westward three years later when the city opened a new natatorium at Alki Beach; Luna Park was never rebuilt.

In 1947 the City of Seattle acquired the property formerly occupied by Luna Park, as an extension of the public beaches lying west of Duwamish Head. Even today, at a minus tide the stubs of the pilings that supported the park stand out above the tideflat. Boaters approaching the head should be aware of a shoal, marked by a light and fog signal, which extends out for ¼ mile.

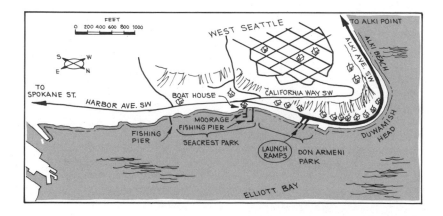

Scuba divers at Duwamish Head

SEACREST PARK

Park area: 4 acres; 2,200 feet of shoreline
Access: Land, boat
Facilities: Restrooms, benches, picnic tables, boathouse, fishing piers, transient moorage, concession, tackle, bait, boat rental, outboard fuel
Attractions: Viewpoint, picnicking, fishing, boating, scuba diving

In 1971 the City of Seattle acquired the property lying along Harbor Avenue SW, southwest of Duwamish Head, and developed imaginative plans for a premium waterfront park, complete with a 700-boat marina, fishing pier, boathouse, promenade, and salmon-rearing pens. Unfortunately, plans for the marina ran afoul of Indian fishing treaty rights, and, in addition, the total package substantially outran available funding.

Plans were scaled down, but even in their final form the breathtaking views of the downtown Seattle skyline against a background of rugged Cascade summits make Seacrest a gem of a park. Shoreline restoration began with the creation of a promenade with grass enclaves and benches on which to relax and enjoy the views. In 1989 a boathouse (a reincarnation of the old Seacrest Marina) was added. The parking lot at the boathouse is quite small, but parallel street parking is available the length of the park.

Two fishing piers extend out into the bay, one at the south end of the park, and a second at the boathouse. Inside this latter pier is an F-shaped set of floats for transient moorage. The jumble of offshore pilings from wharfs long forgotten is a favorite spot for skin diving.

To reach Seacrest Park from downtown Seattle, follow the Spokane Street viaduct west over Harbor Island, and then take the SW Spokane Street/Delridge Way exit onto SW Spokane Street. In about a block take the Harbor Avenue/Avalon Way exit. At an intersection in another block, turn right onto Harbor Avenue SW, which parallels the shoreline all the way to Duwamish Head. The south end of the park is reached in about one mile.

DON ARMENI PARK

Park area: 4.3 acres; 1,400 feet of shoreline
Access: Land, boat
Facilities: Boat launch (ramp), restrooms, benches, picnic tables, boat rentals, bait
Attractions: Viewpoint, picnicking, boating, paddling, fishing, scuba diving

Don Armeni Park is a continuation of the theme of Seacrest Park, with similar fishing and beachfront attractions. The park, which lies along the shore just north of Seacrest Park, was named in 1955 for a deputy sheriff, active in youth fishing derbies, who was killed in the line of duty.

Two pairs of launch ramps are at the south end of the park; each pair has a loading float between them. The ramps to the south are to be used

Piers at Don Armeni Park

when launching, and the ones to the north when returning. Boat rentals and a bait concession are found here. The large parking lot at the center of the park is reserved for cars with boat trailers. Smaller areas at either end of the park are available for general parking; parallel street parking is available along Harbor Avenue.

The shoreline not occupied by launch ramps has a landscaped walkway and park benches above a bulkhead. Concrete viewing platforms are at the ends of the park and at either side of the launch ramps.

The beach north of the launch ramps was the site of Luna Park. The former swimming pool from that park was filled with dirt, and now forms a tree-rimmed grass viewpoint extending out from the seawall. This is the only access point to the beach in this area. At extreme low tide an enormous tide flat is revealed, extending all the way to Duwamish Head, and out into Elliott Bay for nearly a quarter of a mile. City dwellers throng here to look for the few remaining shellfish in the area, to search with metal detectors for treasures, or just to squish sand between their toes.

ALKI BEACH PARK

Park area: 154 acres; 10,000 feet of shoreline
Access: Land, boat (shallow draft)
Facilities: Restrooms, picnic shelter, fire rings, art studio
Attractions: Swimming, wading, beachcombing, picnicking, walking,
    biking, sunbathing, point of interest

In 1851 the original settlers at Alki Point gave their community the name of New York. When they were chided about this pretentious name,

Enjoying the water at Alki Beach

they would respond in Chinook jargon "al-ki," which meant "bye-and-bye" or "someday." By 1853 the term had become so commonly used that the area was appropriately renamed Alki.

Alki Beach has long been a favorite Seattle saltwater playground. As early as 1905 the area had a hotel, swimming pool, and dance pavilion. In order to assure availability of a prime public saltwater beach, in 1909 the City of Seattle condemned 3,000 feet of beachfront northeast from Alki Point and erected a bathing and recreation pavilion. A natatorium, opened at the beach in 1934, was a popular spot for many years before falling into disrepair and finally being razed. Today the public beach extends along the peninsula in a continuous strip from Alki Point to the southern extremity of Seacrest Park.

A public beach is a mixed blessing for the local residents, however, as recent years have found noisy, rowdy bands of youths crowding the area on summer evenings, with no effective means of controlling them. Drastically reduced parking, increased police patrols, and a recently passed anti-cruising ordinance may serve to reduce these problems.

Crowds aside, Alki Beach Park is one of the most beautiful sand-covered expanses on the Puget Sound, with striking views across the sound to the Olympics and north to Whidbey Island and Admiralty Inlet. The shore tapers off gradually, and as a result the shallow waters heat enough in the summer to permit reasonably comfortable saltwater bathing. At minus tides the wide sand strip bares some distance out into the sound, exposing a menagerie of underwater life, including moon snails, starfish, anenomes, and perhaps a clam or two.

Restrooms are found above the beach at 57th Avenue West, 60th Avenue SW, and 62nd Avenue SW. Sani-cans are placed at other beach accesses to the east. The building at 60th also houses a Seattle Parks Department art studio program. A picnic shelter is located near 62nd Avenue SW.

ALKI POINT LIGHTHOUSE

The prominent location of Alki Point along the main channel of Puget Sound makes it ideal for a navigational light. The first settlers to live on the point recognized this, and kept an oil lantern burning as a service to passing mariners. In due time the government also realized the value of the point, and in 1887 officially authorized the placement of a lens-lantern, lit by a kerosene lantern and suspended on a wooden scaffold. This primitive but effective signal served until 1918 when the present lighthouse was commissioned.

Alki Point was the best possible duty for the lighthouse keeper stationed here. While other keepers were stuck on remote islands and far-flung beaches, the one stationed at Alki enjoyed all of civilization's ameneties, as well as the social life of the city.

With the automation of lighthouses in the 1970s, one of the two lightkeeper dwellings was taken over as a residence for the commandant of the 13th Coast Guard District. The lighthouse is open for public tours on weekends and holidays from noon to 4:00 P.M.

Cormorants on pilings at Beans Point

3. Bainbridge Island

The next best thing to living on an island is visiting one, and this island is especially easy to visit. Those who don't have a boat of their own need only saunter aboard the ferry, or load kayak, canoe, bicycle, or (horrors!) auto onto the ferry, and, before the hour is over, they will be soaking up island atmosphere. The Winslow ferry from downtown Seattle goes directly to Bainbridge Island; the Edmonds ferry runs to Kingston on the Kitsap Peninsula; and from there it's just a short drive south to the Agate Passage bridge and across the bridge to the island.

The 24-nautical-mile circumnavigation of the island by boat makes a nice leisurely day excursion, with plenty of time for side trips into Dyes Inlet, Poulsbo, or the island's inviting harbors, as the mood strikes. Boating facilities in Port Orchard channel on the Kitsap shoreline, as well as navigational considerations in the channel and Rich Passage, are described in chapter 4.

Bainbridge Island is a favorite with bicyclers. Many roads are level, following the shoreline and offering spectacular marine views, but a few inland roads provide a real hill-climbing challenge—most notably Toe Jam Hill on the southeast point of the island. Boaters or walk-on ferry passengers wanting to tour the island can rent bicycles in Winslow.

The Eastern Shore

EAGLE HARBOR AND WINSLOW

It's hard to imagine that more diverse activities could possibly be packed into a harbor of such small size. Eagle Harbor houses a ferry terminal, ferry maintenance facilities, boat repair yards, a creosote plant, condominiums, yacht club, marinas, a waterfront park, and private homes with docks. Only 2 miles long (and some of that taken up by mudflat), and averaging ¼ mile in width, the harbor and the town along its north shore are the center of activity for all of the island.

Although the Agate Passage bridge on the west side ties the island to the Kitsap mainland, lives are regulated by the comings and goings of the ferry headed for Seattle and big-city jobs. Early weekday mornings find a number of business-suited commuters, both male and female, rowing boats from Eagledale on the south shore of the bay to Winslow on the north, stepping ashore, briefcase in hand, and dashing for the ferry.

Eagle Harbor has been named one of the most polluted bays in Puget Sound, with bottom sediment containing a high percentage of toxic chemicals. The creosote plant is named as the major culprit, but other factors, both past and present, certainly have had a hand in the harbor's condition.

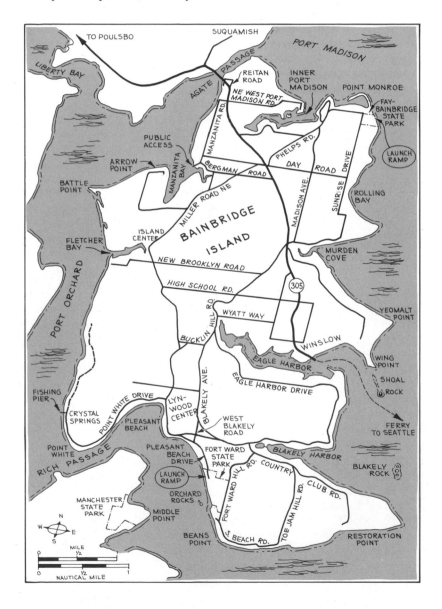

Fish, crabs, and shellfish taken from the bay are considered unsafe to eat.

Winslow does its best to entice travelers to stop and enjoy the town before rushing on to distant destinations. The shopping district is uphill and to the left off Highway 305, immediately after leaving the ferry. A host of stores and businesses along Winslow Way offer opportunities to browse, buy, dine, or wet your whistle. A complete circuit of downtown is just an easy stroll, ending with the green glade of the waterfront park.

EAGLE HARBOR MARINAS

Facilities: Transient moorage with power and water, restrooms, showers, laundry, pumpout station, fuel, marine supplies and repair, groceries, ice, fishing tackle, bait

When entering Eagle Harbor, boaters must use care, as a shoal and rocks extend south for about 500 yards from Wing Point on the north side of the harbor. Follow the channel markers, avoiding the natural desire to head straight into the bay. Good anchorages can be found in 30 feet of water near the west end of the bay, away from the flow of traffic. Anchoring in the bay is limited to seventy-two hours at a time.

Overnight moorage is permitted at the float at Waterfront Park, but there is no power or water on the pier. Winslow Wharf marina on the north shore, west of the yacht club, has transient moorage, fuel, showers, laundry, a chandlery, groceries, a coffee shop, and a couple of restaurants

Sailboat leaving Eagle Harbor

on the wharf. There is no guest dock—all slips are permanent; empty ones are sublet to visitors. Reservations for transient slips are accepted, or check with the dock master on arrival for available moorage.

A second 150-slip marina, on the south shore across from the ferry terminal, does not have fuel, but has guest facilities, including showers, laundry, a hot tub, and a recreation room. Although the marina was originally developed as a condominium dock, there are generally several slips that are uncommitted or available for subletting as guest moorage. Check with the dock master for transient slip assignment: all floats have power and water available. Downtown shopping is only a short row away.

EAGLE HARBOR WATERFRONT PARK

Park area: 8 acres; 1,000 feet of waterfront
Access: Land, boat
Facilities: Picnic tables, fireplace, picnic shelter, restrooms, dock, boat
    launch (ramp), children's play equipment, tennis courts
Attractions: Walking, boating, views

The business district of Winslow is on the hillside above the bay. By some stroke of fortune a stretch of waterfront below the town remained undeveloped, and now has become a pretty little park where tourists and

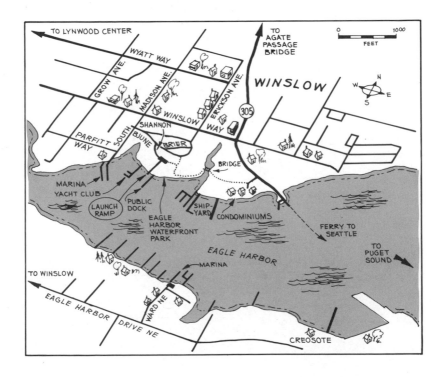

townfolk alike can recreate. To reach the park by foot from the ferry land-ing, walk down a road to the left that serves as an entrance to some condo-minums; shortly it intersects a gravel path, signed to the Waterfront Park, heading west. A short extension of the path continues east, between Scotch broom and a yew hedge bordering the condo property, to the shore just west of the ferry landing. On the route to the west, a wooded ravine and a small backwater bay, crossed by a footbridge, lead to the east end of the park.

Madrona trees overhang the banks, and ivy-covered firs and alders reach upward. Picnic tables and benches at scenic spots provide plenty of excuses to while away some time and watch harbor activity. Kayaks and dinghies weave calmly among yachts, ships, barges, and ferries. Ducks and gulls eye visitors, hoping for a handout, while cormorants look on dis-dainfully.

The beach is gravel and mud, and not inviting for walking, but paths continue along the bank and through the heart of the park to its western edge. Tennis courts, restrooms, and a picnic shelter with fireplace are a block uphill.

On the west side of the park is a single-lane concrete boat launch ramp

Boat launch at Eagle Harbor Waterfront Park

Trail in Eagle Harbor Waterfront Park

and a 300-foot-long float. Moorage on the float is limited to forty-eight hours per week; rafting is not permitted. The zero-tide level is marked on the dock; check the depth and tide level before securing your boat, as a tide flat extends for some distance from the shore. Although the launch ramp is excellent, it may not be usable at an extreme low tide.

From the Winslow shopping district, almost any turn to the south leads to the waterfront park. To drive to the boat launch, turn off Bjune Drive onto Shannon Way, and drive past the Queen City Yacht Club outstation to a parking lot at the end of the road. This lot is restricted to vehicles with boat trailers; additional parking for boat trailers is permitted weekends and evenings on Brier and Bjune avenues.

BLAKELY HARBOR

South along the Bainbridge Island shoreline, 1½ miles from Eagle Harbor, is the quiet little inlet of Blakely Harbor. It wasn't always so tranquil. The harbor once held a booming sawmill that, during the 1880s, was claimed to be the largest in the world; lumber shipped from here graced fine mansions from San Francisco to London.

In 1881, the Hall Brothers Shipyard moved their operation here from Port Ludlow when problems at the Ludlow sawmill threatened the ready supply of finished lumber at that location. The Hall Brother's yard built seventy-seven ships in the years they were in Port Blakely. It was a convenient cycle of events—ships were built of lumber from the mill, and then

Blakely Harbor

many of them carried lumber from the huge mill to markets throughout the world. The five-masted, 225-foot *H. K. Hall*, launched here, could hold one and a half million board feet of fine Puget Sound lumber.

A 1907 fire devastated the mill, and it was rebuilt to only half its former size. The decline in readily available logs, combined with a depressed lumber market, finally led to the mill's closing in 1914. As the mill foundered, the Hall shipyard was moved north in 1903 to Eagle Harbor. For a time Blakely Harbor still held some importance as a ferry landing, but that too was moved to Winslow in 1937, and the harbor settled back into a quiet existence as a residential community.

Pleasure boaters today enjoy the harbor as a good overnight anchorage and an interesting cruising diversion. Private residences rim the bay—some are the remodeled buildings of the old mill and shipyard; all shore lands are private. Numerous rotted pilings and the concrete shell of an old building at the far northwest end of the bay are testimony to the previous life at Blakely Harbor.

Although the bay is exposed to winds from the east, some anchorages can be found along the south shore. The view east to Seattle is stunning, with the Space Needle and downtown skyscrapers looming large.

Blakely Rock, which is marked by a light, lies ½ mile east of the entrance to Blakely Harbor and due north of Restoration Point. A rocky shoal extends 250 yards to the north. The reef is a popular scuba diving site.

Rich Passage and Port Orchard

Bainbridge Island forms the northern boundary of Rich Passage, the narrow channel the ferry must thread on its way to Bremerton. The passage is heavily traveled by pleasure boats; on rare occasions an enormous ship or other Naval vessel heading for or leaving Bremerton fills the channel. Between Point White and Point Glover, at the west end, the channel makes a sharp turn and squeezes down to less than 500 yards wide before opening up into the expanse of Port Orchard. Large vessels will sound one long blast when within ½ mile of Point Glover as a warning to approaching craft.

West of Rich Passage an arm of Port Orchard bends southwest, ending in Sinclair Inlet and the gargantuan Erector Set of the Navy shipyards. The main body of the channel sweeps steadily northward for 9 unobstructed miles between Bainbridge Island and the Kitsap Peninsula, before squeezing through Agate Passage and finally pouring into Port Madison. Navigational considerations and facilities in Rich Passage and Port Orchard are described in chapter 4.

FORT WARD STATE PARK

Park area: 137 acres; 4,300 feet of shoreline
Access: Land, boat
Facilities: Picnic tables, fireplaces, latrines, water, boat launch (ramp),
    hiking trail, mooring buoys, underwater park
Attractions: Historical displays, boating, fishing, hiking, scuba diving

It wasn't until recently, when the lands on the south end of Bainbridge Island were developed as a state park, that many people even knew there had been a military fortification in the area. Visitors are now gradually dis-

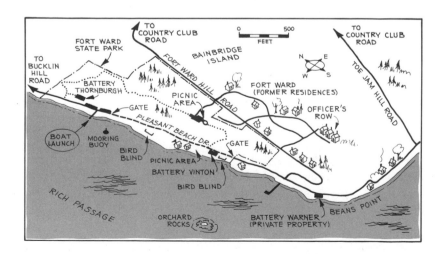

Remnants of Battery Thornburg at Fort Ward State Park

covering this history-rich corner of the island and the richly forested day-use state park overlooking Rich Passage.

Property at Beans Point was purchased by the U.S. Army in 1899; by 1903 construction of buildings and gun emplacements was under way and it was commissioned as Fort Ward. The post, along with the fortifications at Middle Point immediately across the channel, served for twenty years as an inner line of defense to protect the Navy shipyards at Bremerton. Three 8-inch disappearing guns and several smaller rapid-fire guns were installed in four batteries at Beans Point to protect a mine field that was to be laid across the channel. Guns were also planned for Middle Point, but were never placed.

During World War I there seemed no danger of direct attack on Puget Sound, so the 8-inch guns were removed and shipped to France for use there. By 1923 all the guns had been stripped from the batteries; with the "teeth" gone from the fortification, the following year the remaining troops, except for a caretaker detachment, were transferred to Fort Worden at Port Townsend.

The once vital fort was abandoned as an Army post and in 1930 was transferred to the Navy as a recreation site. It saw duty as a Navy radio school and intercept station, and then as a Nike missile site before it was finally surplused. After a brief stint as a children's home, 137 acres of the 480-acre military site was acquired for a state park.

To reach the entrance at the northwest side of the state park, drive west from Winslow to the head of Eagle Harbor on Wyatt Way, then go south on Bucklin Hill Road. At an intersection, where Bucklin Hill Road heads west, continue south on Blakely Avenue. When Blakely Avenue curves east, continue straight ahead on West Blakely Road to Pleasant Beach Drive. Turn left and follow it southeast to the road end in the park.

Just inside the park entrance is a large parking lot and a two-lane boat launch ramp. Launching can be difficult due to the strong tidal current and wakes from passing boats, especially ferries churning by in Rich Passage. The mooring buoy offshore, just north of the ramp, is also subject to channel turbulence.

The bottom offshore is frequented by scuba divers who explore the abundance of sea life on the steep walls. To the south are Orchard Rocks, with anemone-filled grottoes, and perhaps an octopus. Dive with extreme care; use a dive flag and watch and listen for boats when ascending.

At the parking lot a gate prevents driving farther along the service road. The road or the beach can be walked south to the park boundary, passing the park office and a pretty, shore-side picnic area with tables, fireplaces, water, and latrines.

From the picnic area a paved side trail climbs through the forest to the upper park entrance. A few more steps south of the picnic area along the road leads to Battery Vinton, with an informational display and a tip-toe view over a growth of Scotch broom across Rich Passage to Middle Point.

Two unique wooden structures with benches, one midway down the road and the other just south of Battery Vinton, are bird blinds for watching waterfowl in the channel. Along the shore three sets of mouldering pilings, topped by horizontal beams, are "cormorant parking lots," invariably holding a phalanx of these birds craning their necks to watch activity in the channel, or spreading their wings to dry.

From the launch ramp parking lot, another trail goes uphill a short distance to where a side trail leads to the ivy- and moss-encrusted Battery Thornburgh. The main trail continues up to the top of the bluff and heads south to the upper parking lot, through second-growth forest with sword fern and ivy undergrowth. From here the trail from the picnic area can be caught back down to the road. A complete loop hike, including all the sights, is about 2 miles. Do not stray off the paths, as there is poison oak in the area.

The second entrance to the park is at the top of the hill, at the southeast side of the park. To drive there, follow Blakely Avenue east from the West Blakely Road intersection, then turn south (right) on Country Club Road, then right again at Fort Ward Hill Road, which leads to the state park entrance, where there is a large parking lot, picnic tables, fire pedestals, and pit toilets; there are no garbage cans, however. The trails described previously leave from either end of the parking lot.

East of the park boundary are the original buildings of the fort, in various stages of restoration or disrepair. Some carry historical signs telling what they were in an earlier life. All are now privately owned. A tour through this residential area will give an idea of the original size of the fort.

Fort Ward Hill Road can be followed as it continues steeply downhill to the water and the eastern end of the gated park road; however, there is no parking at this end. The concrete remnant of another battery, Battery Warner, along the road to the south, is now on private property.

Continue east on South Beach Road, which follows the shoreline, and a sharp turn to the north brings one to the fabled Toe Jam Hill Road. The name of the hill, it is said, comes from a particularly seedy tavern that was in the area in early times. The libation served by this establishment, instead of being called Rot Gut, was given the even more derisive term of "Toe Jam." The tavern burned in 1903 or 1904, but the name remained for the hill on which it stood.

CRYSTAL SPRINGS

On the southwest corner of Bainbridge Island, in the small community of Crystal Springs, is a long pier that is open to the public for fishing. Even if fish are not interested in being caught some days, the dock is a nice vantage point, with miles of views up and down the channel of Port Orchard and across to Illahee State Park. The pier has no float, but the adjoining beach is quite gentle, so small boats could be beached, or hand-carried ones launched.

Fishing and dropping crab pots from the pier at Crystal Springs

To reach Crystal Springs, follow signs south to Lynwood Center, then turn east on Point White Drive, which curves around the point, and in 2½ miles arrives at the public pier. Parking for a few cars is on the east side of the road in a gravel pull-out. The drive or bike ride around Point White is a scenic one—reason enough to wander here. The road that continues north eventually deadends. To return to civilization one must backtrack to Lynwood Center.

FLETCHER AND MANZANITA BAYS

Gunkholers take note! Two small bays along the west shore of the island offer boaters a quiet overnight anchorage or a spot to drop a lunch hook. Aside from one tiny stretch, the shorelines of both bays are private. Battle Point, the tip of the triangular peninsula separating the bays, was named for a battle of long ago when the local Suquamish Indians and their chief, Kitsap, successfully fought off a band of marauding northern hostiles.

A gravel bar blocks the entrance to Fletcher Bay at mid-tide, and the bay itself is quite shallow, so boats should enter it only during high tide, and then with extreme care.

Manzanita Bay, to the north, offers the best overnight stops, with good protection from southerly blows or, in good weather, placid, star-filled nights. The main body of the bay extends due south for ¾ mile; a short "thumb" trends east. Good anchorages in up to 30 feet of water can be found in either section. The only hazards are submerged pilings about halfway in from the entrance on each side of the bay.

A sliver of public access exists on the north side of Manzanita Bay at a road end, the site of a long-extinct ferry landing. This is a good spot to launch hand-carried boats for exploration of the bay. To reach this access, turn west from Miller Road NE onto NE Bergman Road. In ¾ mile, where the road rounds the north shore of Manzanita Bay, watch carefully for a short, unmarked spur road on the left. The road stub ends in about a block at a bulkhead above the beach; parking space is minimal. Property adjacent to the road and the beach on either side of the road end itself is private. Do not trespass.

Agate Passage and Port Madison Bay

The Agate Passage bridge, at the northwest tip of Bainbridge Island, is the island's only permanent tie to the mainland, freeing it from total dependence on the ferry. Since the completion of the bridge in 1950, old plans for building additional bridges have been periodically dusted off, but the increasing cost of such a project, coupled with the islanders' satisfaction with the status quo, always causes the plans to be shelved once again.

The call for more bridges usually comes from people on the Kitsap Peninsula, frustrated by ferry service, who want bridges to Vashon Island and the south end of Bainbridge, so they can have easier access to ferry ter-

Manzanita Bay

minals on those islands and can swear at three ferries instead of just one.

After their rapid trip through 300-yard-narrow Agate Passage, the waters of Port Orchard pour into Port Madison, a broad, round bay bounded on the south by Bainbridge Island. Point Monroe, a curving sand spit marked by a navigational light, lies at the south point of the entrance to the bay. The spit encloses a lagoon that boats can enter at its west end; however, it is quite shallow and the entrance dries at low tide. Several private homes have been built on the spit, and there are docks on the inner edge.

REITAN ROAD ACCESS

This access directly under the bridge gives a unique water-level perspective on activity in Agate Passage. Traffic roars by overhead, water swirls around the concrete abutments, boats sweep by grandly, given an overdrive assist by the rushing current, and an occasional black head, dripping with water, bobs to the surface. Seals? No—scuba divers!

The primitive access is on the Bainbridge Island side of the channel. Head west on Highway 305 and, just before crossing the bridge, turn north on Reitan Road. The narrow, paved road drops downhill and under the bridge footings. Parking for half a dozen cars is at the side of the road near a powerline tower just northeast of the bridge.

From the powerline tower dirt stair steps lead to a cobble beach dropping off abruptly to the water. The beach south of the bridge is private, but about 300 feet of shorelands to the north are open for public walking.

The access is used by scuba divers who explore the bridge abutments, offshore rocks, and steep walls of the channel. Since the tidal current can reach six knots, only experienced divers should use the area. Those skilled enough to handle the flow thrill to a roller-coaster ride around and over rocks and past the encrusted pilings of the bridge.

PORT MADISON COUNTY PARK (KITSAP COUNTY)

A tiny county park just west of Inner Port Madison is, unfortunately, no longer maintained, but the beach does offer the only public access on the Bainbridge Island side of Port Madison. From the water, the park is an overgrown section of land about 600 yards west of the entrance to Inner Port Madison, just west of some private homes.

By land, the park can be reached by turning east off Highway 305 onto NE West Port Madison Road. Follow the street as it curves north and then turns right and becomes County Park Road. The park is immediately west of the intersection of Gordon Road; there is no sign. A gated dirt road goes north into the heavy growth of old cedar and fir. There is room to park one car outside the barricade. A second similarly barricaded road leads into the park from NE Gordon Drive, just where it makes a sharp turn to the east.

There are deteriorating remnants of picnic tables, the frames of a couple of dilapidated picnic shelters with stone fireplaces, and a pair of pit toilets. One wonders at the festive picnics of yesteryear that the little park must have seen. And why not today?

The beach is reached by a primitive, slippery trail leading down the 50-foot clay bank. A pair of parallel planks embedded in the bank form crude handrails in the steepest part. Remember where the trail comes out of the brush at the beach, as the spot is not easily found. At low tides the beach is gradually tapering cobble; high tide brings the water right up to the tree line.

INNER PORT MADISON

The mile-long arm extending south from Port Madison is unquestionably one of the loveliest boating stops on Bainbridge Island. Names around here are a little confusing—to some *this* narrow inlet is Port Madison—never mind that big chunk of water hovering to the north; to others this arm is Madison Bay. But the name by which it is known locally, and by most knowledgeable boaters, is Inner Port Madison. The community on its shore is also named Port Madison.

Port Madison (the town) was once the major commercial center on the island. Not only was it the county seat, complete with a courthouse and jail, but it also had a large sawmill, shipyards, foundry, fish oil rendering plant, and a population of 400 to 600 people: A geography book published at the time described Seattle as "a lumber town across the bay from Port Madison." Since this was a company town, residences were owned by the mill and rented to employees. When the company fell on hard times because of a depressed lumber market, it became heavily mortaged by the

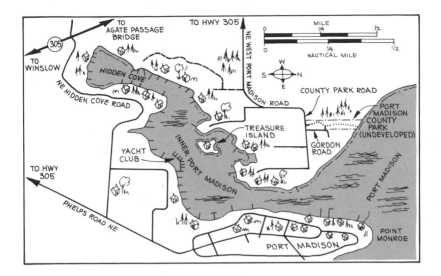

Seattle First National Bank. Eventually the bank foreclosed and took over everything owned by the mill.

Since virtually all the property on the harbor was then in the hands of Seattle First, the bank conceived the idea of developing the property as an exclusive summer resort area. All but the best of the mill buildings were torn down, lots were sold for fashionable summer homes, and metal gates were installed on the road to keep cows from wandering through and destroying the ambience (or depositing their own ambience).

Over the years the summer homes gave way to the gracious permanent homes found along the shore today. The Port Madison Yacht Club has moorages on the bay, and there is an outstation for the Seattle Yacht Club here. The small island midway along the north shore was used as a cemetery during the days of the mill and so was known as Deadman's Island. When a cemetery was established elsewhere on Bainbridge Island, the human remains were moved. High society hit the bay, and the islet was renamed Treasure Island.

Boats entering the bay should hold to the middle of the narrow channel to avoid an old ballast dump lying along the east shore, a remainder from the days when this was a lumber port. Ships arriving in the harbor without a cargo carried a load of rock as ballast to steady them; the rock was dumped when they were ready to take on a load of lumber.

Inside the mile-long bay the only navigational hazards are shoals extending from Treasure Island and a submerged rock marked by a daybeacon lying south-southwest of the small island. Good anchorages can be found throughout the bay, out of the way of traffic, in up to 20 feet of water.

In its last ⅓ of a mile the bay takes a dogleg turn to the south. This far end is known as Hidden Cove. Navigable water continues almost to the head of the bay. There are no public boat facilities on the bay; all shorelands are private.

FAY-BAINBRIDGE STATE PARK

Park area: 17 acres; 1,420 feet of shoreline
Access: Land, boat
Facilities: 36 campsites, picnic tables, fireplaces, picnic shelters, restrooms, showers, boat launch (ramp), volleyball courts, horseshoe pits, children's play equipment, trailer dump
Attractions: Swimming, boating, fishing, beachcombing, scuba diving

The only campground on Bainbridge Island is on its northeast shore, at popular Fay-Bainbridge State Park. The park includes some nicely wooded uplands and one of the prettiest beaches on the island. The beach faces directly on the main channel of Puget Sound, so at times wind and wave action can be severe, and even on hot summer days the water is chilly for swimming; the sandy beach, topped by a row of driftwood and tufts of seagrass, is always a delight, however. At low water the long tide flat holds promise of a few clams for the lucky. The park is heavily used by island residents, and on nice summer days can get very crowded.

For its relatively small size the park packs in a lot of activities. The upper portion of the park has a few picnic sites and some tent camping in grassy areas among the trees. Most of the camping is just above the beach at rather tightly spaced campsites along the southern side of the park, with RV camp areas separate from tenting sites.

On the north edge of the beach is a boat launch ramp and large parking lot. The surfaced ramp ends at the gravel beach line, so launching at mid- to low tide would be difficult. Boats put in here can explore around the corner to the lagoon of Point Monroe and on to Inner Port Madison.

Two mooring buoys offshore are usable for a lunch stop, but the lack

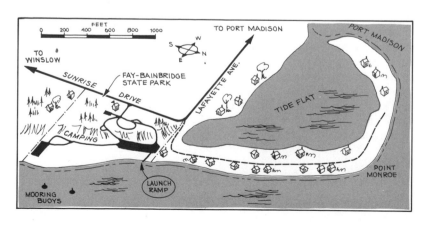

Beach at Fay-Bainbridge State Park

of protection from waves and wakes could make them quite uncomfortable for an overnight stay.

The historical highlight of the park is the large brass bell on display near the entrance. The bell, which was brought from San Francisco about 1883, was purchased by private subscription by the people of Port Madison, and was used in the courthouse there.

By land the park is reached by turning east off Highway 305 4¼ miles north of Winslow onto Day Road, which is signed to the park. When Sunrise Drive is reached, turn north and follow it to the park.

4. East Kitsap Peninsula

The Kitsap Peninsula has the distinction of being bounded on the west by one major waterway, Hood Canal, and on the east by a different large body of water, Puget Sound. With the exception of the major indentation of Port Gamble Bay, the western shoreline of Kitsap Peninsula rolls smoothly along the canal. The eastern edge of the peninsula, however, is heavily convoluted, with numerous bays and inlets pushing deep inland. These sheltered bays, with their miles upon miles of shoreline, lure boaters and beach walkers bent on marine diversions.

Several state and city parks along the shore offer recreation facilities, and a number of towns have marine accommodations and supplies. The shores are heavily populated—one would be hard pressed to find a pristine beach, even in the parks, but the interesting villages and towns along the way compensate for this.

Land travelers usually arrive at the Kitsap Peninsula via ferry, either from Seattle to Bremerton, or from Seattle to Winslow on Bainbridge Island and then by driving or biking over the Agate Pass bridge. Either route is exquisitely scenic, with views of boating traffic on the busy marine highway, the sparkling skyline of the city, and the ethereal presence of Mt. Rainier. The peninsula can also be reached from the south via Highway 16 from Tacoma or Highway 3 from Shelton.

MANCHESTER

Facilities: Dock with float, boat launch (ramp), groceries, ice, service station, bait, tackle

The only public water access between Southworth and Rich Passage is at the tiny community of Manchester. Here the Port of Manchester dock, with its 150-foot-long float, is available for day use by boaters and anglers; overnight moorage is not permitted. Adjacent to the dock to the north is a two-lane concrete launch ramp. The dock also affords expansive views west to the Seattle cityscape, the West Seattle shoreline, and nearby Blake Island, and south to Mt. Rainier.

Car parking at the dock itself is limited to two spaces for handicapped. The closest general parking area is 1½ blocks up the street, north of the Colchester/East Main intersection. The heart of Manchester is a cluster of stores around this intersection.

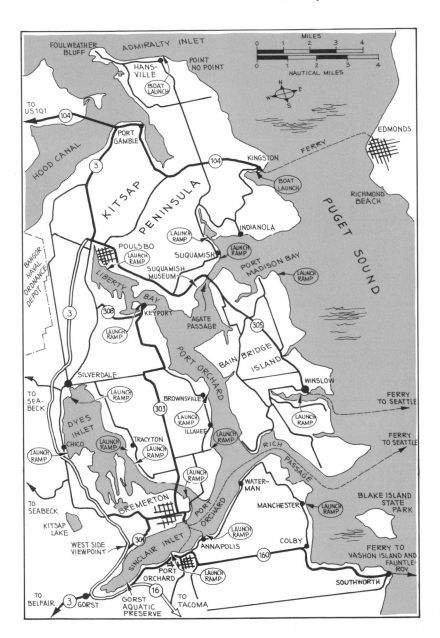

Manchester is most easily reached via the Southworth ferry. From the ferry landing follow State Highway 160 north for 3¾ miles, then turn east on SE Colchester Drive, signed to Manchester and Manchester State Park. The intersection above the dock is reached in another 1¾ miles.

On the beach at Manchester

Rich Passage

Rich Passage is one of the most scenic spots along the route of the Bremerton ferry. Here the channel squeezes at its slenderest point to a mere 500 yards wide, and passengers are treated to close-up views of salty beachfront homes tucked into the green-clad shoreline.

Pleasure boaters should be wary of stiff tidal currents that can be encountered in the channel, especially at the west end. Several rocks lying just offshore are well marked with lights or daymarkers. The largest of the obstacles, Orchard Rocks, lying on the north side of the channel just inside the east entrance, are partially exposed at low tide. Boaters will encounter no problems if they stay in the marked channel, but should keep an eye over their shoulders for ferries bearing down on them.

MANCHESTER STATE PARK

Park area: 111 acres; 3,400 feet of shoreline
Access: Land, boat
Facilities: 53 campsites, picnic tables, fireplaces, picnic shelters, water, restrooms, showers, hiking trails, nature trail
Attractions: Historical displays, hiking, fishing, boating, scuba diving

At the turn of the century, although the United States was not at war, the Army feared foreign ships could sneak into Puget Sound and attack the vital Naval Shipyards at Bremerton. A military station was built at Middle Point on the south shore of Rich Passage to operate a mine field that was to be laid across the channel. By 1910, even before World War I broke out, the technology of the type of mine installed here became obsolete and, since there was no threat of attack, the fort was deactivated; the site was then for a time used for torpedo testing.

During World War II anti-submarine nets were stretched from here across the channel to Fort Ward. The nets were lowered whenever ferries passed. After the installation was no longer needed, part of the military land was taken by the Navy for an oil storage depot; the balance of the property was eventually surplused, and the public got lucky and gained another prime beachfront state park.

To reach Manchester State Park from Bremerton, follow the road paralleling the shoreline around Sinclair Inlet. After going through the small community of Waterman, the road leaves the shore and turns due south. In ½ mile turn west on East Hilldale Road, which is signed to the park.

From Southworth, the terminus of the Vashon ferry from Fauntleroy, the park can be reached by heading west on Highway 160; in 3¾ miles turn right on SE Colchester Drive and follow signs to the park, a total distance of 8 miles from the ferry terminal. When going through Manchester, make sure to take the first right, a short ½ block west of the Colchester/East Main intersection, onto Beach Drive East.

By boat, the park is 10½ miles from Seattle's Shilshole Bay, and 5½ miles from downtown Bremerton or Port Orchard.

The park fronts on a small, shallow cove—not especially good for

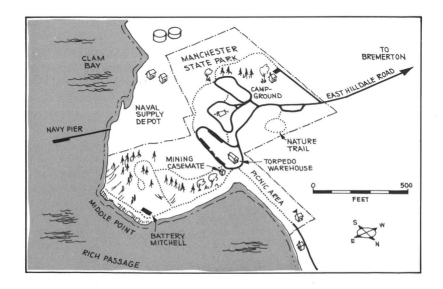

Torpedo warehouse at Manchester State Park

swimming, but an adequate spot to launch hand-carried boats. Underwater rocks off Middle Point are an attractive scuba diving site. The campground, on the hillside above the cove, lies in tall cedar, fir, and aspen, with an undergrowth of sword fern and salal.

The remaining old structures of the fortification—a torpedo warehouse and mining casemate—add to the interest of the park. Informational displays describe the system of placing and detonating the mines, and tracking ships in the channel. The huge brick torpedo warehouse, with gracefully arched windows and doorways, is now a mind-boggling picnic shelter.

Several trails lace the park, connecting the campground with the picnic area and beach; most follow old service roads. A short loop interpretive nature trail is immediately north of the park entrance. Signs advise hikers to stay on trails and avoid brush near the shore since the area contains a heavy growth of poison oak.

A trail leads west from the beach and picnic area to the concrete pit of Battery Mitchell. The Army had planned for the Middle Point fortification to have two 3-inch guns to protect the mine field, but the four batteries at Fort Ward on Bainbridge Island, immediately across Rich Passage, offered ample protection, so guns were never installed.

Port Orchard and Sinclair Inlet

The purpose of geographical names is supposed to be to clarify locations. Unfortunately this is not the case with Port Orchard, as the name refers to (1) the 9-mile north–south flowing channel separating Bainbridge Island and the Kitsap Peninsula; (2) the baylike continuation of that channel that runs southwest to Bremerton; and (3) the small town on the shore of, not Port Orchard, but Sinclair Inlet.

Beach Drive, paralleling the water along the south shore from Rich Passage to the town of Port Orchard, is an ideal bicycle or Sunday-drive route with plenty of places to stop and picnic, birdwatch, fish, or photograph. Monster ferries lumber by, sailboats blow in the breeze, the Naval shipyards look like some enormous Erector Set construction, and above it rise the crystal peaks of the Olympics.

At minus tides the baring shoreline shows interesting lines of parallel rock strata extending diagonally outward from the beach. These are the edges of tilted layers of hard rock that were ground off by an ancient glacier.

WATERMAN

Facilities: Public pier, float, groceries, fishing supplies

In the late 1800s steamers of the Mosquito Fleet stopped regularly at Waterman, on the south shore of Port Orchard, to load bricks from the lo-

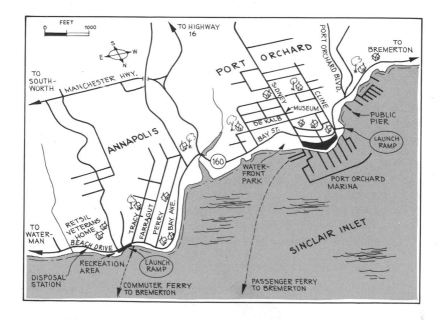

Public pier at Waterman; Bremerton in the distance

cal brickyard and pick up and discharge passengers. The brickyard closed in 1889; in time the steamers ceased calling here and the old piers rotted away. Today the only reminder of the once-busy town is the small multi-purpose marine supply/grocery store sandwiched between the waterfront homes lining the beach drive.

A recreational pier with float has been built at Waterman to serve pleasure boaters, fishermen, and passersby. The 200-foot-long pier, maintained by the Port of Port Orchard, has a fishing platform and a 40-foot concrete float at its end. Moorage here may be a bit bouncy because of swells from traffic on the inlet. At the head of the dock, a wooden deck with a pair of benches fronts a paved, narrow parking area. Next to the shore, wooden stairs give access to the beach, but the beach is public only for the width of the deck above. The store immediately across the road has all the necessary supplies for would-be anglers or spur-of-the-moment picnickers. A public Sani-can is next to the store.

ANNAPOLIS RECREATION AREA

This Department of Game boat launching area is a 200-foot strip of beachfront at the east city limits of Port Orchard immediately next to the

Annapolis–Bremerton passenger ferry dock. The only facilities are a single-lane, surfaced launch ramp, a 100-foot-long float, and a large parking lot for vehicles with boat trailers. The gravel and mud beach slopes outward quite gradually; at low tide the float is aground. There are no restrooms near the ramp area, but there is an RV holding tank disposal station about 200 feet east on the south side of the road.

Just west of the recreation area is the Port of Bremerton Annapolis Dock, used by a small passenger ferry taking commuters to Bremerton. The 300-foot-long dock has a float that can be used for fishing when the ferry is not in. The parking lot at the head of the dock is reserved for cars with permits.

Inspired by the prospects of the naval shipyards about to be built on Sinclair Inlet, the founders of Annapolis named their town after the site of the U.S. Naval Academy in Maryland, and gave the streets names of naval heroes such as Farragut and Perry. The former business center has been annexed by Port Orchard and is now part of that town.

PORT ORCHARD

Port Orchard (the town) is frequently the prime destination for people boating in Port Orchard (the waterway). The town is the antithesis of industrial Bremerton, facing it across the inlet—here life is slow paced, ex-

Port Orchard

cept briefly during shift change at the Navy shipyards, when commuter traffic pours through. The town caters to tourists; its main street, with wooden-canopied walkways reminiscent of the Old West, has an assortment of interesting shops to browse and eateries to try.

Three blocks straight up the hill on Sidney Avenue at the intersection of De Kalb Street is the town's Log Cabin Museum—a case where the building is every bit as fascinating and historic as its contents. Hours are Sunday 1:00 to 4:00 P.M.; Monday 10:00 to 12:00 A.M. The two-story log structure dates from 1913 to 1914; it houses a collection of memorabilia and authentic furnishings.

Port Orchard began its history in 1886 as Sidney, named after the father of town founder Frederick Stevens. In 1903, after ten years of political arm wrestling with the town fathers of Charleston, on the opposite side of the inlet, who decided they wanted the name of Port Orchard too, the name was changed. At that time the shipyard mail was addressed to Port Orchard (the waterway), and everyone was trying to capitalize on it.

From the beginning, Mosquito Fleet steamers were vital to the existence of businesses in Sidney (Port Orchard), but once the shipyards became active they also served to transport workers from their homes on the south side of the bay. The Mosquito Fleet is now just a fond memory, but it

A passenger ferry that runs between Port Orchard and Bremerton

is possible to recapture some of the feeling of that era by hopping the little passenger ferry still running to Bremerton. The boat departs from the terminal immediately east of the marina about every half hour; crossing time is about fifteen minutes. Take advantage of the trip and linger to walk around Bremerton, avoiding parking or mooring woes. A second passenger ferry leaves from Annapolis, on the east side of town, but that boat is primarily used by shipyard workers, and operates only during commuting hours.

PORT ORCHARD MARINA AND WATERFRONT PARK

Facilities: Transient moorage with power and water, diesel, gas, restrooms, showers, pumpout station, picnic tables, picnic shelter

Centerpiece of the town of Port Orchard is the large, modern marina, operated by the Port of Bremerton. Nearly half of the 600-plus slips in the marina are allocated for guest moorage—which soundly attests to the popularity of the town and its facilities as a cruising destination. A long, concrete breakwater cups around the moorage area; entrance is at the west end. The fuel dock and a short guest moorage dock are at gate 1, immediately inside the marina. Gates 2 and 3, the covered moorages in the center, are all

Port Orchard Waterfront Park

permanent tie-ups. The main transient area is along the breakwater and at its western end, adjoining gate 4. In summer late-arriving boaters may have to tie up on the outside of the breakwater, where waves and wakes can make for an uncomfortable stay.

At night the dock gates and doors of the on-shore restrooms by the harbormaster's office are opened by a key card, obtainable from the harbormaster. Water is on the dock, and most moorages have power hookups. Restrooms open to the public, without the use of a key card, are at the west end of the parking lot. Grocery stores, restaurants, marine supplies, and other shopping are only a block's walk away.

Immediately east of the marina is a three-block-long waterfront park and promenade—benches along the way overlook nautical activities. At the far east end of the park is a small pavilion with bleachers that also serves as a picnic shelter when not used by entertainment playing to the bleachers. A wide set of concrete steps leads down to the sand and gravel beach. Take along a tuna sandwich and make use of the picnic tables or shelter at this end of the park.

PORT ORCHARD BOAT LAUNCH AND PUBLIC PIER

Continue west along the waterfront drive to find the city's public boat ramp, immediately across the street from the white concrete block Port Orchard municipal building, at the intersection of Bay Street (Highway 160) and Cline Avenue. The two surfaced launch ramps are separated by a 50-foot finger pier for loading. The adjacent parking lot has space for eight or nine vehicles and trailers.

A commercial boat house lies to the west of the launch ramps, and beyond that, at the intersection of Bay Street and Port Orchard Boulevard, the City of Port Orchard Pedestrian Pier juts into Rich Passage. The 150-foot-long wooden pier includes a couple of park benches and picnic tables. A 90-foot-long float, reached by a ramp, nearly rests on the bottom at low tide. Take advantage of the pier and float for fishing or just dawdling.

GORST AQUATIC PRESERVE

A variety of waterfowl gather at the head of Sinclair Inlet—cormorants perch on old pilings, spreading their wings to dry in the sun, migratory ducks paddle in flocks along the protected shoreline, resting and refueling before continuing on their journey. On the south shore of the inlet twenty-four acres of tidelands have been set aside by the Port of Bremerton and the U.S. Fish and Wildlife Service as a fish and waterfowl refuge.

The preserve is immediately west of the interchange where Highway 160 joins Highway 16. A large dirt parking lot on the north side of the road is marked by a brush-covered sign. A concrete median in the highway blocks access to the lot by eastbound traffic. The shoreline is soggy and densely overgrown—not much for walking, but ideal wildlife habitat. The best way to appreciate the extensive wetlands and possibly view some of the waterfowl is by kayak or canoe, which can be launched at the parking lot at high tide or, when the water is out, in Port Orchard, 5 miles away.

Bremerton

Bremerton is not a tourist town—it is too involved with its job of maintaining Navy ships to be concerned about entertaining guests. The town waterfront has some allure from a distance, with the latticework of the enormous hammerhead crane silhouetted against the pale outline of the Olympic Mountains, and mothballed ships lying in the harbor like snoozing dinosaurs. Up close, however, the oppressive barrier of cyclone fencing and the gritty industrialism of the shipyard sinks in, and visitors leaving the ferry usually hurry on to other destinations.

The local residents are pretty defensive about the shipyard—they know that either directly or indirectly it puts food on the table for nearly everyone in town. In fact, if it weren't for the shipyard, Bremerton might not exist. There were several other well-established towns in the vicinity when Lt. Ambrose Barkley Wyckoff selected a site on the north shore of Sinclair Inlet as the best possible location for a new Navy shipyard. In

Bremerton's Manette Bridge

1891 he purchased 190 acres of land from several property owners, including 86 acres owned by William Bremer. The Bremer property was part of a 168-acre parcel he had previously acquired from his brother-in-law, Henry Hensel. Bremer sold the land to the Navy for less than he had paid for it, feeling the presence of the shipyard would increase the value of his remaining holdings. He built a wharf on the water near the shipyard, cleared and platted forty acres, and named it Bremerton. A town was born.

The Navy yard had its beginnings in 1888 when a commission was appointed to find a site somewhere north of San Francisco for a naval station. Several potential sites in the Puget Sound region were located, but the favored candidates were Port Orchard and Lake Washington. Since the latter site would involve construction of elaborate, expensive, and militarily vulnerable channels and locks, the site on the shore of Port Orchard was selected, and in September of 1891 construction began.

For its first five years the naval station consisted of a wooden Civil

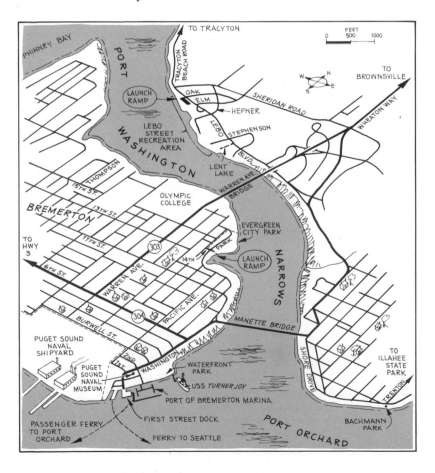

Ships at the Bremerton Naval Shipyard

War gunboat, the USS *Nipsic*, anchored offshore, which served as offices and quarters for the commandant, Lieutenant B. Wycoff. By 1896 an office building, officers' quarters, and the first drydock were complete; however, in 1899 development came to a standstill when the admiral in charge of the Bureau of Yards and Docks decided the station was poorly located and should be closed. The hue and cry of local business interests was felt in Congress, and construction resumed.

In 1904 land was acquired on Dyes Inlet at Ostrich Bay for construction of a Naval Ammunition Depot to assemble explosives and ammunition components into shells for the Navy and Coast Guard, and overhaul ammunition carried by vessels calling at Bremerton for maintenance.

By 1906 a second drydock was needed, and construction of Dock II, the Navy's largest drydock, was completed in 1913. Over the next ten years a marine reservation, hospital, wireless station, several machine and repair shops, and additional quarters and barracks were added. With the outbreak of World War I, the Navy added shipbuilding to the maintenance role of the yard, and a third drydock was constructed. The yard was also designated a training site for naval and marine recruits. Regrading out into Sinclair Inlet (no environmental impact statements in those days) of a large portion of the hillside to the west added thirty-four acres to the installation in 1920.

With the end of the war work, the yard force rapidly dropped from 6,500 to 2,700. Some limited shipbuilding continued, but it wasn't until 1932 that federal spending to relieve unemployment during the Depression funneled money into shore construction. Drydocks were expanded to accommodate the new aircraft carriers, and the hammerhead crane that identifies the yard today was added to handle battleship guns and turrets.

The Nazi invasion of Poland in 1939 triggered a flurry of defense activities, including the addition of a fourth drydock to the yard. Three years later the Japanese attack on Pearl Harbor brought the yard to full round-the-clock operation to meet the immediate demand for naval vessels. With increased ammunition shipments to Alaska and the Pacific, additional ammunition-handling stations with easy rail access became critical, and the Navy acquired the Hood Canal site at Bangor for a naval magazine.

With the end of World War II, the yard began another series of boom-or-bust cycles, dependent on naval maintenance requirements and appropriations. Today the yard is the home of a dozen or so mothballed ships. Active fleet ships still call at the yard for maintenance and upgrades, but shipbuilding here is now nonexistent. The ammunition station at Ostrich Bay has since been converted to the Jackson Park naval housing area.

Currently Keyport has an expanded role as the Naval Undersea Warfare Engineering Station; torpedo testing areas were expanded from Port Orchard to include most of Dabob Bay on Hood Canal. The Bangor facility went through several cycles of activity, with highs during the conflicts in Korea and Viet Nam and lulls in intervening periods. The conversion of Bangor to a home port for Trident submarines brought this area to its present-day mission and condition.

Today many downtown stores are linked to the needs and tastes of shipyard workers and the Navy. Scattered among the blue-collar taverns, bars, and cafes are such Navy-specific enterprises as a uniform supply and a tattoo parlor. The downtown shopping district lies along Pacific Avenue, two blocks from the ferry terminal.

For many years Bremerton had one certified tourist attraction—the USS *Missouri,* on which the Japanese surrendered in World War II, but this was lost when the battleship was reactivated in 1983. Plans to develop new tourist attractions and revitalize the waterfront finally will come to fruition by the summer of 1992 when a new marina and over-water park are completed. The destroyer USS *Turner Joy* has been anchored off Fourth Avenue, and when linked to the new park will be open for tours. The ship will also have remodeled quarters available for use as conference facilities.

PORT OF BREMERTON MARINA

Facilities: Transient moorage with power and water, restrooms, showers, laundry, marine pumpout station

North of the ferry terminal is the First Street Dock, a pretty waterfront facility with picnic tables and park benches. A breakwater that runs north from the end of the dock serves both as the loading platform for passenger-only ferries to Seattle and Annapolis and as protection for the waterfront moorage basin. Behind it are floats with room for 50 to 60 transient boats.

Car parking is available behind the marina office, and on the inner end of the First Street Dock, but auto traffic on First is one-way away from the water, so the area must be approached by a circuitous loop via Washington Avenue and Burwell Street.

BREMERTON WATERFRONT PARK

Pilings support an over-water boardwalk that runs along the waterfront between First and Fourth Avenues. Benches, tables, and planters create a pleasant park and provide places for a picnic lunch or to watch seagulls supervising waterfront activities. At the Fourth Avenue end of the dock, a pier and gangway offer access to the *Turner Joy*. Near the center of the park, at the foot of Burwell Street, is a building with a circular staircase winding up its side to a metal observation platform and a flagpole. Views are south and east across Dyes and Sinclair inlets.

PUGET SOUND NAVAL MUSEUM

For many years a corner of the ferry terminal housed the rather dusty relics of the Puget Sound Naval Museum. In 1986 the museum moved up the hill one block to a brighter, more spacious new location at 120 Washington Avenue. The museum focuses on the history of the Navy yards and ships built there, but it also has displays of ship memorabilia, swords, cutlasses, armaments, mines, and other interesting nautical paraphernalia. The numerous ship models, guaranteed to send small boys into ecstasy, include minutely detailed 15-foot-long replicas of aircraft carriers and plastic see-through builder's models showing all the interior plans.

Ship model at the Puget Sound Naval Museum

The museum expects to be at the Washington Avenue location for only five years, and then it will move to permanent quarters in a as-yet-to-be-constructed waterfront complex. At that new location the museum will expand to represent not just the legacy of the Puget Sound Naval Shipyard, but also the maritime history of the Pacific. It is hoped the growth of the museum will be timed to coincide with the centennial celebration of the shipyard, in 1991.

Port Washington Narrows

The city of Bremerton straddles the ¼-mile-wide trough of the Port Washington Narrows. Two bridges span the channel: near the mouth, Highway 304 crosses on the Manette bridge; midway up the channel the Warren Avenue bridge carries Highway 303. The 3½-mile-long Port Washington Narrows runs between sheer, 80-foot bluffs that gentle out at the northern end. The deep channel has no navigational hazards; however, tidal currents, which can run in excess of four knots, may noticeably affect boat speed and can cause problems for paddle-powered craft.

Aside from the yacht club on the west shore of Phinney Bay, the only commercial marine facility on the Port Washington Narrows or in Dyes Inlet is the Port Washington Marina, located on the south shore of the narrows, west of the Warren Avenue bridge. The marina is difficult to find by land; it is off 15th Street at the end of Thompson Drive. The facility has marine supplies, repair, transient moorage, restrooms, and a laundry, but does not have fuel. Some limited groceries are available nearby.

BACHMANN PARK

On the east side of the entrance to the Port Washington Narrows, at the tip of Point Herron, a tiny park offers an excellent view of traffic shuttling to and fro in the bay and entering the narrows. To reach the park from the ferry terminal, turn right after leaving the unloading area and follow Washington Avenue to the Manette bridge. Immediately after crossing the bridge, turn right and follow the arterial (11th Street) to Trenton Avenue. The park is two blocks to the right, at the end of Trenton.

The park's small wooden gazebo with benches overlooks the water. A breach in the concrete bulkhead allows visitors to reach the water and walk the cobblestone beach, or launch hand-carried boats.

EVERGREEN CITY PARK

Park area: 6 acres; 300 feet of shoreline
Facilities: Boat launch (ramp), restrooms, picnic tables, picnic shelters, water, fireplaces, children's play equipment
Attractions: Boating, fishing

This park is located on the west shore of the narrows, between the two Bremerton bridges, at the intersection of Park Avenue and 14th Street. A

The Warren Avenue Bridge over the Port Washington Narrows

large parking lot adjoins the single-lane, surfaced launch ramp.

The level, grassy park has numerous picnic tables for family picnics. Play equipment for energetic youngsters includes a pair of WWII vintage 3-inch rapid-fire guns to clamber on. The gravelly beach is not inviting for swimming, but is a good spot to try shore fishing.

LEBO STREET RECREATION AREA (LIONS PLAYFIELD)

Park area: 15 acres; 1,700 feet of shoreline
Facilities: Float, fishing pier, boat launch (ramp), picnic tables, fireplaces, children's play equipment, concession stand, baseball diamonds, restrooms, jogging track
Attractions: Fishing, boating, swimming, beach walking

The City of Bremerton and the Lions Club have put a five-block-long stretch of waterfront to its best possible use—a multipurpose recreation complex, appealing to interests ranging from baseball to boating. The park is located on the north shore, near the western end of the Port Washington Narrows. From land, the park is on Lebo Boulevard, which parallels the shore west of the Warren Avenue bridge. Entrances are in the middle of the park at Hefner Road, and at the west end at Oak Street. A third access is at the east end of the park at Lent Lane; here there is only a rough gravel parking lot and a low bank access to the water. Beach walks west from here can

Lebo Street Recreation Area

continue past the park along the shore below Tracyton Beach Road for a total distance of 3 miles. The central section of the park fronts on a sandy beach, perfect for sunbathing or courageously swimming in the chilly waters of the narrows.

Boating facilities at the west end of the park by the Oak Street entrance include a three-lane, surfaced launch ramp and a short concrete float for loading, or for passing boaters to stop at and enjoy the facilities. A long, concrete fishing pier parallels the shore. Benches in a pretty wooden gazebo provide a spot to relax and enjoy the stunning view up Dyes Inlet to rugged Olympic peaks.

The road continuing north from the park, Tracyton Beach Road, follows the shoreline, with numerous spots providing access to the beach. The level, blacktop road, marked as a bicycle route, is ideal for cycle touring, but it is narrow and has no shoulder.

Dyes Inlet

Dyes Inlet is a cruising delight, with fascinating little bays and coves, scenic shorelines, and quiet anchorages. Once past the Port Washington Narrows, the waterway suddenly opens to the 1½-mile-wide inlet, resembling a large, protected lake rather than the open reaches boaters are accustomed to on Puget Sound. The sheltered waters are ideal for kayak and small boat exploration, as well as cruising in bigger boats.

Several deep bays penetrate the southern shore. Phinney Bay, at the northern end of the narrows, hosts the moorages of the Bremerton Yacht Club. The next cove to the west, slender Mud Bay, is well named—it is a tide flat, not navigable by anything but kayaks or dinghies.

Ostrich Bay, the largest cove on Dyes Inlet, is on the southwest corner. Adventuresome boaters will want to follow the narrow slot on the

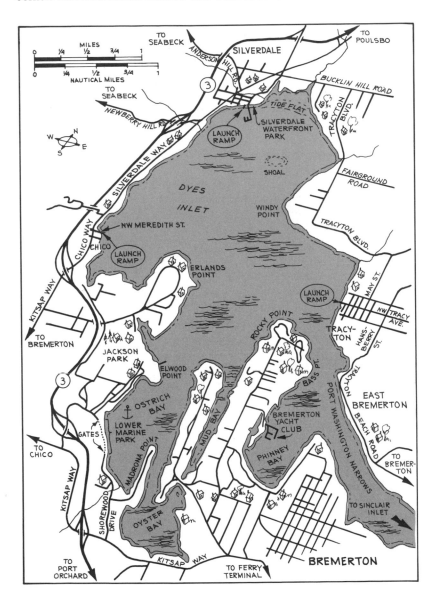

west shore of Ostrich Bay leading into the tiny pocket of Oyster Bay; at extreme low tide there is 6 feet of water midchannel. Good anchorages can be found in either bay. A large rock lies near the west shore, about 250 yards north of the large, abandoned Navy wharf. A ¼-mile section of shore along the southwest side of Ostrich Bay is a Bremerton city park. All other shore land is either private, or part of the Naval Ammunition Depot and the Jackson Park housing for Navy families.

We readily decide there are no ostriches on Ostrich Bay, but oysters on Oyster Bay? Perhaps. Japanese oysters were introduced in the early 1940s by Japanese-American entrepreneurs who established an oyster farm on the east side of Dyes Inlet. The business thrived, but unfortunately with the outbreak of World War II, the owners were confined in an internment camp, and the operation closed. The oysters remained to fend for themselves in the inlet, wherever they could find a suitable environment.

For clam lovers, a prime attraction of Dyes Inlet is a sandy shoal drying at low tide at the northeast end of the bay. When the shoal emerges, the clam diggers descend, armed with shovels and clam guns, to subdue and carry off their booty. It is believed that an ancestor of the abundant Manila clams hitchhiked on the barges bringing in Japanese oysters. Much of the waterfront on Dyes Inlet is private; do not trespass when harvesting shellfish.

TRACYTON LAUNCH RAMP

The village of Tracyton on the east shore of the inlet has a small waterfront access at a boat launching ramp. The single-lane ramp is just off the main road (May Street), at the end of NW Tracy Avenue. Parking for a few cars is nearby, with additional parking along the side of Tracy Avenue. Boats launched here have ready access to the network of bays at the south end of the inlet.

LOWER MARINE PARK

An old road end along the west shore of Ostrich Bay offers a rare treat—public access among prized waterfront properties. The undeveloped city park lies at the end of Shorewood Drive. To reach it, follow Kitsap Way west out of Bremerton; just before reaching Highway 3, turn right onto Shorewood Drive and follow it to its gated end and the parking area.

The abandoned road can be walked all the way to the Jackson Park Navy housing development. Enjoy nice views of the bay through a light screen of trees, or scramble down the 10-foot-high bank for access to the water.

CHICO LAUNCH RAMP

Forsaking Highway 3 and following Chico Way, the scenic shoreline route around the west side of Dyes Inlet, one encounters the community of Chico. In spite of its Spanish sound and the fact that many nearby streets

Blackberry blossoms at Lower Marine Park

have Spanish names, the community was named for William Chico (or Chako), a friendly Indian chief who lived nearby.

Chico was a point of commerce for boats of the Mosquito Fleet and settlers who lived inland on the Kitsap Peninsula; one of the first roads in the area led from Chico to Crosby. Many of the early steamers were shallow-draft and could be beached. Passengers disembarked via a gangplank dropped from the deck to shore; cows and horses destined for pioneer farms were simply booted overboard to swim the short distance to the beach. It wasn't until 1905 that a dock (a raft of cedar logs) was built.

The only public facility at Chico today is a surfaced launch ramp just off Chico Way at the end of NW Meredith Street. The ramp, which is unmarked and evidently not heavily used, has parking space for only a couple of cars along the road. To locate the ramp, watch for Chico Service, a small radiator shop on the west side of the road.

SILVERDALE WATERFRONT PARK

Park area: 4 acres; 600 feet of waterfront
Facilities: Picnic tables, fireplaces, benches, restrooms, water, children's
    play area, horseshoe pits, gazebo, fishing pier, floats, transient
    moorage, boat launch (ramp)
Attractions: Fishing, swimming, boating, beach walking, picnicking,
    paddling

The major attraction on Dyes Inlet is the superb little beachfront park in Silverdale, at the north end of the waterway. A 300-foot-long fishing pier has floats at the end with a capacity for forty to fifty boats. Transient moorage is available, with a three-day limit; moorage fees are deposited in envelopes in a box at the head of the dock. Although the end of the bay is quite shallow, the dock extends out far enough to provide 35 feet of water under the floats at a zero tide. To the north, the extreme head of the bay is a 300-yard-long tideflat.

On the west side of the dock is a two-lane concrete launch ramp. The ramp extends well out into the bay, so there is no problem launching, even at a low tide.

The remainder of the park is grass and a scattering of picnic tables with beachfront views. A low concrete bulkhead rims the beach; at high tide the water comes right up to the bulkhead. Low tide reveals some cobbles and rocks at the high water level, with a sandy swimming beach below. A children's play area, horseshoe pits, and a small wooden pavilion line the east side of the park.

To reach Silverdale by land, follow Highway 3 north out of Bremerton to the marked Silverdale exit. The modern part of town is spread north along Silverdale Way; the original settlement, Old Town Silverdale, with its interesting buildings and waterfront park, is on a point of land on the northwest shore of the inlet. The park is at the end of Washington Avenue. By water, the park is 5½ nautical miles from the eastern entrance to the Port Washington Narrows.

KITSAP HISTORICAL MUSEUM

In the book *Kitsap County: A History*, Fredi Perry writes succinctly: "Nothing much ever happened in Silverdale. Folks made a comfortable living raising cows and chickens and turkeys while others commuted to PSNS. Once the bank was held up."

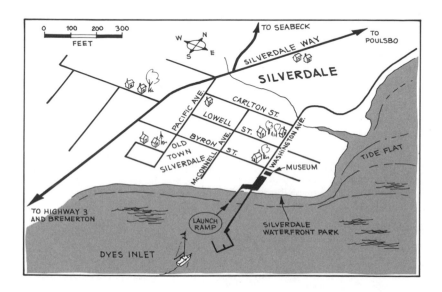

Silverdale Waterfront Park

The history of the town, much the same as other Kitsap Peninsula communities, centered on logging, farming, and eventually was influenced by the military installations in Bremerton, Keyport, and Bangor. The local Kitsap County Historical Museum does a nice job of portraying a town that quietly thrived. The museum is one block from the waterfront park, at the intersection of NW Byron Street and Washington Avenue. The interesting old building housing the museum was formerly the Silverdale State Bank (the one that was held up). Hours are 10:00 A.M. to 5:00 P.M. daily. Off season (between Labor Day and Memorial Day), weekday hours are the same, but weekend hours are 1:00 to 4:00 P.M.

The museum contains an excellent collection of Silverdale memorabilia. One multipart display shows "A Lifeline of Kitsap County" from the time of glaciation, through pioneer settlement, to present time.

Port Orchard Channel and Liberty Bay

Return now to Port Orchard, the long channel flowing north along the back of Bainbridge Island. Superlative boating country, this, with a wide, unobstructed channel enclosed by forested shores and graced at its farthest point with the queen of tourist towns, Poulsbo.

A torpedo testing area is located along the west side of the channel, from Keyport south to Brownsville. Such testing is quite rare, but when it does occur, red lights on Navy range vessels and on top of one of the buildings at Keyport flash a warning. Boaters should not enter the area at that time. Those remaining nearby should shut off boat engines, depth sounders, or any other equipment generating underwater noise, since some torpedoes are guided by sound.

The entrance to Liberty Bay is twisting, and becomes narrow as it rounds Lemolo Peninsula, but there are no navigational hazards. Once past Keyport the channel spreads to ½ mile in width and heads north to Poulsbo, at the end of the bay. Excellent anchorages can be found in muddy bottom in several small coves; those near Keyport and Lemolo offer the quiet protection of the beautiful little bay without the summertime

Sailboat off the shore of Illahee State Park

bustle of the Poulsbo docks; these snug coves, however, do not have any shore access.

Accesses and anchorages in Port Orchard channel along the Bainbridge Island shoreline are described in chapter 3.

ILLAHEE STATE PARK

Park area: 75 acres; 1,785 feet of shoreline
Facilities: 31 campsites, picnic tables, fireplaces, kitchen shelters, group camp, restrooms, showers, water, RV pump out, baseball diamond, children's play equipment, horseshoe pits, hiking trails, boat launch (ramp), fishing pier, float, mooring buoys
Attractions: Boating, fishing, clam digging, swimming, scuba diving, beachcombing, hiking, historical display

A 250-foot bluff above the channel of Port Orchard may seem an unlikely location for a marine-oriented park, but Illahee State Park manages to blend its wooded uplands nicely with its waterfront attractions. The upland portion of the park—campground, group camp, and picnic area—is in timber, with no view of the water. The beauty of the old-growth forest of maple, cedar, and fir more than makes up for the lack of marine vistas. Two 5-inch naval guns mounted on grassy platforms near the park entrance recall the military heritage of the area.

The beach portion of the park is reached via a steeply switchbacking road, or a steeply switchbacking trail—take your pick. Trailered boats that have made it down the hairpin turns of the road will find a single-lane launch ramp adjacent to the parking lot. Floats at the end of a 350-foot fish-

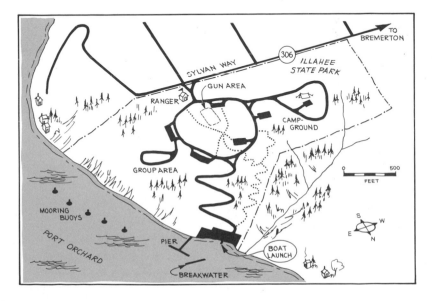

ing pier provide tie-ups for a few boats; a concrete float serves as a breakwater. A few mooring buoys are strung along the shore to the south.

Tidelands south of the pier flare out gently into a sandy beach, delightful for sun-snoozing or wading. A lucky digger may find a clam or two, although the area is heavily harvested. At high tide, water laps against the foot of the bluff.

The park, lying on the north outskirts of Bremerton, is very popular with local residents. To reach it, drive north out of Bremerton on Highway 303 (Warren Avenue) and turn east at a signed intersection onto Sylvan Way (Highway 306), which leads to the park. Highway 304 (Trenton Avenue) can also be taken, but the Sylvan Way turnoff may not be signed.

ILLAHEE

Facilities: Float, groceries, ice, bait, gas (at service station), fishing pier, artificial reef
Attractions: Fishing, scuba diving

To reach the road following the shoreline north along Port Orchard, continue on Trenton Avenue north from the Sylvan Way intersection, and in a few hundred feet, at a Y intersection, turn right onto Illahee Road, which drops down to the water and the small community of Illahee.

Here, a pier with two short floats provides a spot for boaters to stop and pick up supplies. Large boats should approach with care, as the surrounding water is shallow, but small boats should have no problem except during low tides. The dock and floats are closed to the public between 10:00 P.M. and daylight. A grocery store and service station are a short block up the street. The end of the pier spreads out into a broad platform for fishing.

Pilings of the old dock are coated with a forest of fluffy, pastel-colored sea anemones and purple tube worms—paradise for scuba divers who expore the seawalls south from here to the state park, a mile away. Fishing and diving in the area are greatly enhanced by a 300-foot-long artificial reef, marked by buoys, lying 140 feet off the end of the pier. The old tires forming the reef create a habitat for invertebrates that in turn serve as food for a variety of fish, including cod, flounder, rockfish, and salmon. Fish population in the area has more than doubled since the construction of the reef.

BROWNSVILLE MARINA

Facilities: Transient moorage with power and water, boat launch (ramp), groceries, ice, bait, fuel, boat rentals, marine repair, tidal grid, restrooms, showers, picnic tables, fireplaces

The narrow slot of Burke Bay, penetrating the Kitsap shoreline for nearly ½ mile, is too shallow to be attractive to boaters, but the modern, full-service marina on the north shore at the entrance to the bay, operated

Brownsville Marina

by the Port of Brownsville, makes a nice layover for boaters cruising in Port Orchard channel. The 325-slip facility is a surprise either from land or water, since the community of Brownsville is just a smattering of homes along the shore. The marina is on Highway 303, midway between Bremerton and Keyport.

Two breakwaters protect the extensive moorages—stay clear of the red buoys marking cables holding the breakwater. Visiting boaters can reach the fuel dock by entering at the south end of the east breakwater; from here they will be directed to available guest slips. An excellent two-lane concrete boat launch ramp running steeply into the water is south of the fuel dock.

The marina is a pleasant stop, even for nonboaters—the north breakwater also serves as a fishing pier and provides nice views up to Agate Passage and across the busy water highway to Bainbridge Island. On shore is a small park with picnic tables and fireplaces.

As a part of the development of Everett as a carrier home port, the Navy recently arranged a swap of tidelands with the state. Included in this swap is the 2-mile stretch of tidelands between Brownsville and the Keyport Naval Reservation. Although uplands are private, and the beach involved is mostly mud, these new public tidelands open additional beaches for shellfish harvesting.

NAVAL UNDERSEA MUSEUM

Since 1910, when the Navy put Keyport on the map by selecting it as the site for the storage, repair, and testing of torpedos, most of the activity on this tiny peninsula has been hidden behind chain link security fences. An impressive new Naval Undersea Museum is located just inside the gate of the Undersea Warfare Engineering Station—the first time tourists have been invited to share the mysteries behind the fences. At one edge of the parking lot is the *Trieste II,* a huge submersible that set the world's record for undersea descent when it dove to 35,800 feet off of the Guam Trench.

At the entrance to the museum a large hydrospheric globe serves to introduce the museum's theme of the earth as a water planet. Displays include a simulated rock grotto that shows the evolution of undersea technology, and a historical tracing of man's efforts to conquer the undersea realm, from the first Sumerian divers in 650 BC, to the first submarine in 1620, the first hose-free diving in 1865, and finally the landing of the submersible *Alvin* on the deck of the *Titanic* in 1989.

The Orientation Theater features some two dozen scale models of undersea vehicles. Pings, groans, whistles, and other underwater noises provide a background in the Artifact Hall, where a black scrim simulates ocean-bottom visibility. Behind it, a number of full-sized underwater vehicles are spotlighted, including several versions of torpedos, sonic buoys, a cable-controlled recovery vehicle, a one-man human-powered submarine, a dive bell, and others.

Submersible Trieste *at the Naval Undersea Museum, Keyport*

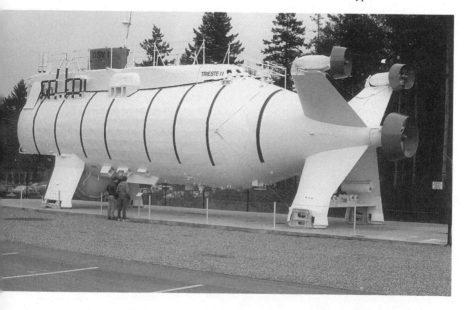

PORT OF KEYPORT MARINA

Facilities: Transient moorage, boat launch (ramp), restrooms, gas (at service station), groceries, ice

A small marina offering some limited boating facilities lies just west of the Navy installation. A few overnight moorages are available on the floats. A single-lane surfaced launch ramp is tucked behind the float—its location makes it difficult to spot from the water. To reach the marina from land, turn north at the junction of Highways 308 and 303 onto the road signed to Keyport, and drive to the end of Washington Avenue. The quiet little marina seems a world away from the bustle at the moorages of Poulsbo, just across the bay.

Poulsbo

Even that shrewd old Norseman, Leif Eriksson, would think he had set foot on his native country rather than on some foreign shore if he landed his ship in Poulsbo. "Velkommen til Poulsbo" a sign proclaims, and storefronts decorated with peasant designs echo the greeting. The historic town is not ersatz Scandinavian—it has a deeply rooted Nordic heritage, from the graceful spire of the First Lutheran Church overlooking the town to the fishing fleet moored in its harbor.

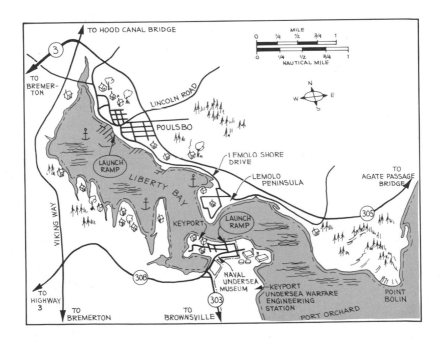

The town was settled in the 1880s by Norwegians from the Midwest, who were drawn here by tales of thickly forested hills and fish-filled bays, so much like their homeland. The first postmaster named the town Paulsbo or "Paul's place," after his home village in Norway, but the U.S. Postal Service, whose errors have had a hand in changing a number of Washington names, misspelled it as Poulsbo, and thus it has remained.

These first settlers were tough farmers and fishermen, well prepared to deal with the rigors of pioneer life. Before the advent of the Mosquito Fleet, it was necessary to row the 20 miles to Seattle, the growing metropolis on Elliott Bay, in order to get provisions. After such a round-trip, an oarsman's hands were frequently so cramped he could not uncurl his fingers for several days. It is claimed that one sturdy pioneer, after crossing the roadless wilderness of the Cascade Mountains with a covered wagon and horses, loaded wagon and team onto a boat in Seattle and rowed them to Poulsbo (oh, for an Evinrude!).

One of the earliest waterfront industries gave the bay its name—a dogfish rendering plant produced the odoriferous oil that was used to grease logging skid roads, and the waterway was officially known as Dog Fish Bay. In the 1890s townfolk petitioned that the name be changed to the more attractive name of Liberty Bay. When the legislature refused, stubborn Norwegians proceeded to use their preferred name anyway, and common usage finally won out.

By land the town can be reached either by taking the Winslow ferry to Bainbridge Island and following Highway 305 across the island and the Agate Pass bridge to Poulsbo, or by driving Highway 3 north from Bremerton and turning south to Poulsbo at the well-marked intersection at the end of Liberty Bay.

By water, Poulsbo lies 13 nautical miles from Shilshole Bay in Seattle, via Agate Passage, or 12 nautical miles from the Bremerton or Port Orchard waterfronts. For boat crews the supreme attraction of the town is the opportunity to browse the shops and haul off bags full of mouthwatering booty from the Scandinavian bakery. Several fine restaurants offer a welcome break to galley slaves.

Poulsbo townfolk love their celebrations, and have plenty of them— Viking Fest, celebrating Norwegian Independence Day, is in mid-May; in summer, Midsommer Fest, the Strawberry Festival, the 4th of July (celebrated with nautical events), and a Boat Rendezvous are scheduled; for the strong-of-stomach there's the Lutefisk Dinner in October. All these festivals (with the possible exception of the Lutefisk Dinner) attract huge numbers of visitors, both by land and water. Scandinavian and Northwest food, crafts, and art are offered for sale, and ethnic musicians and dancers entertain. At such times boating facilities usually are filled, and boats are anchored hull-to-hull at the head of Liberty Bay.

The Marine Science Center, located just east of the marina boat launch ramp, provides classes, teacher training programs, and curricula for the school districts on the Kitsap Peninsula. The building houses class-

Port of Poulsbo Marina

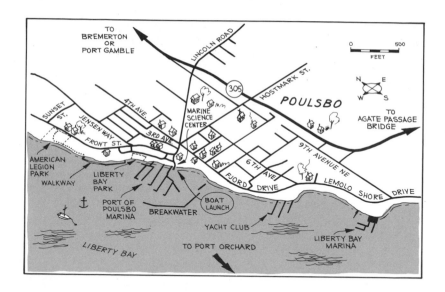

rooms, laboratories, and about a dozen saltwater tanks with marine creatures for touch-and-feel experiences. The center is open for public visits.

POULSBO MARINA

Facilities: Transient moorage with power and water, gasoline and diesel,
   boat launch (ramp), restrooms, showers, laundry, pumpout station,
   tidal grid

Among boaters Poulsbo's reputation lies in its fine waterfront facilities. The marina, operated by the Port of Poulsbo, provides transient
moorage at the downtown docks. Newly improved guest slips on the north
side of the moorage accommodate over a hundred boats. Boaters must get a
key code from the harbormaster to use the onshore restrooms and showers.
A piling breakwater shelters the yacht basin. The south side of the moorage
is filled with the boats of the commercial fishing fleet, and beyond that,
next to the harbormaster's office, is a single-lane surfaced launch ramp.

AMERICAN LEGION PARK AND LIBERTY BAY PARK

Park area: 6 acres; 2,500 feet of waterfront
Facilities: Picnic tables, fireplaces, restrooms, children's play area,
   walking trail
Attractions: Walking, viewpoints

If trolls indeed live under bridges (as is claimed in old nursery tales),
this is certainly the place to find one. Two waterfront parks are linked by
an 800-foot wooden walkway elevated on piers above the shore. Look

Poulsbo marina from Liberty Bay Park

quickly over the edge and you may catch a glimpse of a grizzled troll scurrying out of sight.

Liberty Bay Park is on the downtown waterfront, by the marina. The beautifully groomed and landscaped park has restrooms, picnic tables, fire rings, and large rock erratics for small children to play king-of-the-mountain on. This is the favorite stop (aside from the bakery) for bicycle tourers, who rest on the manicured grass and soak in the atmosphere. Centerpiece of the park is the Rangvald Kvelstad Pavilion, which provides a nice view of bay activity and is also used for concerts, folk dances, and social functions. A statue of a Viking (Leif Eriksson himself, perhaps?) stands guard over it all.

From the north end of the park, the wooden causeway rounds a bluff above the tide and below hillside homes, eventually joining an asphalt path continuing along the bank. Side trails lead down to the mud and rock beach. Shortly, the children's play apparatus and picnic tables of American Legion Park are reached. Here the path turns uphill to a concrete platform overlooking the bay. Return via the beach if the tide is out, or via the road; round trip walk is about 1 mile.

Agate Passage and Port Madison Bay

Agate Passage, with its lofty bridge linking Bainbridge Island and the Kitsap Peninsula, marks the northern entrance to Port Orchard. The tidal current here can reach a velocity of six knots where the channel is squeezed between rocky walls to a mere 300 yards wide. A shoal near the middle of the north end is marked by a buoy. Kelp covers rocks lying near the shore. The passage is frequently used by skilled scuba divers who "drift" dive here—floating and tumbling along the channel as the current provides an exhilarating roller-coaster ride.

The corridor was named, not for the rock hound's prize, although agates can be found along the shore, but for Alfred T. Agate, the artist who accompanied Lt. Charles Wilkes on his surveying expedition of 1841.

In 1905 the U.S. government purchased a section of land on Agate Passage north of where the bridge now stands. The plan was to build a mine control center here and lay mines across the channel, as was done in Rich Passage, in order to protect the Bremerton shipyards from enemy attack. No construction ever took place.

The north end of Agate Passage opens into the lovely round bay of Port Madison rimmed by bluffs and a scattering of homes. All of the Kitsap shoreline facing on Agate Passage and Port Madison, with the exception of part of Miller Bay, was part of the Port Madison Indian Reservation, assigned to the Suquamish and Duwamish Indians in the 1855 Treaty of Point Elliot. Over the years much of the land, especially the waterfront, was sold off, sometimes by federal agents who were empowered to act for individuals they considered "incompetent." Suquamish holdings are now about half of the original reservation, and are largely inland.

SUQUAMISH MUSEUM

Park area: 10 acres; 1,000 feet of shoreline
Access: Land
Facilities: Museum, restrooms, picnic tables, hiking trail

Photos, recorded words, and artifacts serve to tell the story of the Suquamish Indians from the time of the arrival of European explorers through pioneer days. In its major exhibit, "The Eyes of Chief Seattle," the Suquamish Museum uses the words of tribal elders to eloquently evoke not only a time gone by, but a culture nearly lost.

The museum was built by the Suquamish tribe to house and display artifacts discovered by a 1975 archeological excavation at Old Man House. The exhibit also includes items on loan from individuals and other museums. As part of the collection over 2,000 historic photos have been copied for the tribal archives. Museum hours are 10:00 A.M. to 5:00 P.M. daily.

The museum is on the top floor of the tribal center, located on a timbered hillside overlooking Agate Passage. Signs on Highway 305 direct visitors to a turnoff at Sandy Hook Road, which leads to the parking area.

Looking into Agate Passage from the beach of Old Man House State Park

A hiking trail departs from near the museum, looping south in the cedar-scented forest for ½ mile. A few picnic tables on a grassy platform below the building have views of the water; stairs lead down to the beach.

OLD MAN HOUSE STATE PARK

Park area: 0.7 acre; 210 feet of shoreline
Access: Land, boat
Facilities: Fireplaces, picnic tables, pit toilets, water
Attractions: Historical displays, scuba diving, swimming

Enrich a visit to the Suquamish Museum with a stop at the site of Old Man House, now a state park Heritage Area. It is believed that Chief Sealth, who befriended the white settlers, was born in the longhouse that stretched along the shore, although Blake Island also claims that distinction. An informational display at the park tells the history of the longhouse, the largest such structure believed ever to have been built, and shows methods used in its construction. Exact dimensions of the building are uncertain, but it is known to have been at least 500 feet long, and possibly close to 900 feet. It extended far beyond the boundaries of the present-day park, onto what is now private property.

The longhouse was burned sometime after 1870 by federal agents who wanted to discourage communal living and force the Indians to lead a "civilized" life. Some of the large framing posts remained standing for many years; the last is reported to have rotted off and fallen in 1906. Archeological digs show that Indians lived on the site even before the longhouse was built.

The state park is on the outskirts of the town of Suquamish. Just west of the Agate Pass bridge turn north off Highway 305 onto Suquamish Way. In just over a mile turn south on South Division Street and follow rather inconspicuous signs to the park. Parking is on the road end of NE McKinstry Street and just off NE Angeline Avenue South.

The park faces on a beautiful beach with sand at the high tide level, and gravel below (no wonder the Indians chose this spot). There are a couple of picnic tables, a fire ring, pit toilets, and a water faucet; a broad, grassy expanse provides plenty of spots to spread a picnic cloth. No garbage cans or collection at the park; pack it in, pack it out. Scuba divers fre-

Informational display at Old Man House State Park

quently use the park as a put-in for dives along Agate Passage. Boats can easily be beached or hand-launched on the sloping beach, as the Indians did for several centuries. From the water the park can be located by the daymarker on its northern boundary.

SUQUAMISH

Facilities: Fishing pier, boat launch ramp
Attractions: Historic site, fishing

Real estate entrepreneur Ole Hansen purchased the Suquamish waterfront in 1909 from its Indian owner. Hansen renamed the area Silverstrand, subdivided it, and hyped his lots to Seattlites looking to invest in view property. Locals objected to the new name, and one day, as he was arriving with a boatload of prospective buyers, Hansen was startled to find his new, neatly lettered town sign floating in the bay. Suquamish it has been ever since.

The difficulties of early transportation slowed growth of the area, so Hansen did not realize the fortune he had hoped for from the property. He went on to fame as the flamboyant mayor of Seattle, and even hoped to run for president on his ability to see a Bolshevik behind every bush in those Socialist-paranoid times.

A 450-foot-long fishing pier on the Suquamish waterfront offers dynamite views down the throat of Agate Passage, across Port Madison, and up to Indianola. The pier has no float, so boat tie-up would be difficult. To reach it by land, follow Suquamish Way to its end on the south side of town. The path to the pier is adjacent to the launch ramp, and is marked with a sign quoting Chief Sealth's admonition to "love this beautiful land"; the parking area is on an overgrown basketball court across the

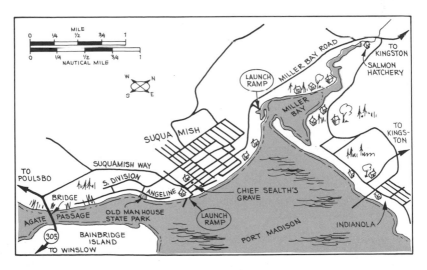

Chief Seattle's grave at Suquamish

street from the town's two taverns. The single-lane, surfaced launch ramp drops down steeply from the parking lot.

Just 1½ blocks up the hill is Memorial Cemetery, where Chief Sealth is buried. The structure surrounding the grave site—four cedar poles topped by canoelike carvings—represents the traditional Indian burial method of putting the deceased in a canoe tied high in a tree. Other interesting old gravestones in the cemetery give insight into life on the reservation. A remarkable number of graves are marked with simple flat stones marked "Unknown." John Kettle, whose grave is located here, is the Indian who Ole Hansen purchased Suquamish from.

St. Peter's, the tiny Catholic church at the edge of the cemetery, was originally an Indian mission, built in the early 1860s. The first building stood about a mile to the south; when the government purchased the land as a military reservation, the church was rebuilt at its present location.

MILLER BAY

Facilities: Marina, boat launch (ramp), gas, transient moorage, fishing tackle, marine repair

The only marine facility on Port Madison is north of Suquamish in Miller Bay. A small marina on the west shore, just off Miller Bay Road,

Miller Bay

has a single-lane concrete launch ramp and boating facilities. A long sand spit extends from the east side of the bay, nearly blocking the entrance. Do not enter at low tide, as the channel and much of the bay hold a foot of water or less at low water. A good anchorage in 6 feet of water can be found just north of the second buoy.

Boaters who enjoy exploring out-of-the-way corners will delight in the quiet little bay ringed by homes. All shoreland is private. A Suquamish tribe salmon hatchery is at the north end; visitors are welcome.

INDIANOLA

The community of Indianola was developed in 1916 as a summer and weekend getaway, but since it was only an hour's steamer ride to Seattle, it didn't take long before property owners who wanted to live here year around and commute to Seattle demanded regular ferry service. Boats were soon shuttling back and forth on regular passenger runs, and eventually even an auto ferry was put in service. Landing or loading could be a real adventure when winter storms whipped the long pier. The ferry service was discontinued when the bridge across Agate Passage was built in 1950.

The 300-yard-long dock used by the ferries was rebuilt in 1972 by the Indianola community and the Interagency for Outdoor Recreation. It serves as a fishing pier and view platform, with views down Agate Passage and

Dock at Indianola

across to Seattle. Pause to imagine a doughty little ferry chugging up to the dock to transport a waiting Flapper-era crowd.

In summer a short float at the end of the pier serves for loading or unloading, but overnight moorage is not permitted. The beach at the head of the pier is for use of residents only. A small grocery store and the post office are on shore nearby. The dock is located at the end of Indianola Road.

The Northern Tip

Beyond Indianola the Kitsap shoreline takes on a different look. Gone are the sheltered beaches and forest-edged channels, as the peninsula sweeps north to its climax at Foulweather Bluff. Beaches here are wild and windswept, with mounds of ragged beach grass and a strand of silvered driftwood deposited by waves from Puget Sound.

KINGSTON

Facilities: Transient moorage with power and water, diesel, gas, boat launch (sling), restrooms, showers, laundromat, Porta-Potti dump, marine supplies and repairs, groceries, tackle, bait, tidal grid, stores, restaurants, picnic tables

The one bit of shelter offered along the northeast side of the Kitsap Peninsula is at Kingston on Appletree Cove. A dredged yacht basin behind a rock breakwater has full facilites for boaters. The forty-slip visitor float is located just behind the rock breakwater. Self-register at the head of the dock, above the fuel float, or at the marina office. Half a block from the head of the dock is a building with restrooms, a laundromat, and a Porta-potti dump. All but the latter are key-coded, with access restricted to registered guests only. A sling launch extends into the basin between D and E

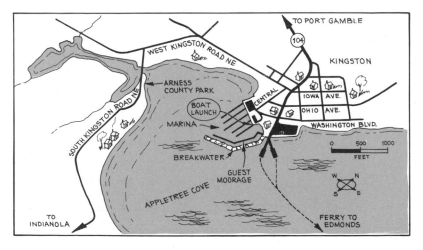

docks of the permanent moorages. There is ample parking for cars and trailers in a large lot at the west end of the marina.

The cove itself is an extremely shallow tideflat; do not stray out of the channel. Picnic tables in a little park above the marina provide a nice over-look of boating activities.

Immediately to the east is the Washington State ferry terminal. Ferries from here zip across the sound to Edmonds, carrying commuters to and vacationers fro. Most visitors' only view of Kingston is from the ferry parking lot. Some wander far enough to buy an ice-cream cone, but all stay within dashing distance of their cars, in case their boat approaches. In addition to the businesses clustered around the ferry landing, a small shopping area is two blocks up the highway, at the top of the hill.

ARNESS COUNTY PARK (KITSAP COUNTY)

Park area: 2 acres; 400 feet of shoreline
Facilities: Picnic tables, fireplaces, Sani-can
Attractions: Boating, picnicking, swimming

Bring out the picnic lunch—here's the place to enjoy it! This little park at the head of Appletree Cove is a pleasant surprise. Small boats can be hand-launched here for paddling about the bay (when there's water in it), and the beach is nice for swimming or wading. If lunch is all you had in mind, just soak in the salty atmosphere.

The park, operated by the Kitsap County Parks Department, can be reached by turning west off Highway 104 in Kingston onto West Kingston Road NE, which curves around the cove. At a Y intersection stay left on South Kingston Road NE and follow it to the park.

EGLON BEACH PARK

It's small, but it is the only public beach for quite a stretch. To find Eglon Beach Park, turn north off Highway 104 at Hansville Road. At the

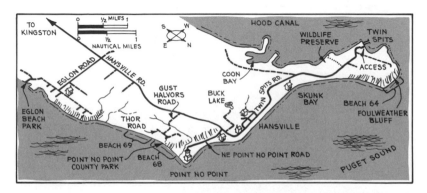

Rock breakwater and marina at Kingston

intersection with Eglon Road turn east, then south at a T intersection. The park is at the intersection of NE Eglon Road and Hoffman Road NE. Park facilities consist of a small picnic area with a fireplace, a Sani-can, and a single-lane launch ramp. There is parking for a dozen or so cars adjacent.

POINT NO POINT COUNTY PARK (KITSAP COUNTY)

Facilities: Latrines, picnic table
Attractions: Hiking, beachcombing, birdwatching

A small county park a little over a mile south of Hansville provides a brief woodsy walk and a route to the beach. To reach it, turn east from Hansville Road onto Gust Halvors Road, marked "Dead End." In about ½ mile, at the T intersection with Thor Road, turn north, and in ¼ mile arrive at the entrance gate of Point No Point County Park. The gate is open from 10:00 A.M. to 8:00 P.M., Wednesday through Sunday.

Beyond the gate a primitive single-lane gravel road continues north through second-growth cedar and alder. Some clearings in the trees could accommodate a blanket-on-the-ground picnic. Just beyond a pair of latrines, the driveable road ends in a turn-around loop.

From here a pleasant ¼-mile hike through light timber leads to the top of the bluff, an overlook of Puget Sound, and a picnic table. Here a picturesque dirt and log staircase leads steeply down the bluff to the shore, arriving near a huge rock erratic that was plonked here by a long-ago glacier.

Stairway from the beach at Point No Point County Park

HANSVILLE AND POINT NO POINT

Facilities: Marinas, boat launch (sling, rail, and ramp), gas, fishing tackle,
bait, restaurant, cabins, boat rentals
Attractions: Fishing, boating, beach walking, light station

Any saltwater fisherman can tell you where Point No Point is—the
area is legendary for its great salmon fishing, either by mooching from
boats drifting just offshore, or by casting from the beach near the point
where the bottom plummets to a depth of 90 feet. Marinas at Hansville and
east along Point No Point Road provide anglers with boat launches, rental
boats, RV campsites, and necessary supplies. For those who would rather
land their salmon at the supermarket and spend their recreational hours
walking the beach, there is plenty of opportunity for beachcombing, too.

Hansville is reached by turning north off Highway 104 onto the Hansville Road; from there you can't miss it. Don't expect posh resorts—the
weathered little town is for dedicated fishermen and vacationers who prefer
the sting of salt air to the swank of tennis courts.

The first settlers here were Anton Husby and Hans Zachariasen. Locals insist (with a straight face) that Husby was a teetotaler, but the other
man enjoyed his spirits, and when local Norwegian loggers came to town,
they soon learned that "Husby von't drink vith you, but Hans vill!"—and
thus the town got its name.

In Hansville turn right on NE Point No Point Road and follow it past
private homes to a resort. Parking is a problem—the resorts have space for
those paying for their facilities, and the lighthouse at the end of the road
has a parking lot for people visiting the light station, but people just want-

Salmon fishing off Point No Point

Beach and glacial erratic at Point No Point

ing to walk the beach must fend for themselves, parking where they think they will least offend residents.

Walk down the road to the lighthouse to reach the shore. Two DNR beaches lie just around the point to the south. Beach 68 is 3,036 feet long, and Beach 69, to the south of it, is an additional 2,420 feet. The public lands on both of these beaches are below the mean high water level—do not trespass on upland property. Shellfishing is not good here, because of heavy wave action from the sound. Near the end of the public beach are the stairs descending from Point No Point County Park and the giant rock erratic. Piles of driftwood in the soft sand provide convenient nooks for watching the scenery, reading, or snoozing.

POINT NO POINT LIGHTHOUSE

Point No Point is well named, as it is only a minor protuberance on an outward bulge of the west side of the Kitsap Peninsula; however, it serves admirably as a site for a navigational marker. The Point No Point lighthouse dates from 1880, when a lantern was first hung in the tower and a bell used as a warning signal.

The building was constructed in late 1879, and orders had been given for it to begin service on New Year's Day of 1880. Unfortunately, although the lighthouse was completed, window glass for the lantern house had not yet been delivered. Orders were to be followed, however, and the lighthouse keeper and his assistant spent a hectic month struggling to keep

Point No Point Lighthouse

the kerosene lantern lit through gales of the dead of winter until the glass finally arrived and was installed.

Personnel will provide tours of the lighthouse between noon and 4:00 P.M. Wednesday through Sunday.

FOULWEATHER BLUFF

Facilities: Marina, boat rental, boat launch (sling), gas, transient moorage, cabins, groceries, tackle, bait

The Kitsap Peninsula ends in the dramatic headland of Foulweather Bluff. Here waves and wind batter the shore from every direction, sculpting the bluffs and depositing sand and silvered driftwood on the beaches. The beach on the north, below the 200-foot-high bluff, is designated as DNR Beach 64. A 3,364-foot strip of tideland, ending at the northeast corner as the shore turns toward Skunk Bay, is public below the mean high water level. The beach drops off quite steeply, with no shellfish in evidence; its main attraction is the opportunity for a front-row seat on the ever-changing maritime scene in Admiralty Inlet.

There is no approved public access to the DNR beach other than by boat, but people have been known to use the public beach access at Twin Spits and walk around to the north side of the bluff at low tide. To reach the beach access, follow the road out of Hansville as it curves west and becomes Twin Spits Road; continue west to its end next to Twin Spits Resort. Hand-carried boats can be put in at the road end. The resort has groceries, necessities for boaters and anglers, fuel, and a sling launch.

Overhanging madrona at Foulweather Bluff Wildlife Preserve

FOULWEATHER BLUFF WILDLIFE PRESERVE

Park area: 93 acres
Facilities: Hiking trail
Attractions: Beachcombing, birdwatching

Since you are in the area, slip around to the west side of the Kitsap Peninsula for a nice little nature walk. The Nature Conservancy has a 93-acre preserve in marshland south of the bluff. The trailhead is on the Twin Spits Road, 3 miles from Hansville. Look for a small turnout on the south side of the road, 800 feet east of the Skunk Bay Road intersection; an inconspicuous sign marking the trailhead is nailed to a tree.

A short hike through the forest leads to the rock and gravel beach. Waterfowl and shorebirds abound. Since this is a sanctuary, camping, fires, clamming, and pets are not permitted; the park closes at dusk. Boats launched at Twin Spits can easily be paddled the mile south to the preserve—the marsh is easily spotted from the water.

At high tide the beach is not exposed, but low water reveals a wide rock and gravel shelf with marvelous tidepools to explore. The view is south to Port Gamble, Hood Head, misty Olympic peaks, and the inviting corridor of Hood Canal—but that's for another chapter.

5. Hood Canal

In Puget Sound country, where inlets and bays and meandering channels are standard fare, this 1½-mile-wide watery finger is unique. Straight and true, it flows southward along the foot of the Olympic Mountains for over fifty miles before bending sharply to the northeast for the final fifteen miles of its course.

Captain George Vancouver, who, on his voyage of discovery in May of 1792, was the first European to visit this body of water, named it Hood's Channel in his journal, but for some reason Hood's Canal was written on his charts, and "Canal" it has remained ever since. In reality it is a fjord— or as close to one as can be found here in Washington State.

The canal was carved by the advances of massive ice sheets that flowed over the area for a period of 1.5 million years. When warming weather caused the northward retreat of the glaciers, several glacial lakes were formed, including Lake Hood. This lake drained to the east through Clifton Outlet into today's Case Inlet. As the glacial melt freed the Strait of Juan de Fuca of ice, the waters of the region dropped and rushed to this

Tidelands at the Skokomish River estuary

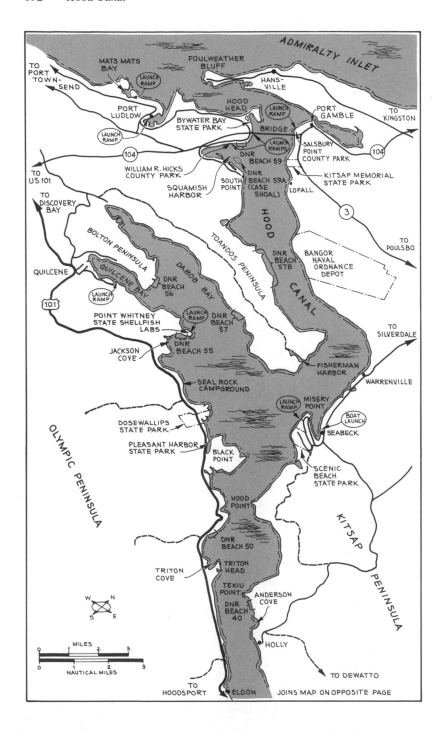

new avenue to the sea. Hood Canal took on its northerly saltwater opening of today, with its connection to Case Inlet but a memory.

Hood Canal boasts some of the region's most spectacular scenery year around, as seasonal changes paint the nearby rugged peaks, glacier-carved valleys, and timbered shorelines. Eight state parks and several other public parks distributed along the length of the canal make this an ideal destination for campers or for boats ranging from kayak to cruiser. Recreational pursuits are an equal attraction, with an abundance of fish to be had for the taking, either by rod or scuba gear—but first check the Washington State Department of Fisheries brochure for gear restrictions and closed areas.

Another prime reason for visiting the canal is to invite to dinner one of the area's most important inhabitants—a succulent little gray critter that delights the palate and slides down the gullet with the greatest of ease—the Pacific oyster. Clams, crabs, and spot shrimp are other forms of canal wildlife that lure thousands of eager gourmets each year. The generally rocky beaches, however, dictate a lot of hard work for the harvest. The best chance for finding oysters and clams is at the public tidelands that are boat access only. Those beaches that can be reached from land are heavily harvested.

Cruise innocently into the canal in late May and you may think you

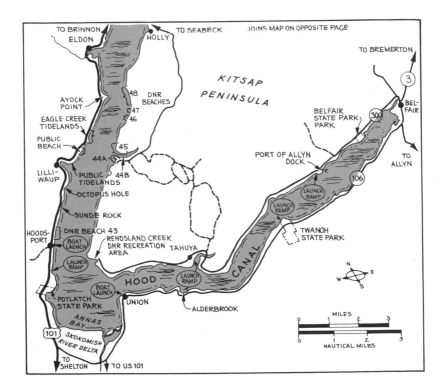

Shrimping at the Great Bend of Hood Canal

have stumbled into a nautical convention. It is then that the month-long, closely regulated Hood Canal sport shrimp season opens, and residents and out-of-staters alike flock here to harvest this delicacy. Spot shrimp, which have white spots on their reddish-brown shells, are the largest species to be found in Puget Sound, reaching nearly 9 inches in size. They are caught in net traps called "pots" that are set in 200 to 300 feet of water. The best spots for catching shrimp are in Dabob Bay and the south end of the canal from Hamma Hamma to Union. Special regulations apply to shrimp fishing in Hood Canal; a stiff fine can result for those failing to comply. Before planning a shrimping expedition be sure to check the state Department of Fisheries brochure listing these regulations.

Although the nautical distance to Hood Canal from the major population centers on Puget Sound is less than the distance to the San Juan Islands, far fewer boaters cruise these waters. While most boaters enjoy the solitude, it can also cause inconveniences—there are fewer commercial facilities to serve boating needs. The small towns of Seabeck, Hoodsport, and Union each have some marine amenities, grocery stores, and restaurants; a few additional commercial marinas are at other spots along the shore.

U.S. Highway 101 parallels the west side of the canal for almost its entire length, with plenty of places for recreational access to the shorelands. The eastern shore is wilder, and roads touch down to water in only a few spots. Once around the Great Bend, civilization sets in with a vengeance on both sides of the canal, with elbow-to-elbow homes (both vacation and year-round) and a proliferation of "private property, no

Hood Canal and surrounding mountains

trespassing" signs.

Beaches along the canal are typically narrow, dropping off quickly to a depth of 80 fathoms or more. Low, sandy points occasionally thrusting outward below the steep hillsides extend for only a couple of hundred feet. The sole exceptions are the wide alluvial fans formed at the mouths of the major rivers draining the Olympics. Here mud and sand deposited by the rivers can extend out into the canal for as much as ¼ mile at minus tides. While shores along Puget Sound are generally gray, here they are a pleasing light tan, with a high-tide band of sparkling white oyster shells.

Because of the narrowness of the underwater shelf, very few docks, either public or private, are built at the northern end of the canal, and good anchorages can be found only at a few limited bays and coves. Stops must be planned accordingly.

At the turn of the century, when settlements along the shoreline were primarily limited to logging camps, these camps relied on rafts anchored in deep water where the steamers of the Mosquito Fleet would stop to unload supplies. Barrels of crude oil for greasing the logging skids were rolled overboard and picked up by the logging boom man to be towed to shore. Horses for the logging camps were pushed over the side to swim ashore.

During times of extreme tide change, the tidal current in Hood Canal can exceed 2.5 knots, causing some problems for small boats. Although usually quite benign, weather can also be a concern, for the steep hills surrounding the channel serve as a funnel for winds, and storms can be furious.

Admiralty Inlet

The mouth of Hood Canal opens into Puget Sound at Admiralty Inlet. Two bays along the Olympic shore, Mats Mats and Ludlow (one snug, one generous) are interesting to boaters or shore visitors.

A series of hull-claiming rocks lie just off the entrance to Mats Mats Bay and extend south for a mile to the entrance of Port Ludlow. These rocks are especially hazardous since they lie in the path of boats running between Port Townsend Canal and Hood Canal. Klas Rock, at the northern end, is covered at extreme high water. It lies ¼ mile from shore and is marked by a lighted buoy on the north side and an unlighted one on the south. Colvos Rocks, ¾ mile farther south, are also marked by a light; a second light shows the end of a shoal running southeast from it. Snake Rock, which is unmarked, is 300 yards offshore, southwest of Colvos Rocks.

MATS MATS BAY

Access: Land, boat
Facilities: Boat launch (ramp), Sani-can
Attractions: Boating, paddling, fishing

Whoever invented the term ''gunkholing'' surely had Mats Mats Bay in mind. It is the ideal little cranny for the adventuresome to explore, with a twisting, timber-shrouded channel opening up into a round little lagoon.

The entrance to the channel lies ¼ mile west of Klas Rocks on the southwest shore of Admiralty Inlet. Upon entering the narrow dredged

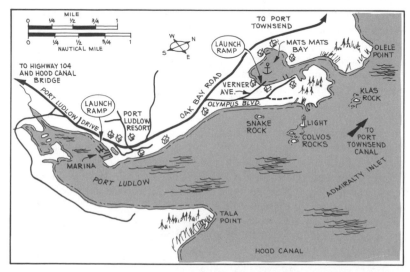

Port Ludlow Marina and peaks of the Olympic Mountains

Boat launch at Mats Mats Bay

channel, align with the range located at the west end of the first leg of the channel. The shallowest portion, 5 feet at mean low tide, extends from the dogleg where the channel turns southward to where it opens into the bay itself. Proceed cautiously, staying midchannel in this section! Once inside, good anchorages can be found in the bay in 5 to 12 feet of water.

All shoreline is private except for a small park and launch ramp operated by the Port of Port Townsend at the southern end of the bay. This ramp can be reached by land by turning east off Oak Bay Road 1¼ miles north of Port Ludlow onto Olympus Boulevard. In ¼ mile turn left onto Verner Avenue, which is signed to Boat Haven. In ½ mile the road dead-ends on the shore of Mats Mats Bay.

Here there is a very nice little park with a single-lane concrete launch ramp, an adjoining boarding float, and latrines. Although the ramp and float extend about 150 feet out into the bay, at low tide the water recedes well beyond their end, leaving a long mudflat, and making the ramp unusable.

PORT LUDLOW

Access: Land, boat
Facilities: Transient moorage with power and water, boat launch (ramp), restrooms, showers, laundry, groceries (limited), fishing tackle, bait, marine supplies, diesel, gas, tidal grid, boat rental, bicycle rental, restaurant, resort, golf course, tennis and squash courts, swimming pool, children's play area
Attractions: Boating, paddling, fishing, bicycling

Over the course of history Port Ludlow has worn many hats. It served first as the site of a lumber mill and shipyard. After the death of the owner,

Colvos Rocks

the original mill ran into difficulties caused by a lengthy probate of the estate, and the shipyard was forced to relocate to Port Blakely to be near a reliable source of lumber. The Puget Mill Company (Pope and Talbot) purchased the foundering sawmill in 1878. After five years of rebuilding and improvements, it became one of the most productive in the area.

In time a dwindling lumber supply and a depressed market forced the mill to close. The small village remaining served for a while as a terminal for a ferry running from Foulweather Bluff. It has now changed hats again and is a posh resort for vacationing and conferences.

For many boaters the Port Ludlow marina is not just a stopover on the

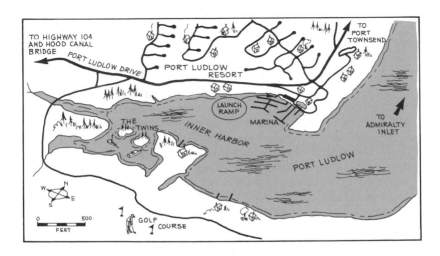

Bay behind The Twins in Port Ludlow

way to somewhere else, but a destination in itself, with great things to do on shore for both adults and children. Visitors can maneuver paddle boats on the resort lagoon, indulge in a spirited game of croquet on the grassy lawn, rent bicycles and tour the quiet byroads, have a round of golf on the resort's 18-hole course (one of the best in the Northwest), or just lie in the sun and enjoy the ambience. The swimming pool, unfortunately, is only for resort guests.

To reach the bay by land, cross the Hood Canal bridge and turn right immediately on Paradise Bay Road, or continue west on Highway 104 and in 3½ miles turn right on the Beaver Valley Road. From either road, signs will direct the way to Port Ludlow. The marina, restaurant, and resort facilities are located at the northeast corner of the inner harbor. The launch ramp, which is usually not signed, can be reached from the west end of the parking lot above the marina store. The steep, narrow, rock and gravel ramp drops into the tide flats west of the marina.

By water, the entrance to Port Ludlow is about 24 nautical miles from Seattle's Shilshole Bay, or 12 nautical miles from Port Townsend, via the Port Townsend Canal. Colvos Rocks lie near the middle of the wide entrance, but they are well marked and easily avoided.

Even without the handsome resort and marina, Port Ludlow would make a dandy overnight stop—offering boaters dozens of good spots to drop a hook all along the shore. The broad outer harbor takes a 45° dogleg to the west, and becomes the inner harbor, on which the resort marina fronts. Channel markers guide the way into the inner harbor.

The special delight of Port Ludlow, however, is the tiny bay at its extreme southwest end, tucked behind two tiny wooded islets. Enter this hidden cove through the small channel between the two islands—the eastern channel between the smaller of the two islands and the shore has many snags and rocks. Be wary also of a rock lying off the south end of the smaller island.

Once inside you will find bombproof anchorages for even the worst of weather, or tranquility for calm summer nights. Don't plan on solitude though, for the spot is well known and heavily used. The little islets, The Twins, are lovely to look at, but are used by boaters to drain their dogs, so any trip ashore may be hazardous to your Topsiders. At present the shoreline around the bay is private, but mostly undeveloped. Recently boating interests actively lobbied the state and raised over ninety thousand dollars to acquire this land in an attempt to prevent it from being logged or subdivided, so the cove would remain natural. Unfortunately, the state failed to support the effort with any financial commitment and, tragically, the shore now seems destined for subdivision.

Hood Canal Bridge—The Eastern Approach

PORT GAMBLE

Access: Land, boat (bay only)
Facilities: Grocery store, historical buildings and museum
Attractions: Sightseeing, picnicking

It is certainly appropriate to begin a tour up Hood Canal with a stop at Port Gamble, a town that played a vital role in this area's early history. A. J. Pope and William Talbot (whose names still linger hereabouts), along with Cyrus Walker, founded the town in 1853. Here they built a company town and a small sawmill; both remain. The mill has been enlarged and modernized several times; however, many of the homes kept closer ties to their Victorian pasts and have been historically preserved.

The town's general store is a fascinating clutter of old and new, selling kerosene lanterns and butter churns along with tourist novelties and pantyhose; some groceries and deli sandwiches are also available. A museum on the second floor displays over 14,000 shells and marine fossils from around the world. Picnic lunches can be enjoyed just above the beach in a grassy area that has several tables and provides a sweeping view of the bay and Hood Canal. Signboards around the town give highlights of the town's history, while the historical museum, located in the basement of the

Port Gamble

general store, traces in more detail the story of the mill and the people who shaped this country. The museum is closed in winter.

Although commercial boats call at the mill to load lumber and wood products, nowhere on Port Gamble Bay is there a public shore access for pleasure boats. The bay, however, does offer boats heading up the canal a pleasant overnight stay, with excellent anchorages in 3 to 5 fathoms. Water immediately outside the entrance to the bay is quite shoal; boaters can locate the dredged channel entrance by heading for the outermost of two channel markers on pilings by the entrance. From there, a range located on

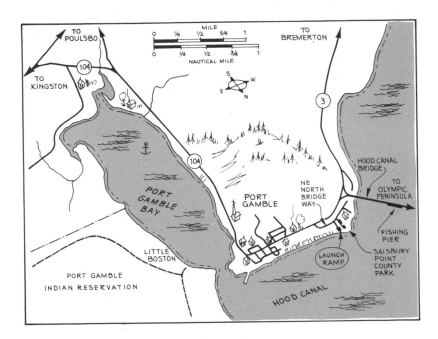

a small point of land about a mile to the north can be used to line up on the channel. Be wary of numerous deadheads that can be found in the bay. Favored anchorages are in the small bight on the east shore at the southern end of the bay.

On the east side of the bay, the sandy spit on the Port Gamble Indian Reservation that holds a deteriorated pier was the site of Little Boston, an early Indian village. These Indians called the bay "Teekalet"—"brightness of the noonday sun." The launch ramp on the spit is reserved for tribal use.

SALSBURY POINT COUNTY PARK (KITSAP COUNTY)

Park area: 5.6 acres; 520 feet of shoreline
Access: Land, boat
Facilities: Boat launch (ramps), picnic tables and shelter, fireplaces,
    children's play area, nature trail, water, restrooms
Attractions: Picnicking, swimming, hiking, boating

A small park just off the northeast end of the Hood Canal Bridge provides easy access to the canal for fishing, boating, and scuba diving. Salsbury Point County Park lies ½ mile northeast of the turnoff to the bridge on Highway 104, and ¾ mile west of Port Gamble. From Highway 104 at a "county park" sign turn west onto Wheeler Street NE, which immediately turns south and becomes NE North Bridge Way. In a short distance, Whitford Road NE leads west to the boat launch ramps. A parallel road just to the south leads to the picnic grounds.

The boat launch consists of two ramps, each about three lanes wide. A voluntary contribution is asked for use of the launch. There is ample parking for cars and trailers at a lot above the ramps and along the sides of Whitford Road. A few picnic tables are found here. The caretaker's house is between the two areas of the park.

At the entrance to the day-use picnic area is a parking lot and a signed nature trail leading into the woods. This area was logged during the 1850s to provide lumber for the mill at Port Gamble. The trail shows many examples of early logging techniques, such as springboard notches.

The timber gives way to an open grassy area and sandy beach. Numerous picnic tables with fireplaces are located throughout the park. The beach slopes gently enough to allow wading or swimming during warm temperatures. The picnic area is closed on Wednesdays and Thursdays, and open from noon to 8:00 P.M. other days of the week.

The park is a favorite access point for scuba divers who explore bridge abutments and cables of the Hood Canal Bridge, just a quarter mile to the southwest. The swiftly flowing current brings nourishment to extraordinary numbers of feather duster worms, plumose anemones, sponges, and other filter-feeding invertebrates. The growth of this marine life is so heavy that it must regularly be cleaned from the bridge cables, or they would break from the weight. Due to the severity of the current, only experienced divers should dive here, and only at slack tide.

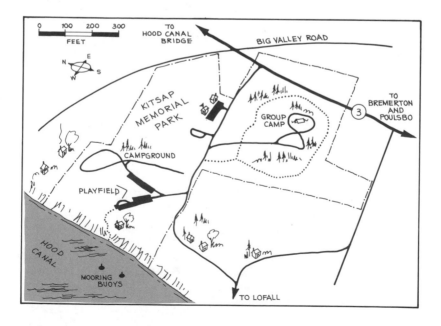

Trail to the beach at Kitsap Memorial State Park

KITSAP MEMORIAL STATE PARK

Park area: 58 acres; 1,800 feet of shoreline
Access: Land, boat
Facilities: 43 campsites, group camp, 2 mooring buoys, picnic shelters, picnic tables, fireplaces, restrooms, showers, baseball diamond, volleyball court
Attractions: Camping, picnicking, boating, swimming, scuba diving, hiking

Summer afternoons find this waterfront state park jammed with local people using the numerous facilities. The park's location, close to Kitsap Peninsula towns, makes it the perfect spot to have a family outing or a scout troop campout. For boaters, the park is a nice place to stop and enjoy an onshore barbeque after a day's recreation on Hood Canal. The two mooring buoys offshore provide a handy spot for large boats to tie up.

Kitsap Memorial Park is located just off Highway 3, 21 miles north of Bremerton and 6 miles north of Poulsbo. By boat, it is 2¼ nautical miles southwest of the Hood Canal Bridge. Small boats can easily be carried the short distance from the parking lot down to the beach for launching.

The park's forty-three campsites are all situated in a forested area away from the water; some are tightly packed along the edge of a large playfield, but most are strung along a more spacious loop to the north. The day-use picnic area, with tables, fireplaces, and shelters, is on the embankment above the beach. A short trail, bordered by Scotch broom and madrona, drops down to the beach from the picnic area.

At high tide the water covers the sandy upper portion of the beach and reaches to the base of the log bulkhead. Low tide exposes boulders and barnacles—difficult for walking in bare feet, but holding some promise of shellfish.

HOOD CANAL BRIDGE AND FISHING PIER

Access: Land
Facilities: Fishing pier
Attractions: Fishing

Most famous of the man-made features of the waterway is the 1¼-mile-long Hood Canal Floating Bridge, located (usually) at the northern entrance of the canal. Built over a four-year period, and finally opened in 1961, the bridge is constructed of a series of twenty-three floating concrete pontoons, linked together. Similar floating bridges had been built on Lake Washington in Seattle, but never before had one of such size been put on saltwater, where it would be affected by tidal changes of up to 18 vertical feet, as well as by heavy currents and waves. In February of 1979, during a period of extreme tidal current, a violent gale smashed down from the north and destroyed the western half of the bridge.

The trusty state ferry, which had shuttled between Lofall and South Point prior to the building of the bridge, was pressed back into service for another four years while the bridge was reengineered and rebuilt. Reopened in 1982, the bridge now serves as an important transportation link between Puget Sound cities and the Olympic Peninsula, as well as a handy butt for local jokes. Originally operated as a toll bridge, the bridge was declared toll-free in a 1985 court decision.

The bridge serves not just for transportation, however—it also functions as a dandy fishing platform. A 6-foot-wide cantilevered walkway gives access to pontoons on the east end. Parking is on the north side of the east end of the bridge where there is space for about thirty cars. The walkway follows the north side of the bridge at treetop level for a few hundred yards before descending a winding staircase to the fishing pier. Whether you are planning to fish or not, a stroll along the upper walkway provides broad views out to Admiralty Inlet and Hood Canal, and knee-weakening views to the water and bridge pontoons below.

The safety rail surrounding the pier has frequent spots for holding rods, and a number of fish cleaning stations. Chunks of broken concrete have been dumped below the pier to form an artificial reef that attracts bottom dwellers such as rockfish and lingcod. The site provides a deep-water fishing opportunity without the necessity of a boat.

Fishing off the Hood Canal Bridge

Hood Canal Bridge—The Western End

BYWATER BAY STATE PARK AND SHINE TIDELANDS

Park area: 135 acres; 23,500 feet of shoreline
Access: Land, boat
Facilities: Boat launch (ramp), 20 campsites (primitive), latrines, *no water*
Attractions: Beach walking, birdwatching, fishing, clamming, crabbing

The almost-island of Hood Head, lying close to the western shore of Hood Canal, encloses a mile-long tide flat appropriately named for what it is: a bywater bay. Such bays are formed by the action of waves building a sandspit.

A 130-acre parcel of lushly forested waterfront land facing Bywater Bay and Hood Canal is being held by the state for possible future development as a park. The area is open to public use now, but has no amenities, and usage is limited to beach areas. A second 5-acre section of beachfront south of the main parcel is open as a primitive campground.

To reach the camping area by car from the west end of the Hood Canal Bridge, turn northeast onto Paradise Bay Road, then immediately turn right on Termination Point Road, a narrow track leading downhill to a Y. The right leg of the Y ends in a boat launch ramp. The single-lane concrete ramp dropping steeply into the water is usable at all tide levels.

The left leg of the road goes to a parking area and twenty primitive campsites spread along an open meadow above the shore; pit toilets are found in the trees above the beach. The adjacent beach is sandy and gently

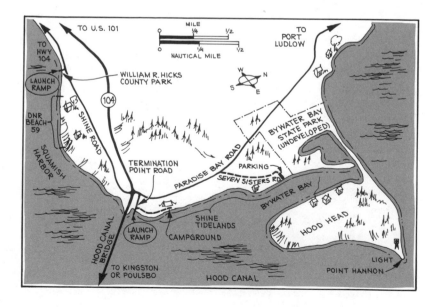

sloping. All of the tidelands from here north to Hood Head are managed by the state Department of Natural Resources and are open for beach walking and clam digging.

The car access to the larger section of the park is farther north. Continue on Paradise Bay Road for ½ mile and turn right onto Seven Sisters Road. Follow the one-lane, unpaved road for another ½ mile to a dirt parking area next to the bay with room for about a dozen cars. Property adjoining the road is private, but the road end permits public access to the beach. Camping is not permitted here.

Bywater Bay, which nearly dries at a minus tide, is one of the prime crabbing areas on the canal. Dungeness crabs are the prize catch here; however, the less meaty red rock crab are just as tasty and do not carry legal restrictions on size or sex.

Explore the bay and adjacent lagoon by walking the beach. The long stretch of beach along the north shore of Hood Head and halfway down its east side is also public below mean high tide levels. Note the differences between the intertidal marine life found on the wave-washed north side and that seen in the protected bay and lagoon.

WILLIAM R. HICKS COUNTY PARK (JEFFERSON COUNTY)

Park area: 0.7 acre; 460 feet of waterfront
Access: Land, boat
Facilities: Boat launch (ramp), picnic table, fireplace, latrine
Attractions: Clamming, crabbing, oyster picking, boating, birdwatching

Hood Canal offers very few boating detours along its narrow length; Squamish Harbor is a notable exception. The bay lies hard to the starboard immediately after passing under the Hood Canal Bridge. A lighted beacon near the northern shore marks Sisters Rocks.

Navigational caution in Squamish Harbor is imperative, as lying along the southeast side is Case Shoal, a large gravel bar filling nearly half the broad bay and drying at a minus tide. The shoal is marked by a nun buoy #2 at its southern end, a marker on a piling on the north, and a small floating buoy between. Water is adequately deep along the north shore and offers some good anchoring possibilities; however, the bay is quite open and doesn't provide much shelter when strong winds kick up.

Midway along the northern shore of the bay is William R. Hicks County Park, which has a one-lane concrete launch ramp, a single picnic table, a latrine, and parking for five to ten cars. Since the ramp runs down to a gradually sloping gravel beach, it is not usable at low tide.

To reach the park by land, turn south onto either end of Shine Road, either just after crossing the Hood Canal Bridge, or 2½ miles farther west. The park is on a spur road a little over a mile from either turnoff; however, the sign identifying the park is visible only when approaching from the west. Shine Road parallels the north side of the bay, with views out to the

Heron in Squamish Harbor

water through red-barked madrona and, in summer, wild peas and fire-weed.

The Squamish Harbor tidelands are a popular foraging area for dozens of great blue herons that nest nearby. As gracefully as dancers they wade in tidepools hunting for stranded fish.

SQUAMISH HARBOR DNR BEACHES

The major attraction of Squamish Harbor is a pair of DNR beaches offering some of the best opportunities for clam, crab, and oyster harvesting on the canal. Take along a sturdy shovel and lots of determination, and try to dig for the geoducks said to be plentiful here.

Beach 59. On the north shore, DNR Beach 59 is a 2,800-foot strip beginning directly below a steep, 100-foot cliff and running westward. It can be reached by boat or by walking the beach from the county park boat launch area at low tide.

Beach 59A. The second DNR beach, 59A, includes all the tidal area of Case Shoal, which at a minus tide offers several acres of prime shellfish gathering for butter, horse, and littleneck clams.

SOUTH POINT

Before the coming (and the second coming) of the Hood Canal bridge, South Point was a ferry landing. The old dock pilings offer some scuba diving possibilities, while the shallow sandy beach below the bulkhead on the east side of the lot tempts exploration for crabs and clams. Surrounding

Clamming on the beach at Squamish Harbor

property is private.

To reach South Point, drive on Highway 104 to the end of Squamish Harbor; 3 miles west of the Hood Canal Bridge turn left on South Point Road. In less than 3 miles the parking lot at the old ferry terminal is reached. Views south down the canal include the ominous structures of the Bangor nuclear submarine base. The attractive little boat moorage behind the peninsula just north of South Point is private.

Bangor Vicinity

The presence of the U.S. Navy nuclear submarine base on Hood Canal at Bangor, and the publicity during the infrequent nuclear protest blockades, may cause some pleasure boaters to avoid the canal altogether. Boaters will encounter no problems while cruising in the vicinity of Bangor if they hold close to the western shore, staying well clear of the posted military areas lying on a 5-mile strip along the east shore. Movements of the submarines are kept secret, but on rare occasions one may be seen. The sight of one of these steel leviathans with a conning tower as tall as a four-story building cannot fail to stir deep emotion, ranging from awe to anger, depending on one's political predilection. If a submarine is sighted, boats must keep 1,000 yards' distance.

A naval operations area is located in this portion of the canal from approximately Lofall to Hazel Point on the Toandos Peninsula, and in Dabob Bay. Such operations are rare; however, when they are underway, flashing green lights are shown when caution is required for boaters, and flashing red lights when the area is closed to navigation. If no lights are flashing, operations are not underway. Consult navigational charts for the exact location of the operations area and the warning lights. Boaters may also receive instructions by radio. Any total closure is usually only for a few hours. Failure to observe warning lights may result in a torpedo-sized opening in one's hull.

Toandos Peninsula

This 12-mile-long forested spine separates Dabob Bay from the main channel of Hood Canal. The interior of the Toandos Peninsula offers little for tourists—a single main road runs the length of the ridge, with all views obscured by dense forest, and the few road ends touching water are all on private property. A private camping club holds a large section of waterfront and timbered uplands along the southeast end.

DNR BEACHES 57B AND 57

Precipitous cliffs surrounding the Toandos Peninsula rise steeply for 200 feet, and below water the seawalls drop off as sharply to depths of 25 fathoms or more. Two narrow, cliff-bound DNR beaches on either side of the peninsula offer boaters several miles of shore access at low tide. DNR Beach 57B is a 12,050-foot strip on Naval Reservation property along the west shore of Hood Canal. It can be located by spotting the Brown Point light, which is approximately in the middle of the beach. Beach 57, facing on Dabob Bay, is a 3,280-foot strip of tidelands running south from Tabook Point. Both of these rocky beaches hold oysters and a variety of clams.

FISHERMAN HARBOR

Fisherman Harbor is a narrow slot in the bluffs at the foot of the Toandos Peninsula resembling, perhaps, a fjord for elves. Merely a cozy 200 yards wide, the cleft extends for ¾ mile between rocky walls.

Venturesome boaters do enter Fisherman Harbor, but only during high tide; a sandspit extending from the west shore across the entrance is nearly bare at low water. After crossing the entrance shoal, turn to the west at a right angle, keeping within 10 or 15 feet of the sandspit—the shore drops off sharply on this side. Follow the spit for almost its full length, then turn north, following the west shore into deep water. Once inside, several tight anchorages can be found in adequate depths of water.

The tidelands on either side of the entrance to Fisherman Harbor are designated as Toandos Tidelands State Park. Oysters and clams can be taken at low tide on this 10,455 foot-long stretch of sand and gravel beach.

Exploring DNR Beach 56 on the Bolton Peninsula

Dabob and Quilcene Bays

The forked arm of Dabob Bay, thrusting northward between steep, forested walls of the Olympics, provides a pleasant digression from Hood Canal's "main street." Here is found an even greater sense of remoteness; the intrusion of civilization is slight, and much of the shoreline remains just as natural as when it was first seen by early settlers.

Although to many people the names of Dabob Bay and adjoining Quilcene Bay are synonymous with gourmet oysters, the bays are also noted for their commercial production of oyster seed. The seed (juvenile oysters) are grown here in long net bags called cradles, which are suspended from logs floating in the water. The harvested seed is sold to oyster growers throughout the world.

Stores on Quilcene Bay have freshly shucked, commercially grown oysters for sale; or several public beaches on Dabob Bay are accessible by boat for those who thrill to stalking the wild ones. Jackson Cove, lying midway along the western shore of Dabob Bay, has a section of rocky ledge offering at low tide some promise of oysters. The public area, DNR Beach 55, is a 2,791-foot strip on the east side of the bay, lying along Pulali Point. Some clams can be found on the gravelly northern half of the beach. Boy Scout Camp Parsons is immediately adjacent to the beach, so it is heavily used by youngsters from the camp; there is no public access to the beach through the scout camp. Jackson Cove has space for several nice boat anchorages in a rocky bottom.

DNR Beach 56, a 2,400-foot rocky tideland at the tip of the Bolton Peninsula is one of the best spots to find oysters, as well as clams. The beach, directly below Red Bluff, is easily located by spotting a house at the top of the bluff. The public shore is immediately east of a drainage flume coming down from that house.

Every year from the end of May to mid-June, Dabob Bay sees a major invasion by eager shrimp fishermen. The bottom configuration of the bay is especially suited to the lifestyle of shrimp who spend their nights in 100 to 200 feet of water and move into deeper trenches during the day.

Since the tidal currents are weaker here than in the rest of Hood Canal, the steep, rocky underwater walls from Point Whitney to Seal Rock are prime scuba diving areas. Octopus, lingcod, and free swimming scallops inhabit crevices in the basalt ledges.

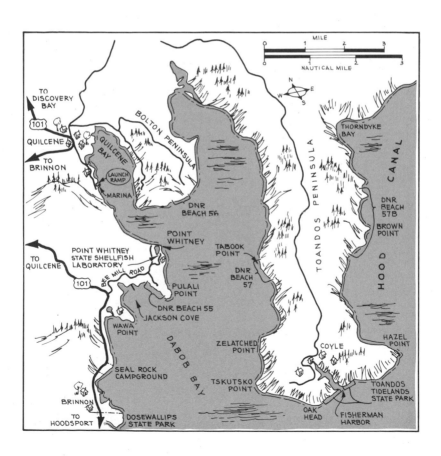

POINT WHITNEY STATE SHELLFISH LABORATORY

Area: 10 acres; 2,000 feet of shoreline
Access: Land, boat
Facilities: Boat launch (ramp), float, restrooms, laboratories
Attractions: Educational displays, swimming, clams, oysters, fishing

An interesting wayside stop along the western shore of Dabob Bay puts tourists in closer touch with the shellfish they hunt in Hood Canal. The labs located here are responsible for setting the state regulations for the harvesting of shellfish. This facility also raises juvenile geoducks for enhancing the local population. The buildings, which are open during normal business hours, are not geared to visitors, but an interpretive display located outside near the restrooms explains the biology of intertidal life, and the reasons why regulations are imposed.

To reach the labs, turn off Highway 101 8 miles south of Quilcene or 2¼ miles north of Seal Rock Campground onto Bee Mill Road, signed to Camp Parsons. Continue past the scout camp, staying on Point Whitney Road to the labs, in 2½ miles. A single-lane, gravel launch ramp is at the road end, with adjacent parking for several cars. Boaters who stop by can land small boats at the lab's pier, which has a short float.

A sandspit encloses a saltwater lagoon used to grow algae to feed the lab's shellfish. The bay side of the spit is open to the public for shellfish gathering, beachcombing, and swimming. Since Dabob Bay is shallower than the rest of Hood Canal, the water here is generally much warmer. To the north, public land ends at the end of the sandspit, but on the south the open beach continues for several hundred more feet onto the tidelands of the navy operations area, marked by a white wooden tower on the bluff.

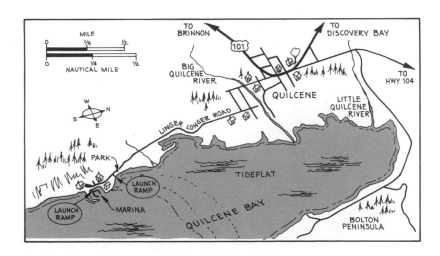

QUILCENE BAY MARINA

Access: Land, boat
Facilities: Boat launch (ramps), fuel, transient moorage (limited),
    restrooms, showers, picnic tables, fireplaces, swimming beach,
    groceries (in Quilcene)
Attractions: Picnicking, swimming

Both Dabob and Quilcene bays dwindle out into long, mucky tidal flats, not lending themselves to carefree boating. Midway into Quilcene Bay, just where the water begins to shallow, is a small marina and a water-side park. The marina, operated by the Port of Port Townsend, has a basin with space for about thirty-five boats. A single-lane concrete launch ramp is located inside the protection of the marina's rock breakwater, although it may not be usable at very low tides.

The south side of the rock jetty protects a roped-off swimming area on a gently sloping beach (no lifeguard). A small day-use park on the north side of the oyster company jetty has Sani-cans, a few tables, and fire braziers for an afternoon picnic. A second launch ramp located at the park

Quilcene Bay Marina

is usable only at high tide, as it leads out to a mudflat at lower tidal levels. One of the two oyster companies located here offers fresh oysters for sale.

The town of Quilcene itself is at the head of the tidal flat, and has no water access. To reach the bay from Quilcene, turn off Highway 101 at signs pointing to Quilcene Boat Haven, and follow Linger Longer Road to its end in about 1½ miles. For boaters in need of supplies, the town is a long but pleasant trudge along Linger Longer Road with roadside blackberries in season, and some salty views across the end of the bay.

Dosewallips

SEAL ROCK CAMPGROUND

Park area: 30 acres; 2,700 feet of shoreline
Access: Land, boat
Facilities: 41 campsites, picnic tables, fireplaces, restrooms
Attractions: Scuba diving, beachcombing, oysters, clams, swimming

Near the mouth of Dabob Bay the boundaries of the Olympic National Forest dip down to touch saltwater. Here, along the shore, is Seal Rock Campground—the only Forest Service campground in the nation where oysters can be gathered.

The campground lies 10½ miles south of Quilcene on Highway 101. The camping area is in two loops in fine, old-growth forest on a low bluff

Herons on the beach at Seal Rock State Park

above the shore at the north end of the park. Handicapped access points with beach views are provided along the lower section of the campground area. Stairways lead down the embankment to the beach.

On the south, the road terminates at the day-use picnic area. A few picnic sites are located on the edge of the bluff above the beach, but most are in timber on the hillside above the parking area. The upper beach ranges from cobble to boulders, all liberally covered with oyster shells. At low tide it tapers out gently for several hundred yards to gravel and mud at the lower levels. The park has no easy access for boaters; the only option is to anchor out and land small boats on the rocky beach.

DOSEWALLIPS STATE PARK

Park area: 425 acres; 5,250 feet of shoreline
Access: Land, boat
Facilities: 153 campsites, group camp, picnic tables, fireplaces, restrooms, showers, hookups, trailer pumpout, hiking trails
Attractions: Beachcombing, boating, paddling, hiking, fishing, birdwatching

The Dosewallips River, which originates in glaciers of the high Olympic peaks, meanders into Hood Canal at the mile-wide alluvial plain of Brinnon Flats. The estuary created here holds a thriving intertidal community of saltwater invertebrates, fish, and shorebirds. Search the tideflats carefully to see how many kinds of life you can find, but treat every crea-

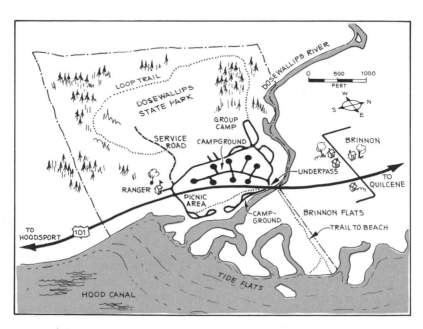

Trail to the beach at Dosewallips State Park

ture with care; each is a part of the web of life. The best exploring is at low tide; wear rubber boots for wading channels and squishing through the tide flats.

The park lies south of Brinnon on U.S. 101. The camping area is divided into two sections. The older section of the campground, containing twenty-four sites without hookups, is located along the Dosewallips River on the east side of the highway. The access road to these campsites runs under the bridge, and the low clearance prevents use by tall RVs. The newer campsites, many with complete hookups, are on the west side of the highway in a grassy flat broken up by planted evergreens. The picnic area is on the east side of the highway, near the salt marsh.

An upland hiking trail starts near the shops at the entrance to the campground area and wanders through the forest along the park's western boundary before returning to the group camp area. Walk quietly and perhaps spot some of the blacktail deer, elk, raccoon, beaver, or skunk known to frequent the park.

The marsh at the east side of the picnic area is heavily overgrown and laced with muddy channels, so it does not afford any easy access to the beach. To reach the beach, cross the river on a narrow walkway along the east side of the bridge, and find the trailhead on the northeast side of the bridge.

The trail follows the park boundary eastward, first through a thicket of brush, alder, and cedar, then shoulder-high blackberries. In little over ¼ mile vegetation tapers down to sow thistles, Puget Sound gumweed, and beach grass as the trail breaks out to the wide, flat beach. Shallow, mud-rimmed, saltwater channels give way to rock and cobble extending outward for another ¼ mile at minus tides.

The vast tideland lies waiting to be explored. Watch for great blue herons, loons, and dozens of other waterfowl frequenting the area. Unfortunately, pollution makes the shellfish unsafe to eat.

Access to the park by boat is difficult, due to the huge tideflat.

The Kitsap Peninsula Shoreline

Traveling south along Hood Canal, the eastern shore, which is the Kitsap Peninsula, becomes wilder. Land accesses are limited to half a dozen sites, joined together by isolated roads through the densely timbered hills of the peninsula. The common starting point for land trips is Bremerton, which can be reached by ferry from Seattle, or via Highway 16 from Tacoma.

Seabeck

SEABECK

Access: Land, boat
Facilities: Marina, boat launch (hoist), boat rentals, transient moorage,
    bait, fuel, groceries, restaurant, fast food, post office
Attractions: Boating, fishing, scuba diving

One of the oldest towns in the state, Seabeck was founded in 1856 when a sawmill was established at the site. The town prospered as a lumber and shipbuilding center until a fire leveled the mill in 1886. Since the nearby timber supplies were nearly exhausted, the operation moved to Hadlock, rather than rebuild at Seabeck. The population quickly deserted the town, and the mill dock was used as a landing place for a small resort, which also failed after a short period.

Today Seabeck is a favorite spot for fishermen—the waters of the canal just west are one of the premium salmon fishing spots in the state. An artificial reef placed just northwest of the tip of Misery Point provides excellent fishing for rockfish, lingcod, and other bottom fish. Fishing from the marina dock is permitted for a fee. The smooth bottom of the bay, with its many old pilings, makes Seabeck Bay a popular scuba diving site.

Seabeck Bay is the only noteworthy moorage spot south of Port Gamble along this side of the canal. The Indian name for it was "Kah-mogk,"

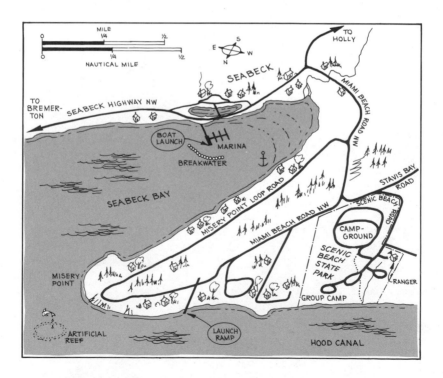

meaning "quiet waters." The bay is well sheltered on the west by the long finger of Misery Point; however, it has little protection from strong northerlies. The marina located here has solved this problem quite uniquely by chaining a mass of huge, surplus iron ring-buoys together to create a floating breakwater north of the marina.

To reach Seabeck, take State Highway 3 north from Bremerton to the Newberry Hill Road/Silverdale exit. Head west on Newberry Hill Road, which joins Seabeck Highway NW in 3 miles. Follow the highway another 1½ miles to Seabeck. Total distance from Bremerton is about 13 miles. Most of the parking in Seabeck is along the road; when shrimp season or fishing derbies are on, the space can be jammed.

MISERY POINT LAUNCH RAMP

Facilities: Launch ramp, Sani-cans, fishing reef
Attractions: Fishing, scuba diving

An excellent public launch facility operated by the Department of Wildlife between Seabeck and Scenic Beach State Park is heavily used by shrimpers and salmon fishermen. An artificial reef, placed to attract bottom fish, lies just a stone's throw to the east off the tip of Misery Point.

To reach the launch ramp, continue south from Seabeck on Seabeck Highway NW to its intersection with Miami Beach Road NW, ¼ mile from Seabeck. The intersection is signed to the park and boat launch. Turn right onto Miami Beach Road NW. At a Y intersection in ½ mile turn right, and follow signs to the single-lane paved ramp.

The area is open for use between 4:00 A.M. and 10:00 P.M.; overnight parking and camping are prohibited. A spacious parking lot has room for thirty cars with trailers above the ramp. Sani-cans are found at the entrance to the launch site. Property on either side is fenced and private.

SCENIC BEACH STATE PARK

Park area: 90 acres; 1,600 feet of shoreline
Access: Land
Facilities: 52 campsites (no hookups), group camp, picnic tables, picnic shelter, fireplaces, restrooms, community center, children's play area, volleyball court, horseshoe pit
Attractions: Camping, picnicking, walking, beachcombing, scuba diving, views

Scenic it is, with awe-inspiring views up the imposing glacier-gouged valleys of the Dosewallips and Duckabush rivers on the west side of the canal, and north to Dabob Bay and the steep walls of the Toandos Peninsula. Sunsets silhouette the darkening peaks against a rosy sky, or morning mists engulf the phalanx of hills and peaks in nuances of gray.

In late May the scenic beauty is enhanced by masses of the pink blossoms of native rhododendrons. The park is said to have more rhododen-

Sailboats in a cove at Scenic Beach State Park

drons than any other in the state; most bushes are to be found on the campground loops. Call ahead to the park ranger to find if they are at the height of their bloom, and enjoy them along the road on the drive to the park as well as in the park itself.

Campsites, located on a double loop on the west side of the park, are pleasantly isolated by tall Western hemlock and dense underbrush. The main picnic area lies in a small fir-studded meadow above the beach. The trail to the beach can be found at east side of the picnic area.

Farther east across a gully is a large grass field and an orchard. Here is the "Emel House," built in 1912 and currently used as a community center. Joe Emel, Sr., who owned thirty acres of what is presently park land, operated a resort and boathouse on the site, which he called "Scenic Beach." The log cabin on the south side of the gully was built by his son. Following Emel's death, the property was purchased for a state park.

The park's gently sloping beach is mostly gravel and cobblestone below a steep bank, with access via a short trail from the picnic area. Very little beach is visible at high tide, however, as the water laps up against the bluff and bulkheads. This is a favorite area for scuba divers who swim out from shore. Hermit crabs, sea pens, sea cucumbers, and striped nudibranchs are but a few of the animals found on the sandy bottom. Extreme low tide reveals some of these creatures to beachcombers.

To reach Scenic Beach State Park, drive south from Seabeck, as described for the Misery Point Launch Ramp, above. Instead of turning right at the Y intersection, bear left and follow signs to the park in another ½

224

Rhododendrons at Scenic Beach State Park

mile. The park is open from April 1 to October 1. Because of its nearness to Bremerton, it is very popular with Kitsap residents.

EAST SHORE DNR BEACHES

Some short sections of beach along the east shore between Point Misery and the Great Bend offer some limited opportunities for harvesting shellfish. None have upland access (because of private land), and so can be reached only from the water.

DNR Beach 40. Existing as a beach only at low tide, DNR Beach 40 is a 2,145-foot strip of mud-to-sand, offering opportunities for oysters, mussels, clams, and crabs to those who can beach a boat or anchor off and come ashore by dinghy. The beach lies between a cluster of homes north of Anderson Cove and a row of pilings extending far into the water 2,500 feet farther north.

DNR Beaches 48, 47, and 46. One long and two smaller beaches provide an opportunity to gather oysters and clams at low tide. All three beaches are cobble; their boundaries may be marked by black and white DNR posts. Beach 48, immediately across the canal from Ayock Point, is 9,072 feet long, and lies below a steep, wooded cliff about 300 feet high. Beach 47, which is 900 feet long, lies 500 feet south of Beach 48 beneath extremely steep timbered banks. Another 600 feet farther south is Beach 46, 1,643 feet long. It lies below a recently logged area.

DNR Beaches 44A and 44B. Two short stretches of beach are located on the south side of Dewatto Bay. Both are gravel, sloping to sand and mud, where oysters, clams, and crab are found. Beach 44A, 514 feet long, surrounds a point at the southwest entrance to the bay. Beach 44B, 713 feet long, lies along the next curve of the beach, inward into the bay. The bay itself is very shallow, with most of the inner bay drying at a low tide.

The Olympic Shoreline

PLEASANT HARBOR

Park area [state park]: 0.8 acres; 100 feet of shoreline
Access: Land, boat
Facilities [at the state park]: Dock, Sani-can; [at the marina]: transient
    moorage with water and power, groceries, restrooms, showers, fuel,
    swimming pool, hot tub, laundry, fishing supplies, picnic pavillion
Attractions: Boating, fishing

In summer evenings when nighthawks sweep across the bay, capturing insects in their open beaks, and the last rays of light glimmer across the darkening water, "pleasant" barely begins to describe this harbor. A bit more than ½ mile long and 300 yards across, this snug little evergreen-rimmed cove is one of the few well-protected niches on Hood Canal. Located on the west side of the canal just across from Seabeck, the harbor is hidden behind Black Point, and is reached through a narrow channel lying on the north side of the point.

Pleasant Harbor shelters a short dock that is billed as a "State Park," and a sizable commercial marina/resort complex. The second dock just inside the harbor entrance is the principal facility of Pleasant Harbor State

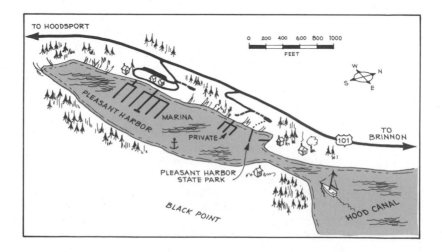

Park. The float has room for about six boats, but has no power or water. The only other amenities of the park are a few garbage cans located at the head of the dock and a Sani-can a bit up the road at a small parking area. Private property bounds both edges of the property, leaving about 100 feet of beachfront for the park. Just beyond the state park float is a private marina, whose floats are plainly posted.

The commercial marina at the west end of the harbor more than compensates for the Spartan nature of the state park. Six long sets of floats are capable of accommodating more than 200 boats, and although some are filled with permanent residents, ample transient moorage is usually available. Onshore facilities provide most of the necessary amenities. If the marina is full, or if boaters do not want to take advantage of its facilities, the harbor has generous space to anchor in about 5 fathoms of water.

To reach Pleasant Harbor by land, follow U.S. 101 along the west side of Hood Canal to 1½ miles south of Brinnon. A gravel road, signed to the marina, drops downhill to a road looping around the grocery store, with parking at the top side of the loop.

Pleasant Harbor Marina

The road to the state park leaves the highway at a deserted grocery store slightly less than ¼ mile north of the marina. Kayaks or inflatable boats could be carried down to the float and put in for exploration of the bay and shore of Hood Canal.

TRITON COVE STATE PARK

Facilities: Launch ramp, dock and float, picnic area, restrooms

A privately-owned trailer park north of Hoodsport was acquired by State Parks and Recreation in 1990. The upland portion of the park, the old trailer parking area, has been converted to picnic sites. A steep single-lane concrete launch ramp drops very steeply into the water, and has an adjoining float off a dock.

WEST SHORE PUBLIC BEACHES

Property owners along the west shore of Hood Canal zealously guard their tidelands and the tasty critters they harbor. Visitors will do well to heed posted property; however, a number of brief sections of beach lying just below Highway 101 are open to the public for gathering shellfish.

The glaciers that gouged out Hood Canal carved deeply into bedrock along this portion of the canal, and the rocky ledges now lying underwater paralleling the shoreline are a scuba diving mecca, home to a kaleidoscope of marine animals that love niches and crannies. Divers should be aware that although the tidal current might be weak near the surface, it can be much stronger at greater depths, as it flows through the subterranean canyons.

Low tide at Eagle Creek Tidelands

Gathering oysters at Eagle Creek

DNR Beach 50. Located 2 miles southwest of the outflow of the Duckabush River, and ½ mile southwest of McDaniel Cove, DNR Beach 50 is 2,610 feet long. The north half of the beach is almost nonexistent, as rock slabs taper steeply into the water. The south half of the beach is on the alluvial fan of Fulton Creek; the sand here harbors oysters, clams, geoducks, and crabs for the harvest at low tide. Although the beach lies just below the highway, the bank is so steep the upland approach is hazardous; it is best reached by boat.

Eagle Creek Recreational Tidelands. Directly across the road from a tavern on the south side of Eagle Creek, 2¾ miles north of Lilliwaup, are extensive tidelands that dry out about 2,000 yards at a minus tide. The rocky beach is an excellent harvesting spot for oysters. There is parking for about fifteen cars alongside the road south of the Eagle Creek bridge. When the tide is out and oysters are prime, numerous cars are usually parked here. The beach north of the creek is private.

Lilliwaup Public Beach. One mile north of the town of Lilliwaup is a 900-foot-long rocky beach immediately adjacent to the highway. A sign identifying this as public beach is only visible to southbound traffic. A roadside pull-off provides ample parking; steep trails lead down the bank to the beach.

Mt. Washington, as seen from Hood Canal, bears the profile of George Washington.

Lilliwaup Tidelands. As Highway 101 continues northbound from Lilliwaup, the highway bends west around Lilliwaup Bay. At the end of the bay, ½ mile from the town, as the road curves northwest again, a 4,122-foot rocky stretch of public beach lies below the bluffs. Although the beach and adjoining bluffs are owned by the State Parks and Recreation Commission, the area is not developed. Parking is at an unmarked gravel pullout above the bluff. Crude access trails have been worn into the bluff from either end of the parking area. Very steep underwater rock walls below the beach are favorite sites for scuba diving.

Octopus Hole. This offshore rock ledge is not officially a public beach by any means, but it is an immensely popular scuba diving spot with de facto beach access. The rock ledge, in about 30 feet of water, is riddled with cracks and holes providing homes for wolf eel and octopus. The area can be visited by divers of any skill level; tidal currents are minimal. Limited roadside parking is found above the beaten trail to the beach. The site is 3¼ miles north of Hoodsport, and 1¼ miles south of Lilliwaup.

Sunde Rock. An offshore rock 2 miles south of Lilliwaup is of interest primarily to scuba divers. The top of the rock is exposed at all times, but it is the myriad ledges lying below the water, with their wealth of fish, numerous kinds of crabs, and colorful starfish, anemone, and nudibranchs that attract divers. A turnout on Highway 101 just north of mile marker 330 has parking for several cars. A short trail leads to the beach; respect private property flanking the path.

The Great Bend

HOODSPORT

Access: Land, boat
Facilities: Transient moorage, marine supplies and repairs, boat launch
(sling), groceries, ice, restaurants, fuel, scuba air fills, shopping,
motels
Attractions: Fishing, shrimping, scuba diving, salmon hatchery

Hoodsport is the only town of any size on Highway 101 between
Shelton and Quilcene. It marks the beginning of the Great Bend of the
canal as it heads westward, and also the beginning of greater population.

The community of around 600 residents is oriented to the tourist
trade, with numerous gift shops, restaurants, and motels catering to visitors
touring the Olympic Peninsula. In late May, during shrimp season, the
town is crammed with sport shrimpers who set pots in offshore waters for
the big prawns.

The Port of Hoodsport dock provides transient moorage for pleasure
boaters who want access to shoreside facilites. Caution: the innermost section of the three-fingered float almost rests on the mud at a minus tide. Immediately south of the port facility is a marina with a sling launch, floats,
repair facilities, and marine supplies.

A salmon hatchery operated by the Washington Department of
Fisheries located immediately north of Finch Creek in Hoodsport is open
for public viewing. Outdoor rearing tanks can be visited at any time; the
hatchery office is open from 8:00 A.M. to 4:30 P.M., weekdays. The 600-
foot-long gravel beach in front of the hatchery is public and may be ac-

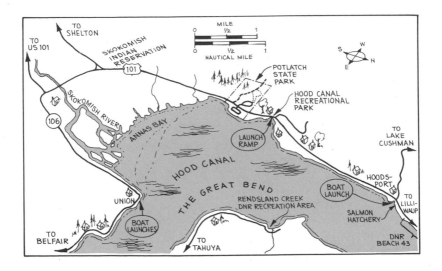

Digging clams at Hoodsport

cessed from the north side of the hatchery. Saltwater fishing is restricted in a radius of 100 feet from the confluence of Finch Creek.

DNR Beach 43, lying immediately adjacent to the highway ¼ mile north of the center of Hoodsport, just north of the town limits, is accessible from both land and water. The cobblestone beach is 2,951 feet long; adjacent beaches are private. At low tide find oysters, clams, mussels, and crab, although the area is heavily used because of its closeness to the town. The beach also provides a scuba diving access. Parking space along the highway at this point is very limited.

HOOD CANAL RECREATIONAL PARK
(CUSHMAN PARK)

Park area: 4.7 acres; 1,000 feet of shoreline
Access: Land, boat
Facilities: Picnic tables, fireplaces, restrooms, boat launch (ramp)
Attractions: Picnicking, fishing, boating, swimming

Tacoma City Light, which operates the large hydroelectric plant 2½ miles south of Hoodsport, provides this day-use picnic area and launch ramp immediately across Highway 101 from their facility. A large parking lot, ample for seventy-five to eighty cars and trailers is adjacent to the highway. Beyond the lot is a wide grass strip with fruit trees, evergreens, and about fifty picnic tables. Generator flywheels and other castoffs from the hydro plant are mounted at several places in the park as decoration and for kids to scramble on.

The long cobblestone beach is open for wading or swimming. A two-lane concrete launch ramp drops steeply from the southeast corner of the parking lot down to the water.

POTLATCH STATE PARK

Park area: 57 acres; 9,570 feet of shoreline
Access: Land, boat
Facilities: 37 campsites, picnic tables, fireplaces, restrooms, showers, trailer dump, swimming beach, mooring buoys
Attractions: Camping, picnicking, swimming, clamming, boating, scuba diving, hiking

Potlatch State Park, a small facility along Highway 101, 3 miles south of Hoodsport, occupies the site of a former private resort. The park's campground lies on the west side of Highway 101, and the picnic area and beach on the east. A single campground loop has thirty-five sites (eighteen with hookups) and two primitive walk-in spots. The wooded campground isn't particularly spacious, so privacy between campsites is limited.

A short trail leaves the back of the campground, joins a service road, and then loops back to its beginning. The woodlands attract a variety of critters such as squirrels, skunk, rabbits, deer, and mountain beaver.

The picnic area is a large, open, grass field overlooking the beach. The beach below tapers gently into Annas Bay and varies from rock to gravel and mud. Offshore are five mooring buoys for visitors arriving by water. Although clamming is a favorite sport here, the beach is heavily dug, and a sturdy shovel is necessary to find the few remaining shellfish

Curious harbor seal in Hood Canal

down through the rocky cobbles. Seals are frequently seen cavorting in Annas Bay, and waterfowl frequent the salt marshes.

The Skokomish (meaning "River People") originally inhabited the river delta and adjoining valleys at the southern end of Hood Canal. The Point No Point Treaty of 1855 set aside a portion of their land as a reservation, which they were to share with the Toandos and Chimakum Indians. Although the broad flat north of the Skokomish River delta was a traditional gathering site, it was not included as part of the reservation.

It was here that the Skokomish held their "potlatches"—ceremonies popular among Northwest Indians in which the host chief proved his status and wealth by giving away or destroying vast amounts of his possessions. These elaborate ceremonies often required years of preparation, with dances and songs to be rehearsed, speeches to be composed, and offerings of furs, blankets, food, oil, ornaments, and slaves to be amassed.

UNION

Access: Land, boat
Facilities: Marina, transient moorage, groceries, ice, boat launch (ramp
　　and hoists), fuel, restaurant, bait
Attractions: Boating, fishing

The small community of Union lies on a point of land east of the delta of the Skokomish River, where Hood Canal makes its hook to the north-

Union

east. The town consists mostly of a few businesses catering to recreational boat traffic on the canal and tourists on the highway.

There are two marinas at Union, and they and adjoining businesses provide full facilities for visitors. Immediately west of the marinas is the Mason County public launch area, a two-lane concrete ramp. Adjacent parking is limited.

Union is 5 miles east of the Highway 101 on State Highway 106 East, or 24 miles southwest of Bremerton on that same highway.

The South Shore

Once past the Great Bend, the nature of the Hood Canal shoreline changes drastically, becoming wall-to-wall cabins, beach houses, and year-round homes, and the water becomes busier with small pleasure craft and water skiers. Pollution in the ever-more-shallow water, along with the population density, make for slimmer pickings of shellfish at the few available public accesses. In short, here civilization has virtually conquered the natural state of the waterway.

The shoreline on either side of the canal in this reach is most often approached by land from Bremerton. Follow State Highway 304 west out of Bremerton to where it joins State Highway 3 as it skirts the north shore of Sinclair Inlet. Continue southwest on Highway 3 for another 10 miles to reach Belfair, a small community at the far east point of Hood Canal. Here at a Y in the highway, Highway 300 heads down the north side of the canal and in ½ mile, at a second Y, Highway 106 heads down the south side.

If approaching from either the north or south via Highway 101, turn onto Highway 106 at either of two intersections in the Skokomish Indian Reservation, or just south of it.

ALDERBROOK INN

Access: Land, boat, floatplane
Facilities: Resort, conference center, restaurant, swimming pool, hot tub, sauna, shops, golf course, transient moorage (power, water), paddle boat and sailboat rentals, tennis courts, volleyball, badminton, horseshoes, children's play area
Attractions: Swimming (saltwater and pool), golfing, boating, hiking, scuba diving

Whether touring Hood Canal by boat or car, visitors cannot miss the striking facilities of Alderbrook Inn, located on the south side of the canal 13 miles southwest of Belfair on Highway 106. By boat, the dock at the inn lies on the south side of the canal, 2 miles east of Union.

Alderbrook, one of the finest resorts in western Washington, has complete resort and conference facilities, and a justifiably renowned dining room. Reservations are recommended for stays at the rooms or cottages of the resort. Guest boat moorage is available on 1,200 feet of floating dock

Waterwheel at Alderbrook

(for a fee). A small additional charge is made for use of the indoor swimming pool. The resort has neither groceries nor marine supplies; the closest spot for these is Union.

Near Alderbrook, just south of the Union Post Office, is an ancient waterwheel, one of the first built in Mason County. Situated just off the east side of the road on private property, the historic wheel with its decrepit wooden flume still functions despite the ravages of age. Walk from Alderbrook, or park at the post office and walk along the road (being careful of traffic) to view it.

TWANOH STATE PARK

Park area: 182 acres; 3,167 feet of shoreline
Access: Land, boat
Facilities: 52 campsites, RV hookups, group camp, restrooms, showers, picnic tables, fireplaces, kitchen shelters, dock, 7 mooring buoys, boat launch (ramp), marine pumpout station, swimming beach, wading pool, bathhouses, tennis court, horseshoe pits, hiking trails, concession stand
Attractions: Boating, fishing, swimming, hiking, camping, picnicking, scuba diving

Flanked by miles of beachfront homes and near the population centers of Bremerton, Port Orchard, and Shelton, Twanoh State Park has many of the features of a well-developed city park, yet it manages to blend in the camping and hiking found in more remote state parks. The park is 7½ miles southwest of Belfair on Highway 106. The highway splits the park into two sections: on the south the camping and hiking area, and on the north the picnic grounds and beach.

Campsites along the single loop road are fairly open, separated by second-growth cedar with sparse underbrush. Only nine of the campsites have hookups. The park is open to camping from April 1 to September 30.

An interesting feature of the park is numerous large cedar stumps with springboard notches, remnants of the 1890s when the area was first logged. Many of the park buildings—built with large stones and heavy timbers— were constructed in 1936–37 by the Depression-era Civilian Conservation Corps.

Although Twanoh is best known for its beach, most of the park consists of densely wooded hillsides above the small stream flowing through the park. A 2-mile-long hiking trail swings through this area, with a shorter 1¼-mile loop option. Both ends of the loop start at the parking lot west of the campground.

The west leg of the trail is a fire road climbing steeply through moss-covered cedar to top a 350-foot-high ridge. Here is the option of the short or long loop, with the short trail dropping steeply downhill in a series of switchbacks through fir and hemlock forest to the east side of the loop just

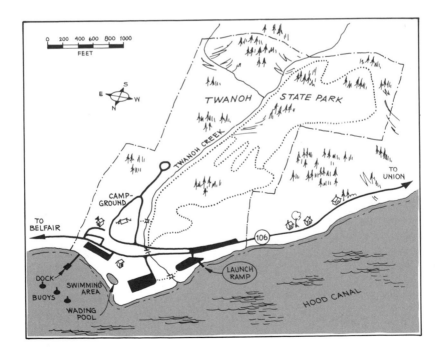

above the creek bed. Continue on the longer loop to break out onto an open hilltop covered with huckleberries. From here the trail drops gradually downhill to the south park boundary, then switchbacks down to the bank above the creek. As the trail follows the creek downhill, the moist forest sprouts devil's club, ferns, and moss. The shorter loop trail joins in at an open grassy spot, and the converged trails continue along the creek back to the parking lot.

The park's day-use area, on a small point protruding into the canal, is open 6:30 A.M. to dusk, year-round, although most of the facilities (such as restrooms) are available only in the summer. A small creek divides the area into two; each section has a parking lot and picnic facilities. The two-lane concrete boat launch ramp is at the west section of the park. The eastern section has a roped-off swimming beach with two floats; a shallow wading pool for toddlers has been scooped out of the gravel beach near the swimming area.

At the southeast corner of the park, a 40-foot-long float extends off the end of a dock. The float is quite close to shore; approach cautiously at low tide. Five mooring buoys are spaced offshore for visiting boaters.

The beach at Twanoh State Park

The North Shore

BELFAIR STATE PARK

Park area: 62.5 acres; 3,720 feet of shoreline
Access: Land, boat (shallow draft)
Facilities: 184 campsites, RV hookups, restrooms, showers, picnic tables,
    fireplaces, swimming beach, bathhouse, trailer dump
Attractions: Picnicking, camping, beachcombing, scuba diving,
    crabbing, fishing

The farthest reach of Hood Canal dwindles down to a shallow tideflat that bares at the hint of a minus tide. Belfair State Park, the largest park on the canal, is located at this end, 3 miles west of the town of Belfair, on State Highway 300. The park provides an interesting combination of freshwater and saltwater shoreline, as two good-sized streams, Big and Little Mission creeks, flow through it to reach the canal.

Because of the shallowness of the water, only small boats can approach the park, and even those with care, lest they become mired. The advantage of the tideflat, however, is that water flowing over it warms more quickly than that in deeper portions of the canal, making it ideal for summertime wading and swimming. A saltwater lagoon formed in a diked-off area at the mouth of Big Mission Creek provides an even warmer and more protected bathing spot.

Camping is in two distinct areas. The loops of the older section of the park are in old-growth Douglas fir and rhododendrons; however, these sites have no RV hookups. Many of the campsites in the newer section of

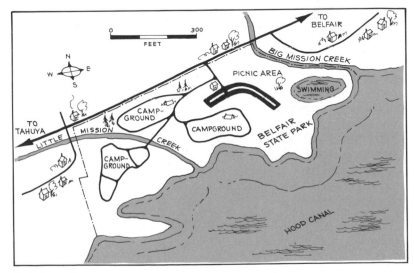

BELFAIR STATE PARK

Belfair State Park

the park have hookups, although they are more in the open. Camping is permitted year around, although the park hours vary by season. Picnic sites are on the east side of the park, scattered along a grass strip between the parking lot and Big Mission Creek.

A rock bulkhead defines the park shoreline. The beach below is gravel baring to sand and mud at low tide. Seagulls, ducks, and geese populate the shore, while woodpeckers and a variety of other birds inhabit the wooded upland areas.

The tiny peninsula that juts out from the shoreline on the west edge of the park, according to Indian legend, carried supernatural powers that caused people loitering there to become possessed. Its Indian name meant "Snail Woman," an evil person who carried a large basket on her back, and who stole children and ate them (no child psychologists back in those days!). She was transformed into the tiny snails with shells on their backs that can be found there today.

PORT OF ALLYN DOCK AND LAUNCH RAMP

Area: 30 feet of shoreline
Access: Land, boat
Facilities: Dock with float, launch ramp, Sani-can
Attractions: Boating

West on State Highway 300, 1½ miles from Belfair State Park, a small bulge of land provides a site for a dock and launch ramp operated by the Port of Allyn. The ownership seems a bit incongruous, since the town

Port of Allyn dock

of Allyn lies 8 miles away on Case Inlet, at the end of Puget Sound, but one cannot complain of the existence of this fine, well-maintained facility.

The launch ramp and dock are separated by a two-block-long section of private beach homes; the caretaker lives next to the single-lane, concrete boat launch ramp. The dock extends out to a U-shaped float that has room for about fifteen boats. Although the area is intended primarily for day use, overnight moorage is permitted after registering with the caretaker. All adjacent beach is private.

From land, the dock may be identified by a sign "Caution, Pedestrian Crossing—Boat Ramp Ahead." Parking and a Sani-can are at a pull-off across the road from the head of the dock. More parking is available opposite the launch ramp.

TAHUYA

Facilities: Bait, fuel, transient moorage, boat launch (ramp), boat rentals, RV camping

The community of Tahuya surrounds a pretty little bay at the mouth of the Tahuya River. Just west of the residential area is a commercial resort with camping and boating facilities and supplies, and a dock with floats. It can be reached by land by driving 12½ miles southwest of Belfair on North Shore Road, the county road extension of State Highway 300.

The melodious name "Tahuya" is an Indian word meaning "that done." It refers to some memorable (but since-forgotten) event that took place here long ago.

Driftwood on the beach at Rendsland Creek

RENDSLAND CREEK DNR RECREATION AREA

Area: 8 acres; 1,405 feet of shoreline
Facilities: Sani-can
Access: Land, boat (shallow draft)

A small undeveloped section of land owned by the Department of Natural Resources is located at the far southwest point of the Kitsap Peninsula, just across Hood Canal from Hoodsport. The area consists mainly of a small peninsula covered with stumps and driftwood at the mouth of Rendsland Creek. South of the park property is a tiny bay, with rows of private homes fronting the opposite shore.

The area is 18½ miles southwest of Belfair on North Shore Road, the county road continuing on from Highway 300. There is parking space next to the road for three or four cars.

Appendices

A. *Emergency Phone Numbers and List of Contacts*

All western Washington cities and counties use 911 as an emergency number. The following phone numbers are listed as additional contacts for *non-emergency* situations.

All numbers are area code 206.

SHERIFFS AND POLICE

Jefferson County: (Port Townsend) 385-3831
King County: (Seattle) 296-3311 or 1-800-344-4080
Kitsap County: (Port Orchard) 876-7101
Mason County: (Shelton) 426-9766
Snohomish County: (Everett) 259-9393

COAST GUARD

Everett: USCGC *Point Doran* 252-5281
Seattle: Emergencies 286-5400
      Other 442-5295

U.S. CUSTOMS

Everett: 259-0246; after hours and weekends: 1-800-562-5943
Seattle: Private yacht arrivals
      (weekdays and Saturday, 8:00 A.M. to 5:00 P.M.): 442-4678
      (evenings, Sundays, and holidays): 1-800-562-5943

RADIO CONTACTS

Marine VHF: Coast Guard distress or hailing—Channel 16
      Coast Guard liason—Channel 22
      Coast Guard Vessel Tracking Center—Channel 14 (1 watt only)
      Hiram Chittenden Locks—Channel 13 (1 watt only)
      Marine Operator: Everett—Channel 24
                 Tacoma—Channel 28
                 Seattle—Channels 25 and 26

NOAA Weather Service—Channel WX1
Seattle Ship Canal Bridges—Channel 13 (1 watt only)

OTHER CONTACTS

Red Tide Hotline: 1-800-562-5632
Whale Hotline (to report sightings or strandings): 1-800-562-8832

FERRIES

Washington State Ferries Information:
(Seattle) 464-6400 or (toll free) 1-800-542-0810 or 1-800-542-7052
Bremerton–Winslow schedules: 464-6990
Edmonds–Kingston schedules: 464-6960

WASHINGTON STATE PARKS

General information regarding the state parks is available from Washington State Parks and Recreation Commission, 7150 Cleanwater Lane, Olympia, WA 98504. Toll-free number for information or reservations (Memorial Day through Labor Day): 1-800-562-0990.

Belfair: NE 410 Beck Road, Belfair, WA 98528. Phone: 478-4625.
Dosewallips: P.O. Box K, Brinnon, WA 98320. Phone: 796-4415.
Fay-Bainbridge: 15446 Sunrise Drive NE, Bainbridge Island, WA 98110. Phone: 842-3931.
Fort Ward (satellite to Fay-Bainbridge): 15446 Sunrise Drive NE, Bainbridge Island, WA 98110. Phone: 842-3931, 842-4041 (seasonal).
Illahee: 3540 Bahia Vista, Bremerton, WA 98310. Phone: 478-6460.
Kitsap Memorial: 202 NE Park St., Poulsbo, WA 98370. Phone: 779-3205.
Manchester: P.O. Box 36, Manchester, WA 98353. Phone: 871-4065.
Potlatch: Route 4, Box 519, Shelton, WA 98584. Phone: 877-5361.
Scenic Beach: P.O. Box 7, Seabeck, WA 98380. Phone: 831-5079.
Twanoh: East 12190 Highway 206, Union, WA 98592. Phone: 275-2222.

OTHER PARKS

Bremerton Department of Parks and Recreation: Sheridan Park Recreation Center, 680 Lebo Blvd., Bremerton, WA 98310. Phone: 478-5305.
Discovery Park: 3801 W. Government Way, Seattle, WA 98199. Phone: 386-4236.
Edmonds Parks and Recreation: 700 Main St., Edmonds, WA 98020. Phone: 775-2525.
Everett Parks and Recreation: 3002 Wetmore, Everett, WA 98201. Phone: 259-0311.

Jefferson County Parks and Recreation: Lawrence and Taylor, Port Townsend, WA 98368. Phone: 385-2221.

King County Parks and Recreation Division (general information): 2040 84th SE, Mercer Island, WA 98040. Phone: 296-4232.

Kitsap County Parks Department: 1200 NW Fairgrounds Rd., Bremerton, WA 98310. Phone: 692-3655.

Seal Rock Forest Campground: Quilcene Ranger Station, Quilcene, WA 98376. Phone: 765-3368.

Seattle Parks and Recreation Department (general information): 600 4th, Seattle, WA 98104. Phone: 684-4075.

Snohomish County Parks and Recreation Division: P.O. Box 310, Monroe, WA 98272. Phone: 339-1208 or 743-7504.

MUSEUMS

Bremerton Naval Museum: 130 Washington Ave., Bremerton, WA 98310. Phone: 479-7447.

Edmonds Museum: 118 5th Ave. N, P.O. Box 52, Edmonds, WA 98020. Phone: 774-0900.

Firefighters Museum: 13th St. Dock, Everett Marina, Everett, WA 98201. Phone: 259-8709.

Kitsap County Historical Museum: 3343 NW Byron St., Silverdale, WA 98383. Phone: 692-1949.

Port Gamble Historic Museum: Port Gamble, WA 98364. Phone: 297-2426.

Suquamish Museum: P.O. Box 498, Suquamish, WA 98392. Phone: 598-3311.

OTHER

Point Whitney State Shellfish Laboratory: Brinnon, WA 98320. Phone: 796-4601.

Seattle Aquarium: Pier 59, Seattle, WA 98101. Phone: 625-4358.

B. Charts, Maps, and Tide Tables

CHARTS

Sketch maps in this book are intended for general orientation only. When traveling by boat in waters covered by this book, it is imperative that the appropriate nautical charts be used. The following list of charts covers the area included in this book. They may be purchased at map stores or many marine centers.

NOAA Chart 18445 SC, Puget Sound—Possession Sound to Olympia, including the Hood Canal. (Scale 1:80,000—folio of charts including some detailed insets.)

NOAA Chart 18441, Puget Sound—Northern part. (Scale 1:80,000)
NOAA Chart 18448, Puget Sound—Southern part. (Scale 1:80,000)
NOAA Chart 18443, Approaches to Everett. (Scale 1:40,000)
NOAA Chart 18473, Puget Sound—Oak Bay to Shilshole Bay. (Scale 1:40,000)
NOAA Chart 18476, Puget Sound—Hood Canal and Dabob Bay. (Scale 1:40,000)
NOAA Chart 18449, Puget Sound—Seattle to Bremerton. (Scale 1:25,000)
NOAA Chart 18458, Hood Canal—South Point to Quatsop Point including Dabob Bay. (Scale 1:25,000)
NOAA Chart 18477, Puget Sound—Entrance to Hood Canal. (Scale 1:25,000)
NOAA Chart 18444, Everett Harbor. (Scale 1:10,000)
NOAA Chart 18446, Puget Sound—Apple Cove Pt. to Keyport Agate Passage. (Scale 1:10,000)
NOAA Chart 18450, Seattle Harbor, Elliott Bay, and Duwamish Waterway. (Scale 1:10,000)
NOAA Chart 18452, Sinclair Inlet. (Scale 1:10,000)

MAPS

USGS topographic maps are not required for any hiking described in this book, but the 7½' series maps are both useful and interesting. Those covering areas in this book are: Belfair, Bremerton East, Bremerton West, Brinnon, Duwamish Head, Eldon, Edmonds East, Edmonds West, Everett, Hansville, Holly, Hoodsport, Lake Wooten, Lilliwaup, Lofall, Marysville, Mukilteo, Port Gamble, Port Ludlow, Poulsbo, Quilcene, Seabeck, Seattle North, Seattle South, Skokomish Valley, Shilshole Bay, Suquamish, Tulalip, Union.

For detailed street maps the following are useful:

King, Snohomish counties—Thomas Brothers Maps
Bremerton, Port Orchard, Silverdale, Poulsbo, Winslow, Kitsap County—
    King of the Road Map Services.

TIDE TABLES

Tide Tables—19__, West Coast of North America and South America. NOAA (published annually).

Tidal Current Tables—19__. Pacific Coast of North America and Asia. NOAA (published annually).

19__ Current and Tide Tables for Puget Sound, Deception Pass, the San Juans, Gulf Islands, and the Strait of Juan de Fuca. Island Canoe, Inc., Bainbridge Island. (Extract from the above NOAA tables for local areas.)

C. Quick Reference to Facilities and Recreation

Some kinds of marine recreation, such as boating, fishing, and beachcombing, are found throughout Middle Puget Sound and Hood Canal; however, others are more specific to particular areas. The table on the following pages provides a quick reference to the facilities and activities in the major areas covered by this book.

Marine Services include fuel and marine supplies and repair; in some places they may be of a very limited nature.

Shopping/Food generally includes groceries, cafes or restaurants, and a varying range of other types of stores. These too may be of a limited nature.

Floats/Buoys refers to marinas with transient moorage as well as to public facilities at marine parks.

Launch Facilities may be only shore access for hand-carried boats. Hoists and slings are always located at commercial marinas. Ramps may be at either commercial or public facilities.

Points of Interest includes historical or educational displays, museums, and self-guided nature trails.

Some facilities listed may be entirely at commercial resorts or marinas; some may close in the off-season. For detailed information read the description of specific areas in the text.

[ ] = Freshwater
Launch Facilities: H = Hoist; R = Ramp; C = Hand Carry

	Marine Services	Shopping/Food	Moorage/Docks/Buoys	Charters/Rentals	Launch Facilities	Fishing Pier	Shellfish	Paddling	Scuba Diving	Swimming	Beachcombing	Camping	Picnicking	Walking/Hiking	Point of Interest
1. POSSESSION SOUND AND EDMONDS															
Tulalip Bay Marina	•	•	•		R			•						•	•
Ebey Slough Launch Ramp					R										
Langus Waterfront Park			•		R			•						•	•
Port of Everett Marina	•	•	•	•	H										•
N & S Marine View Parks									•	•					
Marine Park			•		R								•		
Everett Jetty Park		•										•	•	•	
Howarth City Park												•	•	•	

	Marine Services	Shopping/Food	Moorage/Docks/Buoys	Charters/Rentals	Launch Facilities	Fishing Pier	Shellfish	Paddling	Scuba Diving	Swimming	Beachcombing	Camping	Picnicking	Walking/Hiking	Point of Interest
Mukilteo	•	•	•	•											•
Mukilteo State Park					R					•			•		
Picnic Point County Park									•	•	•		•		
Norma Beach				•											
Meadowdale	•	•		•	H	•									
Meadowdale Beach County Park											•		•	•	
Port of Edmonds Marina	•	•	•	•	H										
Edmonds Underwater Park					C				•	•	•				•
Edmonds Public Fishing Pier		•				•							•		
Marina Beach					C		•	•	•	•	•		•	•	
2. THE SEATTLE AREA															
Richmond Beach County Park									•	•	•		•		
Boeing Creek Fishing Reef															
Carkeek Park										•	•		•	•	
Golden Gardens					C			•	•	•			•	•	
Eddie Vine Boat Launch		•			R										
Shilshole Bay Marina	•	•	•	•	H	•									•
Hiram M. Chittenden Locks													•		•
Ship Canal Fish Ladder															•
Commodore Park					C			•					•		•
Fishermen's Terminal	•	•													•
Ship Canal Public Accesses					[R/d]			•					•		•
Gas Works Park								•					•		•
Lake Union Public Accesses	•	•	•	•	[R/d]			•	•				•		•
Portage Bay Public Accesses	•				•			•	•				•		•
Discovery Park							•				•		•	•	•
Smith Cove Park											•		•		•
Elliott Bay Marina	•	•	•	•	H	•									
Elliott Bay Park		•				•							•	•	•
Myrtle Edwards Park													•	•	•
Downtown Seattle Waterfront	•	•				•		•					•		•
Pier 23 Fishing Pier						•									
Harbor Island Marina	•	•	•												
First Avenue South Boat Launch					R										
Duwamish River Access Points					C		•	•					•	•	•
Seacrest Park		•				•		•	•	•	•		•	•	•
Don Armeni Park		•			R						•		•		•
Alki Beach Park		•			C		•	•	•	•	•		•		•

	Marine Services	Shopping/Food	Moorage/Docks/Buoys	Charters/Rentals	Launch Facilities	Fishing Pier	Shellfish	Paddling	Scuba Diving	Swimming	Beachcombing	Camping	Picnicking	Walking/Hiking	Point of Interest
3. BAINBRIDGE ISLAND															
Eagle Harbor and Winslow		•				•									•
Eagle Harbor Marinas	•	•	•												
Eagle Harbor Waterfront Park		•			R				•		•		•	•	
Fort Ward State Park		•			R			•	•		•		•	•	•
Crystal Springs					•										
Reitan Road Access									•		•				
Port Madison County Park											•		•		
Fay-Bainbridge State Park		•	•		R		•	•		•	•	•	•		•
4. EAST KITSAP PENINSULA															
Manchester		•			R	•									
Manchester State Park									•		•	•	•	•	•
Waterman		•	•		•										
Annapolis Recreation Area		•			R										
Port Orchard	•	•	•	•	R	•							•		•
Downtown Bremerton	•	•											•		•
Evergreen City Park					R								•		
Lebo Street Recreation Area		•			R	•				•	•		•		
Tracyton Launch Ramp					R										
Lower Marine Park											•			•	
Chico Launch Ramp					R										
Silverdale Waterfront Park		•			R	•	•	•		•	•		•		•
Illahee State Park		•			R	•				•	•	•	•	•	•
Illahee		•	•				•			•					
Brownsville Marina	•	•	•		R	•							•		
Port of Keyport Marina	•	•	•		R										•
Poulsbo		•								•					•
Poulsbo Marinas	•	•	•		R		•						•		•
American Legion & Liberty Bay Parks													•	•	
Suquamish Museum													•	•	•
Old Man House State Park										•	•	•	•		•
Suquamish		•			R	•									•
Miller Bay	•				R										
Indianola		•	•												
Kingston	•	•	•	•	H								•		
Arness County Park											•	•	•		
Eglon Beach Park					R						•	•	•		

	Marine Services	Shopping/Food	Moorage/Docks/Buoys	Charters/Rentals	Launch Facilities	Fishing Pier	Shellfish	Paddling	Scuba Diving	Swimming	Beachcombing	Camping	Picnicking	Walking/Hiking	Point of Interest
Point No Point County Park											•		•	•	
Hansville and Point No Point	•	•	•	•	H/R						•				•
Foulweather Bluff	•	•	•		H							•			
Foulweather Bluff Wildlife Preserve											•			•	

5. HOOD CANAL

	Marine Services	Shopping/Food	Moorage/Docks/Buoys	Charters/Rentals	Launch Facilities	Fishing Pier	Shellfish	Paddling	Scuba Diving	Swimming	Beachcombing	Camping	Picnicking	Walking/Hiking	Point of Interest
Mats Mats Bay					R			•							
Port Ludlow	•	•	•	•	R			•		•		•	•		•
Port Gamble		•											•		•
Salsbury Point County Park					R			•					•	•	•
Kitsap Memorial State Park			•					•		•	•	•	•	•	
Hood Canal Bridge and Fishing Pier						•			•						•
Shine Tidelands					R		•	•			•	•	•		
Bywater Bay State Park											•			•	
William R. Hicks County Park					R		•						•		
Fisherman Harbor							•	•							
Point Whitney Shellfish Laboratory					R		•			•					•
Quilcene Bay Marina	•		•		R		•			•			•		
Seal Rock Campground					C		•		•	•	•	•	•		
Dosewallips State Park											•	•	•	•	
Seabeck	•	•	•	•	H		•								•
Misery Point Launch Ramp					R		•								
Scenic Beach State Park				•					•		•	•	•	•	•
Pleasant Harbor	•	•	•					•		•			•		
Triton Cove State Park					R								•	•	
West Shore Public Beaches							•		•	•	•		•		
Hoodsport	•	•	•		H		•		•						
Hood Canal Recreational Park					R					•			•		
Potlatch State Park			•		C		•		•	•	•	•	•		
Union	•	•			R/H										
Alderbrook Inn		•							•	•	•				•
Twanoh State Park			•		R	•		•	•	•		•	•	•	
Belfair State Park										•	•	•	•	•	
Port of Allyn Dock and Launch Ramp				•	R										
Tahuya	•	•			R								•		
Rendsland Creek DNR Area												•			

Index

About the authors:
Seattle residents, the Muellers have been active in the outdoors around Puget Sound for over thirty years. Both Marge and Ted are long-time mountain climbers and worked with Mountain Rescue Council; they have also instructed in mountain climbing through the University of Washington. More than a decade ago they added sailing to their round of interests and, with their two children, began wandering the inlets and outlets of the Sound year round.

Researching and writing the *Afoot & Afloat* series took the Muellers more than eight years, and included visits to every beach, bay, island and "point of interest" covered in the text, plus many hours spent in libraries and museums and contacting land management agencies for historical and useful information.

The Muellers' first book, *Northwest Ski Trails,* was also published by The Mountaineers.